Praise for *Telling Tales Out of School*

'I've increasingly come to the view that schooldays should come at the end, rather than the beginning, of one's life, when we have at least a modicum of the wisdom and experience necessary to deal with so many life-changing decisions. But then maybe we'd lose some of the surreal serendipity of schooldays, so vividly recaptured in *Telling Tales Out of School*. A rich compendium of shared confusion.'

– MICHAEL PALIN

'This is a delightful and compelling collection of stories about something we've all had to go through. From the very first page it brings back all the pangs and pleasures of school, teased out by the quiet, sympathetic and highly effective professionalism of Jonathan Sale.'

– JOHN SIMPSON

'The most interesting chapters in any successful person's life are not the ones at the end in the section called Meetings with Important People but the ones at the beginning headed Early Struggles. More interesting still, perhaps, are the even earlier stages of their lives which are remembered in this book, at school and university, before any of them had even the beginnings of an idea how their story would turn out.'

– MICHAEL FRAYN

To Ken — best
wishes from Jonty

TELLING
TALES
OUT OF
SCHOOL

JONATHAN SALE

The Robson Press

First published in Great Britain in 2014 by
The Robson Press (an imprint of Biteback Publishing)
Westminster Tower
3 Albert Embankment
London SE1 7SP

ISBN 978-1-84954-773-4

10 9 8 7 6 5 4 3 2 1

A CIP catalogue record for this book is available from the British Library.

Set in Stempel Garamond

Printed and bound in Great Britain by
CPI Group (UK) Ltd, Croydon CR0 4YY

MIX
Paper from
responsible sources
FSC
www.fsc.org
FSC® C020471

*To my partner Diana Aubrey and
my children Rebecca, Peter and Jessica,
all of whom are class acts*

CONTENTS

INTRODUCTION

One of them was told that he just wasn't university material, the other that unless he got O level maths – at his sixth attempt – he could not take up his exhibition to Cambridge. And that's just two presenters of *University Challenge*. Bamber Gascoigne pulled up his socks academically and Jeremy Paxman did his stuff mathematically; both show that it's possible to have a second chance at school and university.

Good or bad, there is always a moment. (Six moments, in the case of Paxman: getting the right answer was as hard as getting a response from Michael Howard.) Actor Tom Conti had a sudden moment after leaving school that steered his life in a new direction. Walking down a corridor with the intention of enrolling in a music course, he noticed a sign pointing to the drama department. On a whim, he changed direction and his life took a dramatic turn.

Paddy Ashdown had a tough life in the Special Boat Service and an even tougher time as leader of the Lib Dems. I'm not saying it was a life-changing moment but his first skirmish, with his over-strict primary school headmistress, deserves celebrating as an indication of how he was shaping up. He locked her in the stationery cupboard and ran away. 'One to watch,' she may have thought, 'and not in a good way.'

How did creative people develop their creativity? Actors, singers, sportsmen and women: who or what lit their fire? Broadcasters, entrepreneurs and scientists: who pulled their strings? Writers, comedians, campaigners, politicians and directors: who turned the key in their ignition?

We may not know it, we may not like it, but our schools are crucial in what we are and what we do. There are primary teachers who encouraged us with gold stars and scary maths teachers who frightened us off figures forever. Even if we are reacting against our teachers, that's still an influence they are having on us.

'You take your school life with you all your life,' the writer Kate Figes told me. 'My own school life is still very vivid to me.' One of those vivid moments involved, aged twelve, having to defend her mother's new book on feminism from the attacks of her forthright classmates. A tough gig. No wonder she went home in tears. Maybe it's not strange that she is a writer herself: *Life After Birth* and *Couples*, among other titles.

Over a fifteen-year period I have been engaged in a weekly series of interviews, mainly for *The Independent*, on memories of school and, where applicable, art school, drama school and university. They are on the whole the kind of people sufficiently well known to appear on *Desert Island Discs*, with whole lives and careers sufficiently interesting to talk about.

My aim in this book was to avoid the use of the word 'celebrity' (that didn't last very long, did it?) on the grounds that it seems the wrong term for people like Doreen Lawrence, who is a public figure because of the admirable way in which she has created the Stephen Lawrence Charitable Trust to conjure something positive from the worst event that can happen to a mother. On the other hand, it is not a crime to be a celebrity and the word describes most of the people in the book. The word 'interesting', however, describes them all. Being a boring celebrity, I hope you'll agree, should certainly be a criminal offence.

Among those who let me make withdrawals from their memory banks were Meera Syal, Rory McGrath, John Simpson, Gina Yashere, Konnie Huq, Gary Lineker, the Astronomer Royal, Zippo the Clown and one third of Monty Python. They feature in the selection made for this book, together with 230 other well-known and interesting men and women who have made the most of their talent and potential. These are people who may not be typical – they have chosen to stick their heads above the parapet – but many of their experiences at school and university are similar to those undergone by the rest of us.

Drawing on their memories, I have compiled a kaleidoscope of experiences that contributed to their development and careers. Some of these incidents are unique. Actress Jean Marsh remembers being told that the little girl who sat next to her in class had just been killed in the Blitz. Others ring only too true for us all: not knowing where the loos are on your first day (with predictable results for John Humphrys). Robert Winston had the problem of mistaking his form order for his marks; he confessed to his mother that he never got more than a '1' or '2'. Pat Cash ran home twice – on his first morning.

Dragon James Caan flogged leather jackets from his father's shop during break – and added a mark-up which dad didn't know about. Toyah Willcox was one of several who thought that their first day at school was a one-off; they didn't realise that you went back the next day, and the day after and…

How did these singular individuals fare during their childhood and young adulthood? Did their academic performance have any bearing on what they ended up doing? Were the seeds of success planted in the playground – or stunted?

What emerged during the interviews were fascinating personal stories and revealing insights. It brought up a range of questions. What were the sparks that lit their fire? Were they a teacher's pet or a teacher's pest? Which opportunities did they seize? What did they miss? Their answers provide us with significant hints, clues and examples.

Some showed an early talent. As a toddler, Simon Schama was so brilliant that he got fed up with his parents showing him off to their friends; he refused to utter a word and put himself on a 'speech strike'. A prophetic primary school teacher told novelist Margaret Forster, 'You'll be a writer.'

Others dug themselves out of trouble. The pupil suspended for shoplifting (Clare Balding, since you ask) ended up as head girl; at university she became union president, while simultaneously leading another life as a leading amateur jockey.

Education gave some of the interviewees a springboard to a charmed life: (Lord) Chris Patten became the last governor of Hong Kong and then Chairman of the BBC Trust. Mind you, another ended up in Guantanamo Bay, though he doesn't blame his school for that.

While our country's most creative and interesting individuals were sometimes found at the top of the class like Melvyn Bragg, many weren't. They were at the bottom or not in it at all, having bunked off ('Where's that Bradley Wiggins? Down the bike sheds again?') to pursue interests which were nowhere on the curriculum. Indeed, a report card of As does not necessarily make a rocket scientist.

Billy Bragg and David Bailey were told by careers masters that all they could look forward to was, respectively, the Ford Dagenham production line and digging holes in roads. One teacher told Helen Sharman that she was hopeless (she only became Britain's first female astronaut, a real rocket scientist) while Edward Fox's father was informed by an actor friend that his son would never make it in the profession.

The chance of developing one's potential is often a hit-and-miss affair. Young Steve Redgrave's teacher noticed his big hands. So? Well, it's a clue that you're going to have a big body, which is just what is needed when a school is looking for a rowing eight. Three members of his school rowing club made it to the 1988 Olympics – that was some teacher.

Chris Packham was prompted by his junior school teacher to write to *Blue Peter* to ask about the location of Dartford Warblers (Dartford, perhaps?) and has been filmed poking around in hedgerows ever since.

Another fluke: by misreading the instructions at the top of the question paper, Terry Jones messed up the A level he needed to get into the university of his choice, only to end up at another where he met and teamed up with Michael Palin, fellow-Python-to-be.

The paths taken in these colourful lives resemble school food: sometimes nourishing, sometimes bin-worthy. Here is a handy morsel from Myleene Klass: she moved to a school where to hold your head high you needed to own a horse; she didn't, so she bought the sort of coat that you wore if you did. Science-hating Kathy Sykes listened carefully to the new teacher who advised her not to drop physics O level; she is now a broadcaster and Professor of Sciences and Society at Bristol University. Paula Radcliffe spent more time training than many students do studying – but she still went to the lectures, did the work and got a First. The worst pupils, who left school with no qualifications, often turn into the parents most liable to beg their children to get on with their homework.

One of the most reassuring tales comes from Queen guitarist Brian May. His father was most worried when Brian, after a successful school and university career, was finishing his PhD on interstellar dust – and suddenly declared he was abandoning both thesis and financial security by joining a band. It turned out that he was exchanging stardust for rock stardom and Queen got to the top – of Buckingham Palace during the Jubilee celebrations, in the case of their guitarist. Decades later Brian blew the dust off his thesis. It passed.

The lesson to be learnt from this is that there is a point where parents have to take a back seat as children work out the route of their lives and careers. This is not, of course, to say that we should allow four-year-olds to play on motorways if they feel like it, but that we have to let twenty-year-olds get behind the steering wheel. The one happy moment in *Babbitt*, Sinclair Lewis's 1922 novel about a prosperous American conformist who tries to kick over the traces, is when his son throws up his college career and becomes an engineer. Conversely, there are also novels to be written – and they surely have been – about lads who horrify parents by leaving jobs in engineering for a university place.

Whatever the new path taken, youngsters who start bands should be reminded that they are unlikely to make a living by playing lead guitar. Brian May had the rocket science to fall back on. So the parents who insist on qualifications are probably right too.

CHAPTER 1

NURSERY SEEDS

t's hard to detect promise in a playgroup. 'I always knew Miranda was going to be Prime Minister when I saw her re-arranging the spades in the sandpit into colour-coordinated groups.' No, probably not. We parents are kidding ourselves if we think we find signs of potential captains of industry, or even of small yachts. We have to wait.

It's like the journalist on the *Sunday Times* who handed his colleague (this, children, was back in the days of 'pieces of paper' and 'typewriters') the article he was working on and asked, 'What do you think of it so far?' There was one word on the otherwise empty sheet: 'The'. To this the response is 'Fine, as far as it goes,' or 'Try a slightly different angle.'

The kids in a kindergarten have scarcely got to the 'T' of their development, let alone the 'The'. They may take into adulthood only a single snapshot of memory from that period, like a lonely photo in an empty album. The picture may be fading and unreliable but it is what they are left with and it is important. Often it is not so much the incidents hanging around in the brain that are extraordinary but the fact that you remember so slight an event in the first place.

*　*　*

Playing with girls was a problem for Richard Whiteley when he went to Mrs Wighteman's kindergarten in Baildon, near Bradford. The future presenter of *Countdown* was one of a dozen toddlers who pottered about in a wooden shed in her garden.

'There was an Elsan chemical toilet and, in an effort to ingratiate myself with Sheila Biggs, who was crying, I put Felicity Norris's doll down it.' Unlike the doll, this enterprise did not go down very well and Richard learnt that you can't please all of the women all of the time.

He made up for this later by pleasing a lot of the women a lot of the time. I refer, of course, to the lady viewers who sent him those unsuitable ties as tokens of their affection. He was also referred to as 'Nightly Whiteley', to which he would reply, 'No, I'm Nearly Yearly.'

Our most eminent science fiction writer Brian Aldiss was also in trouble with the ladies at an early age:

> At Miss Mason's kindergarten in East Dereham, Norfolk, we discovered a delicious game. The boys were cows and the girls were milkmaids – and would 'milk' us. Unfortunately I was unwise enough to tell my mother and she rang the headmistress.

The dairy farm was closed down but there is sometimes a certain joyful sauciness in his stories that might be an echo of this early agricultural experience.

Krishnan Guru-Murthy was so affectionate that they called him 'Lover Boy'. It is not a term of endearment that is often used by his interviewees on *Channel 4 News* but it is how the staff thought of him at his playgroup. 'I used to hug and kiss the teacher and, if I forgot, I made my mother drive me back.'

'They were terrorists!' recalls actress Maria Friedman. She was referring not to the other kids at the kindergarten but to the staff, whom she had no desire at all to hug and kiss. After all, they put Sellotape on her mouth because she talked too much. She has since made up for having her voice stolen by putting it to good use, in, for example, *Casualty* and Andrew Lloyd Webber's musical *The Woman in White*.

Her family moved to England when she was five but her formative (or de-formative) years were spent in Germany, where her father was the lead violinist of the Bremen Philharmonic. While the teachers in question bore little resemblance to the Baader-Meinhof Gang who would soon be open for business, one can see why Maria might make the comparison.

Things did not improve in the season of goodwill. The 'terrorists' laid on a Father Christmas to help celebrate the day when the school reports came out. This turned out to be a mixed blessing. For a start, the reports were not sent to the family homes but read out there and then. Worse, Father Christmas bore two sacks: one with good presents for the A-list kids with good reports and the other with bad presents for the B-list with bad reports. The kindergarten's verdict on Maria's personality and performance was 'You're bossy and talk too much,' so there was no question of which bag would contain her Christmas present. Santa handed her a plastic frying pan.

From then on, it was downhill all the way as far as schools were concerned. Fortunately she had a wonderful mother, an art historian who lectured at the British Museum and could say, 'Don't they know anything about child psychology in Germany?' in five languages.

The millions of readers of the *Horrible Histories* series might perhaps form the impression that author Terry Deary is no fan of authority but a paid-up member of the Awkward Squad from birth. And the readers would be dead right.

> At kindergarten in Sunderland, I soon learnt that teachers were the enemy. I got a very nice Dinky Toy bus for my fourth birthday and was running it along my desk. The teacher called me to the front and got a cane out of the cupboard and I was beaten.

'I'm not bitter, you know…' he added bitterly.

Andrew Collins, the former editor of *Empire* and co-writer of *Not Going Out*, didn't give his playschool a chance. Keen on not going out even at that age, he shouted and screamed so loudly at playschool that he was taken away immediately and never went back.

There were tears too on Gail Porter's first day at nursery school in Edinburgh – her mother's – because she screamed so loudly she had to be driven away. After that, however, the little girl loved it and indeed her subsequent 'Big Schools'.

Oona King, who was a London MP until edged out by George Galloway, was another dissatisfied customer. She went to a north London nursery on a Tuesday and was presented with a plate of spinach. One doesn't have to be a child psychiatrist to work out how well that went down. Not at all, of course. Nonetheless, the next day she found herself sitting in front of a plate of spinach – the same plate of spinach. Incredible. The green slime was there again on Thursday, and on Friday, at which point her mother arrived and took her away.

After that, she had a great time at her schools. She does approve of nursery places being offered to all three- and four-year-olds – 'as long as there's no spinach!' And, one might add, the teacher is properly trained.

At least spinach is good for you. 'One of my school memories is being force-fed custard and throwing up,' said comedian Gina Yashere. 'I didn't touch custard again until I was about seventeen.'

Olympic breaststroke champion Duncan Goodhew found it difficult to keep, as it were, his head above water. 'I have fairly savage memories of Miss McTavish's in Middleton-on-Sea, West Sussex. I remember fidgeting. She put me in the corner and at one point she tied me to my chair.'

Elizabeth Filkin would not have stood for this nonsense. She is the former Parliamentary Ombudsman who, as a punishment for asking too many awkward questions of dodgy MPs, was told to reapply for her own job. She promptly walked out. This is exactly what she had done at her kindergarten in Keynsham, Somerset, where there seemed to be nothing on the syllabus except dancing.

To the horror of her mother, she declared, 'I'm not going back there!' on her first – and only – day. That was it until it was time for her to go to Keynsham Infants, an excellent establishment where dancing was less dominant.

Playwright Stephen Poliakoff went to a 'pre-prep' school in Chelsea. It closed down long ago but one episode has stayed in his mind ever since.

'I have a haunting memory of the headmaster's wife saying

goodbye to us and bursting into tears, which was the first time I had seen that happen to an adult; she died shortly afterwards.'

Booker Prize-winning novelist Penelope Fitzgerald looked back on her kindergarten years as being the only time she was really happy at school. Her schools after this were so awful that she could not even denounce them in her books, because the very thought of those freezing dorms cast her into a deep depression. Thank heavens, then, for her kindergarten: 'We walked over Hampstead Heath to a dairy to watch and draw cows.' (Yes, this was a long time ago; no good trying to order a daily pint there now.)

Another novelist, Clare Francis, remembers the elevating aspect of her kindergarten. The smallest children sat at the front and the benches behind rose up in tiers as if it was the auditorium of a tiny theatre. You ascended as you got older, being prevented from banging your head through the ceiling only by your transfer to the next school. This may or may not have given Clare her head for heights, but it is certainly a fact that she became acclimatised to shinning up masts as she sailed single-handedly across the Atlantic – the first British woman to do so.

Young Michael Rosen, our one-time Children's Laureate, never reached these heights, certainly not on the climbing frame at Tyneholme Nursery School in Wealdstone, Middlesex. 'I could never climb the chimney,' he admits. He couldn't pronounce it either, referring to it creatively as the 'chimbley-pock.' He was therefore particularly impressed by his friend Jimmy, who could cope with the word – but then Jimmy was upwardly mobile at an early age: 'He wore a suit and put his hands in his pockets, which at three or four I thought was very adult.'

Unlike Michael, presenter Dave Berry did manage to make it to the top of the climbing-frame at his kindergarten in Charlton, south-east London, which was quite a feat on the occasion when he deprived himself of vision by turning his balaclava the wrong way round and pretending he was Spiderman. He didn't see, therefore, the little boy who punched him smack in the face.

Ann Leslie had an ideal start for a foreign correspondent who was to report for the *Daily Mail* from over seventy countries, covering the fall of the Berlin Wall and the release of Nelson Mandela. 'My mother had many marvellous qualities but being maternal wasn't one of them. She preferred to have me off the premises.' Her father was in oil and the family lived in India. At the age of four, she was packed off to boarding school.

'I was always being put on huge, long trains. I went to so many boarding schools.' One could assume she became used to looking after herself from the title of her autobiography – *Killing My Own Snakes*.

Sara Peretsky, author of thrillers set in Chicago featuring feminist private eye V. I. Warshawski, grew up amid nature red in tooth and claw. At Cordley School in Lawrence, Kansas, she was so fond of her kindergarten teacher that she hated being sent out to play house with the other girls and just sat around waiting for playtime to be over. She was a loner – 'I think I grew up in the woods raised by wolves' – and didn't know how to play with other children, as opposed to wolf cubs.

Christopher Timothy, who is best known for looking after tamer animals in *All Creatures Great and Small*, began his education with a walk. He was born in Bala, north Wales, and was sent to a private tutor.

'I seem to remember walking to the tutor by myself at the age of four – and sometimes going into a church school on the way and being allowed to stay until someone noticed.'

The actor Corin Redgrave was another early walker. He went

to Westminster School *twice* – not on two days but in two differ-ent periods of his school life. He was three or four when he first went to that public school after it had been relocated during the war from its usual London premises to a very large old house in Herefordshire. For some reason it had been decided to set up a class for toddlers, which included not only Corin but his sister Vanessa, two of the three children of the actor Michael Redgrave. It was a long toddle to the school premises.

'We had been evacuated to Bromyard, three miles away, and I remember crying with the cold as we walked that long distance.' They returned to London in 1944 and he told me that he didn't think he went to school for a couple of years after that. He was not complaining.

The least stressful pre-school times ever are enjoyed by teenies who don't even have to travel anywhere to go to kindergarten, thanks to their parents who set one up in their own house. Roger Lloyd Pack's parents did just this in their South Kensington house as a way of economising on school fees, an important considera-tion for a couple who were, as their son would be, actors. (Roger continuously had to remind people that 'Trigger' wasn't actually his name, but that of his character in *Only Fools and Horses*.)

'Shadow Poet Laureate' Adrian Mitchell had two years of fun in his own house, which was where his mother held her kinder-garten according to the principles of Froebel. (Froebel? He was a progressive educator like Montessori. Montessori? She was a pro-gressive educator like Froebel. I discovered in my mid-twenties that I went to a Froebel primary. Or maybe it was Montessori.)

Oliver James, the clinical psychologist who earned the thanks of a grateful nation by making Peter Mandelson cry on his BBC2 series *The Chair*, had not one but two parents who were psy-choanalysts. His books include *They F*** You Up* and it was to avoid 'f***ing him up' that his own mother and father set up a nursery school in their home at the epicentre of analysis, St John's Wood, north London. Their worry was that, having three sisters, he would not otherwise be exposed to enough testosterone. 'Unfortunately all the children who came were girls.'

He may well have been exposed to quite enough testosterone – his own – to judge by his conduct at an Evelyn Waugh *Decline and Fall*-type prep school where his uncle was the headmaster. 'On my first day I launched an unprovoked attack on two older boys and had a great chunk of hair pulled from my head.' He then decided to **** off and somehow managed to give school a miss for a year.

Just one event from his kindergarten days remained engraved in Sir Terry Pratchett's memory. There was one kid who would these days be termed a 'difficult' child. When they were told to draw a picture of Goldilocks and the Three Bears, the little boy scribbled away with his red pencil to depict a theme not taken from the conventional telling of the tale. 'Goldilocks Burning up in the Fire' was the incendiary title he chose for his drawing. 'I remember thinking that the human brain was a very strange thing,' said Terry, whose own brain has created the wonderful *Discworld* book series but, sadly, developed Alzheimer's.

On the one hand, it is possible that Barbara Dickson may not have been a very nice little girl: 'When my mother was pregnant with my brother, she tried to send me to a kindergarten at the age of three but the principal said I wasn't a very nice little girl because I put my fingers in my ears during the morning hymn.' On the other hand, it might have been her musical sensibilities (she has an MBE for services to music and her hit singles include 'I Know Him So Well') kicking in at this early age.

'The only thing I remember about my kindergarten in the hall of St Peter's Church in Gorleston, Norfolk, is having cookies and milk while a teacher played the piano,' said Myleene Klass, former member of Hear'Say and a classical pianist. 'We put up our hand if we knew what was being played – "Twinkle, Twinkle, Little Star", for example.' She brought the tune back into her life by performing it on *Music for Mothers*, her first album since having a baby. She points out that this is a pretty classy nursery rhyme, being based on an arrangement by Mozart. It sounds like a good one for pregnant mothers to play to their foetuses.

Letchmore Heath in Hertfordshire was where *Village of the Damned* was filmed (it's about alien children and my partner was in it, as one of the earthlings) but there is nothing damnable about the place itself, or the nursery school where novelist Joanna Briscoe was among the tiny pupils. It is no one's fault that the single memory she has of her nursery is one of those sad, awkward recollections that we are lumbered with, in spite of all the happy events enjoyed during the same period. Needing her mother, as one does, she informed her teacher that 'I want Carol' – she called her parents by their Christian names – and was relieved to be told 'She's over by the doll's house.' However, she was immediately disappointed: it was not her mother but a little girl named Carol who was playing with the dolls.

Michael Palin has a more neutral but equally clear memory of the first day of his travels through private education, which began at the kindergarten attached to Birkdale Preparatory School. He recalls 'the very dark brown paint of the converted house of a Sheffield steel owner; Miss Fossdike taking my hand; the doors swinging to behind my mother.' Early on in his nine years there, he enjoyed geography and maps; one project involved colouring in the rocks beneath the throbbing surface of Sheffield. The series producer involved in Michael's first documentary, Roger

Laughton, was in the year above. The old toddler network. It must be something in the water. Or the rocks.

Oddly enough for a rapper, J-Rock of Big Brovaz had a brief experience of a highly privileged education. He was about three when he was chauffeured to school in Washington, DC, where his father was the ambassador for Ghana. We must hope that he made the most of the high life while it was there, because his family went downmarket after that and in his teens he was to live in an area he describes as 'very ghetto' where he had to carry a gun. (Did he use it? 'Not really,' he replies – ever the diplomat.)

If you had to look for an under-five education that was both privileged and yet diametrically opposed to the J-Rock experience, you might well point to Gelek Rimpoche, the great-nephew of the thirteenth Dalai Lama. Born in Lhasa, Tibet, he was picked out shortly after his birth as a possible reincarnation of the Panchan Lama, Number Two to the Dalai Lama. At the age of three, however, he was downgraded, decreed to be the reincarnation of an abbot: 'I'm not among the highest lamas but not the lowest: upper-middle-class in British terms!'

Although he was, theologically speaking, practically of *Downton Abbey* status, he began his education as a monk by living in a cave with his teacher. He had one-to-one tuition; he couldn't yet read, so, at an age when British kids would be hearing nursery rhymes, he listened to and repeated long Buddhist prayers and mantras. He perfected the art of sleeping not only while standing up but while reciting his homework, a skill from which many of us would have greatly benefitted during our teenage years.

In these less innocent days, it seems incredible that a three-year-old girl would be sent off to kindergarten in the charge of only a five-year-old brother. Yet this is how crime novelist Minette Walters began her educational career, when their mother put them on the bus to Hill Side in Scarborough. 'We wore labels with our names and address on them in case we got lost en route.' Paddington Bear springs to mind – and not in a good way. Still, she learnt to read, so the worrying trek paid off.

After briefly being a latchkey kid at grammar school, Minette was sent to a boarding school sixty miles away from the home of her mother, who rarely visited. Fittingly, the uniform here resembled the dress of Orphan Annie. 'I don't think our relationship recovered.'

'I went on a speech strike.' Simon Schama's revelation about his early vow of silence surprised me. It would have astonished his French teacher at secondary school, who called him 'the gasbag'. It would also astonish all who admire his fluency in *A History of Britain* and his other BBC2 series. Yet when he was very young, he got fed up with being wheeled out by his proud parents to show off his incredible memory. He could remember everything. When he was at an age when merely reading the words on the labels of potted plants would have been pretty smart, his idea of a good time was memorising the Latin names, a skill which, to his regret, has since departed.

He dug in his little heels and refused to be the Mr Memory – or rather, Master Memory – of Westcliff-on-Sea. He refused to utter a word, except to the gardener (presumably to make sure that the potted plants kept coming) who was sworn to secrecy. His parents decided he must be mad and packed him off to a psychiatrist, who asked, 'Why are we so silent?' Simon refused to answer.

Some of us missed out on the nursery and kindergarten scene. When broadcaster Anna Ford was three, she wondered where her brother Adam went every day. Pooh Bear had the same query about Christopher Robin, whose front door had a message stating 'Gon Out Backson', later replaced by the more correct 'Gone

Out Back Soon' which showed that the local infants' school in the 100 Acre Wood was up to scratch.

The Fords lived in the vicarage half a mile from the village with the pedestrian name of Boot in what is now Cumbria. 'I followed him up the road to Boot Primary School but the teacher said that, as I was three, I would have to come back when I was four, so I sat down on the step and she gave me a crayon and paper.' Anna wrote 'Back Next Year' on it, or would have done if she could have spelt it.

Bernard Hill realised he was missing out on the school action and tried to go a year early. Like Frodo in *The Lord of the Rings* (Bernard was in the film but not as a hobbit) sneaking into Mordor, the eager four-year-old slipped into the stream of five-year-olds in his street heading for St John Bosco in Moss Side, Manchester. The priest with the register blew his cover, however, and promptly sent him home: 'No, you don't come this year, Bernard.' What is the opposite of truanting, that is, going to school when you shouldn't be? Anyway, no punishments were involved. Those, as we shall see, would come later.

Shirley Anne Field acted in a series of noteworthy films – *The Entertainer*, *Alfie* and *My Beautiful Laundrette* among them – but her earliest education was also notable for the fact that she went to 'big school' before she went to a nursery school. She was born in the East End of London just before the beginning of World War Two, which, as well as being incredibly dangerous, was not a very good career move.

'My dad was missing in action – or just missing – and my mother had no one to look after me.' While the poor woman carted her baby son with her to the factory where she did her war work, Shirley's two older sisters took her to their school, where she sat out of the way at the back of the class. When her sisters were old enough to be evacuated, Shirley went to a nursery school at the end of the road. Until it was bombed. Fortunately she herself was soon evacuated and went to an elegant nursery near Godalming, Surrey. Here they had to waddle across gravel wearing nothing but sun bonnets. This was supposed to toughen them up. 'I don't know if it did; now I wear shoes when I walk across gravel.'

After two years of nude gravel endurance, she was ready for 'big school' again, this time in her own right. The gravelly matron presumably thought that the mother of naughty Shirley was not up to coping with her, so she arranged for the National Children's Homes to care for her instead. The five-year-old was packed off in her new clothes to her new school, travelling by herself through a war zone – i.e. England during World War Two – expecting to be met by her family. It wasn't in fact her family who were waiting on the platform but the head of the 400-strong school who took her to Edgworth, north of Bolton. And Shirley Anne remained there for a decade.

The differences between kindergarten, play school, nursery and nursery class need not detain us here. The point is that for many this is when their boat was launched into the educational rapids. If the water is too choppy, this will be a bad start for the whole voyage. With a bit of luck, these will be quite slow rapids. Anyway, under-fives don't have to turn up every morning and afternoon; they don't by law have to be in a kindergarten at all. Toddlers can toddle off until a primary school has them legally in its grip. But it's still a crying (or grizzling) shame when things go wrong.

It's wonderful when they have an enjoyable and educational time (in that order), a useful preparation for the years of being gathered together every day with an adult who isn't their parent and children who aren't their siblings. And for some it is particularly precious: those for whom it is the only form of schooling they actually liked.

CHAPTER 2

THE FIRST DAY OF THE REST OF YOUR SCHOOL LIFE

This was it. It wasn't like playgroup, where you could take the next pedal-car out. This was it for the following decade. At least. Make that two decades if, instead of quitting classrooms as soon as is legally possible, you clung on to university for a second degree or even a PhD.

It is easy to forget how confusing everything is in those early days. Coming from a home where cooking was pretty basic, children's author Jacqueline Wilson was reduced to tears by the school dinners: she'd never come across anything as sophisticated as stew or mince.

On the plus side, some of the experiences in this new world are joyful and stay with you forever. The first day I went into Byron House, Cambridge, was also the first day I came across Pooh Bear. The class were sitting in a semi-circle while the teacher read the first story in *The House at Pooh Corner*. This became one of my favourite books and I re-read it for some time. When I say 'for some time', I mean that in my first year as a student we used to sit around and read it into a rare tape recorder which one of my technically-minded friends possessed. We all took different parts and I was the narrator, which required less acting ability. My second job was on *Punch* magazine, the one much earlier held by A. A. Milne; I like to think that the venerable roll-top desk where I sat had been where Pooh's creator sat years before.

Unlike me, Pat Cash is not one to sit around, being as fast a mover on his first day at school as he became on the tennis court later. Having delivered him to Our Lady of Good Counsel Primary in Melbourne, his mother suddenly saw him shooting past her on the way home. (If this had been a tennis match, the score would have been fifteen-love to Pat.) She caught him (fifteen-all) and took him back to the care of Our Lady (fifteen-thirty). The sympathetic teacher put him by the window so that he could look out at the world but he crawled through it and scampered away (thirty-all). He was caught again (thirty-forty) and given some good counsel: 'My mum said she would belt me within an inch of my life.' (Game, set and match to Mrs Cash.) Fortunately he soon got to like school after that.

Sue Townsend lasted only slightly longer on her first day at Glen Hills Primary, near Leicester: 'I went home at playtime. I thought that was it. I thought I'd stayed a fairly long time, being bored and shouted at.' The late author of the Adrian Mole yarns was not best pleased to discover that there was a lot more where that came from. 'It got worse.'

The catchment area included a posh neighbourhood and other people's fathers worked, for example, at the Foreign Office, and not, like hers, in a factory. She was one of the 'children from the rabbit-hutches', i.e. the enclave of prefabs on the unfashionable side of the main road, and was not as well spoken, well dressed or well moneyed.

Her legs were slapped as a punishment for not being able to read. She associated this somehow with the Queen, whose picture happened to be just above where she sat, and she was a republican for all her life. The slapping (unsurprisingly) did not instil the ability to read, but the mumps did. At eight and a half she was off school for three weeks and turned to some *Just William* books from a jumble sale: she worked out what the captions to the illustrations meant. Then she was off into the landscape of the printed word as fast as William's mongrel (fittingly named 'Jumble' in view of the source of the books) after a rabbit.

'I came home at lunchtime on my first day,' says Graeme Garden, one-third of the classic comedy series *The Goodies*. 'My mother was very surprised.' It was nothing to do with 'the really smashing village school' in Broughton, near Preston. It was just that when the classes stopped for lunch, he assumed that this was it for the day, which is what you would expect from the creator of Radio 4's *I'm Sorry I Haven't a Clue*.

So, singer and actor Toyah Willcox, how was your first taste of school? 'It was possibly the worst day of my life.' At four and a half she was dressed in 'this excruciatingly uncomfortable uniform' that she hated. Her mother drove her to Edgbaston Church of England College for Girls and left her there but, since Toyah simply screamed and screamed, she had to come back. Toyah clung to her.

It didn't help that 'the spinster who was our teacher' was without any appearance of warmth. It also didn't help that the lunch of sprouts and sausages was, in words that we hope Toyah didn't use at the time, 'f***ing horrible'. Finally, when her mother returned at the end of the day to collect her, Toyah cheered up: 'I thought that was it, that there was no more school.'

There was in fact more school, fourteen years of it, and she detested the uniform every day.

As Toyah showed, it was an easy mistake to make and young Trevor McDonald made the same one. His father took him to his primary school and popped back later to make sure his son was OK, thus giving him the wrong impression.

'I thought it was a one-off; I'd done it and could retire to a useful career somewhere else.' If anchoring ITN counts as a useful career, Trevor has certainly had one, but first there was the second day at primary school, and the third, not to mention the scholarship exams for secondary school and the place at University College of the West Indies. Education wasn't a barrel of laughs and all the while his poor father worried that his son wasn't headed for a 'proper job' like a lawyer or doctor.

Years later, when Mr McDonald Senior saw youngsters crowding round Trevor for his autograph, he finally accepted it hadn't all been a complete waste of time: 'I hadn't become a total vagrant – or if I had I was a well-known one.'

Splott sounds like the sound effect of an ink pellet scoring a direct hit on a teacher's bald head but is in fact a district in Cardiff, hence Splott Primary School where a rival newsreader on the other channel, John Humphrys, sat at its old, old desks.

'On one of my first days there, I can remember not knowing

where the loos were and not liking to ask – with the resultant disaster when I failed to reach the safety of my home. My mother was very sympathetic.' We've all been there and our mothers were very sympathetic; at least, mine was.

Botanist and broadcaster David Bellamy had no sympathy for a mishap: 'On my first day at school, I shared a double desk with a little girl; she wet the seat and I got the blame.'

There was more to come to make kids wet their knickers. When he was six, the war started and Chatsworth Road Infants in Cheam, Surrey, was in 'Doodlebug Alley'. If your friends missed school, it wouldn't be because of a tummy-ache; it would be because of a direct hit on their house by a flying bomb. A lot of lessons took place in the shelters.

'Then I went to Cheam Juniors, 300 yards away, which had a motley set of teachers who taught us well in impossible conditions.' One teacher had been in the Indian army and the best lesson was when he showed David's class pictures of heads chopped off and impaled by the 'wicked Indians', which would have taken their minds off the 'wicked Germans' flying above them.

Margaret Drabble could have been put off education for life: no Quaker school, no Cambridge place, no graduate wife novels, and no editorship of *The Oxford Companion to Literature* to help out with our crossword puzzles. Her delightful school in the village of East Harding near Pontefract had two teachers, one for the smaller kids and one for the larger children.

She turned up on her first day under the impression that they would be cutting things up and sticking them down – yet the day passed without any action on the sticking-down front! This made her all the more determined to return on Day Two to check it out. This gap in the curriculum was then remedied and young Margaret did indeed get stuck in, both to the handicraft on offer and to the beginning of her sparkling career at school and university.

Malcolm McLaren's first day at William Patten Primary in Stoke Newington, London, was also his last for some time. The Sex Pistols' manager-to-be, he was brought up by his Portuguese-Jewish grandmother, who was by way of being the black sheep, or ewe, of the family. He states that she was related to Danny Kaye, although she is unlikely to have been one of the relatives invited to the Kaye family gatherings. She gave Malcolm two pieces of cotton wool (to block up his ears if he didn't like what the teacher was saying) and a piece of advice (turn your face to the wall anyway).

He went one better. He crawled under the desk, from where he was dragged out, clinging to the leg of a little girl.

'I may have sunk my teeth into her thigh,' he adds ingenuously, as if it were the kind of thing one might not have noticed one was doing at the time.

He did not trouble any school with his presence for two years, which would have suited everyone. His grandmother, assisted by a private tutor, taught him to read and write – and read he did, first *Jane Eyre*, which took him a year, and then a facsimile edition of *A Christmas Carol*. This had Dickens's original crossings-out, as his grandmother, who becomes more intriguing the longer the grown-up Malcolm talks about her, declared that mistakes are very important in the creative process.

When he was eight, it seemed a good time to give school another whirl, this time without the cotton wool in the ears. Granny, whose father was a diamond dealer, paid the fees for Avigdor School in north London. These may not have been very high, as he remembers it as being situated in a prefab building resembling an RAF training barracks converted into one of today's less successful free schools. The afternoon schedule concentrated on religious instruction, so Malcolm tended to give it a miss, not being desperate to learn Hebrew. To his credit, he does not seem to have bitten anyone this time.

Phill Jupitus has a more architectural memory of his own Day One of education. 'I vividly remember walking from the pub (it wasn't a pre-school drink – we lived above it) on the first day at Northbury Infants and Juniors in Barking, Essex. When I went into the classroom I remember running my finger along the dado rail.' He defined the latter as 'a row of tiles three feet above the ground'. Not for nothing is he one of the humorous polymaths of *QI*. Some of us may be vague on the definition but a dado is indeed a moulding thirty-six inches above the floor; it sticks out and protects the wall from chairs pushed against it.

The rail was only the tiniest of details but it stuck in his mind over the years. It also stuck to the wall and was still there when, in a visit packed with emotion, he went back to open a new wing (the Jupitus Extension?) a few years ago.

'School felt like playtime with an informational element,' which sounds like a winning combination worthy of an Absolutely Outstanding classification from Ofsted. 'History was my favourite subject. Being told about Romans and Saxons was a new concept: things had happened *before* the Second World War.'

This historical revelation has left him with a special interest in buying old coins. 'Tactile history. I like beat-up ones. Billy Bragg gave me a coin (he got two for the price of three) from 800 BC with a crude eagle on the back.'

(Let's leave aside the bit about *duo* for the price of *tres*, as we Ancient Romans put it, which I take to be a *jockus*. Without casting aspersions on the worthy singer Billy Bragg, one has to ask if the 'crude eagle' is intended to be the symbol carried by

Rome's legions. If so, one has to point out that according to tradition, Rome was not founded until nearly fifty years later than the alleged coin, in 753 BC, by Romulus and Remus. Or a wolf. Stephen Fry would know.)

Barbara Trapido, author of *Brother of the More Famous Jack*, had an early lesson in the language of apartheid when her family moved to South Africa. On her first day at the all-female, all-white Berea Road Primary School in Durban, they were opening their packed lunches when one of the girls asked, 'Would you rather a native boy [African] or a coolie [Asian] made your sandwiches?'

Still, there was a spiritual element to the school. This was where she found God, in the sense that she had never heard of Him before and now someone would come into the classroom once a day and stick pictures of Jesus on a green beige board. 'I was enchanted,' she recalls.

Publicist Max Clifford's first day at All Saints Junior School in Wimbledon was a PR disaster. 'I had a fight with a boy called Andrew Baxter and he got a bloody nose. He turned out to be the headmaster's son.' He was more successful on behalf of the other kids, however, his first ever clients: 'I had a creative imagination. I would make an excuse for someone who was late or teach them how to get away with it.' Unfortunately, as an adult he has recently failed to use his imagination sufficiently to get away with it on his own behalf.

Fortunately, primary schools seem to leave happier memories than secondary schools. That is not a national scientific survey. It is not even a survey of the hundreds of people I've interviewed. It is just my impression.

Take comedian Phil Cool, who was lucky in both his primary schools: 'Sunny days, flowers and sometimes doing lessons on

the bowling green.' That slightly made up for his clouded memories of his secondary modern.

Maybe primary schools seem to be on the sunnier side of the
street simply because distance adds something to the view and
the memories of our experiences as a five-year-old are that much
further away. Also, there are a lot fewer exams.

CHAPTER 3

PRIMARY COLOURING IN

S
chools are a bit of a shock to a young child. Imagine that you have scarcely stumbled across the concept of work – and then suddenly you are conscripted into an incomprehensible job in which most people are bigger and more clued-up than you. Some of them hit you. Then, after several years of getting the hang of it, you are whisked off to another place of employment where the people are even bigger and brainier, possibly hitting you harder. And there is no question of resignation or a union to complain to.

Substitute 'school' for 'work' and you understand that our

kids may wonder why we conscript them to primary and secondary, or preparatory and independent, school of our (not
their) choice.

It helps that there are many more primary than secondary
schools and therefore there is more likely to be one nearer a
young child's home. David Threlfall of *Shameless* fame lived so
near to his first school that he walked home for lunch. He once
walked back in break as well but that was his mistake. The novelist Iain Banks once ran home when he was upset; it was all of
fifty yards. You can easily walk several times that distance *inside*
secondary schools.

'I don't want to go to school, Mum,' is a heartfelt poem by
Pam Ayres about a child who would rather stay at home with
her mother and toy duck. It ties in with an early memory of hers
about being terrorised at her Church of England primary in Stan-
ford-in-the-Vale, situated in the Vale of the White Horse, and it
is not as idyllic as the location. Her memory is of a big boy at
the top of the school telling her 'I'm going to *poke* fun at you',
emphasising his point in a tactile way by *poking* (you see what
he did there?) her in her bony chest.

'There was much trumpeting' – without the trumpets, which
are expensive – 'when the school library opened. It was only one
shelf.' However, it had precisely what Pam wanted, which was a
book about ponies. *Wish for a Pony* was the first book that she
read for pleasure and it made her look for other books by the
same author. 'Admittedly, Monica Edwards's books were a bit
snobby and made me look down my nose at our council house.'

If it is any consolation to Pam, it occurs to me that traditional
school yarns from Billy Bunter onwards have made everyone feel
their upbringing was downmarket, as they generally feature the
son of a lord in the same dorm who asks them back to a stately

home with a kitchen garden taking up most of the West and North Ridings. Your parents could live in Blenheim Palace and yet these topping tales about sporting heroes at St Chappie's would make you wish your mummy and daddy weren't quite so bourgeois.

Miss Edmonds was the teacher who introduced Pam to Monica Edwards's equine oeuvre. There were three other teachers, one for each of the four classes, and Miss Bedford, who taught Pam's class, had the fearsome reputation of being a tartar and very strict.

'One day I inadvertently tore my exercise book by trapping it in the lid of my desk. I was so terrified that I feigned all sorts of illnesses and for weeks I was away more than I was at school. My mother thought I had appendicitis and got the doctor out.'

Eventually the game was up. On one of the days when Pam actually did go to school, Miss Bedford asked, 'Pamela, will you bring your exercise book?' Pam burst into tears but the now not-so-tartarish teacher merely remarked, 'Oh, that's what it's all about,' and repaired it with sticky tape.

Brian May will go down in musical and monarchical history as one of the few guitarists to have played on the roof of Buckingham Palace: Queen playing for the Queen, the high point of the Jubilee. At Cardinal Road Infants in Feltham, Middlesex, the summit of their ambitions was to sit on the air-raid shelter next to the school. The girls had a game called 'I wish I was …' and one day Brian chipped in with his contribution: 'I wish I was a bum.' He had no idea what it meant.

He soon did: 'We are all going inside,' the teacher snapped. 'Brian May has just used a rude word.'

Life, in the shape of Cardinal Road Infants, had another lesson for him. Few rock guitarists apart from Brian have a PhD on 'zodiacal dust' or indeed any subject, and he was a bright lad even then.

> I remember winning a first prize and being given a book, *Black Beauty*. This coincided with a wart being cut off my finger in a clinic attached to the school. It was agony and I went home in pain. My mother decided to read *Black Beauty* to me and I found it so sad. I found out that there are some things in life that can't be made better.

More cheerful reading matter came at Hanworth Road Juniors: 'My favourite thing was rainy days, when we could stay inside to read comics such as *Eagle*, featuring Dan Dare, Pilot of the Future – a great inspiration.

Brian was good at science and built a small telescope. This school was less welcoming to his other consuming interest: 'Music was my friend from a very young age but music at school wasn't a very good experience for me; we were forced to listen to classical music and told what to think of it.' Some of the lads used to hide round the back of the bike shed – but not, he says now, for cigarettes or girls. The illicit activity involved their guitars, not allowed at school.

Corin Redgrave had much worse luck than Brian May when, at the age of six, he was sent with his sister Vanessa to a state primary. 'This was difficult; my father was now a well-known film star and we were treated as oddities,' he says. They were taken away after a term. Then followed a year of what he remembered as 'an ideal form of school and teaching' in which a Miss Glascott taught eight or nine children in a vicarage. The class included Corin, Vanessa and Matthew, the son of Alec Guinness: three children of two of the most talented actors of their generation, all of whom became actors in turn.

A much bumpier educational ride was the lot of young Oliver James. Coming up to five, he decided to give school a miss for a year before starting again more successfully. He then followed his sisters to a 'truly ludicrous' school called Miss Renee's off Gloucester Road, west London, where they made no attempt to teach you anything.

'There were no boys really, apart from the one whose arm I broke during the daily walk in Kensington Gardens.' (That is one way of remembering your fellow pupils: oh yes, the boy whose arm I broke.) It was beginning to appear that it was the schools, not his parents, who were f***ing him up.

'My father decided that if I was going to pass the exams to Eton, knowledge was required.' (As we'll see later, this was not the conclusion reached by Ranulph Fiennes, for whom Eton was the easy option.) Oliver's father sent him off to an establishment stricter than Miss Renee's, that is, Westminster Under School. 'In my class there were five sons of MPs.' All of them doing better than him.

'My academic performance was atrocious. The head wrote in his report that I was mentally handicapped.' The solution was thought to be a boarding school in Kent, though, if this was supposed to be the answer to his problems, perhaps the wrong question was being asked. Once there, he showed no improvement: 'I was pretty unpopular, being obnoxious, violent and selfish.'

As if things weren't bad enough, he joined the football team, 'and who should come to coach us but Jeffrey Archer'. There then followed a crammer in Sussex of incredible strictness: 'Before breakfast you had to learn twenty Latin and twenty French words.' This seems to have done the trick. 'By some miracle I managed to pass the entrance exam to Eton.'

Actor Siân Phillips also had a rocky start. She grew up in a monoglot household: 'Everything was in Welsh.' This is why she refused to go to a school named Dan-y-Graig in Pontardawe: 'Its name means "under the rock" and it was indeed under what seemed, at the age of five, a massive cliff which I was afraid was going to fall down.' She was frogmarched there but went on hunger strike and her mother finally took her away.

Her fellow Welsh actor Harry Secombe had just a minor hiccup. Brought up on a council estate in Swansea and knighted for services to entertainment in the ground-breaking Goons, Harry did well at school, as did his sibling Secombes: 'We were voracious readers. My brother read *Decline and Fall* when he was ten. My mother didn't allow us to read at table,' he said, adding, 'so I read the sauce bottle.' He had scarlet fever when he was seven. 'My grandfather bought me the Waverley novels, with very small print, to read in hospital.' Walter Scott's books take some getting through, particularly when you are seven and ill. They can't have helped the eyesight problems associated with scarlet fever, either.

'When I came out, I kept getting thumped because I couldn't see the blackboard. I can still remember the first day I got my steel-rimmed spectacles, that wonderful feeling of being able to see things clearly.'

Now less optically challenged, he was able to sit the scholarship exam to Dynevor School. 'My brother was already there; as a prefect he used to leave the back door open for me when I was late. My sister won a scholarship to the girls' secondary school; she married a headmaster,' Harry explained, adding, 'after a suitable interval.'

Meera Syal, co-writer and star of *Goodness Gracious Me*, enjoyed Perry Hall Infants and Juniors in Wednesfield, Wolverhampton, not least because of being able to go with her mother, a teacher there. 'There were only two other Asian kids at the school, both boys, and there was some teasing, as there was with fat girls and boys who wore glasses.' She noticed that in Nativity plays the black kids were always the Three Wise Men – never angels – and that in history lessons India was always taught through the prism of the glorious Raj.

She kept a diary for three of her years at school. 'I've got all the diaries – and they're Sellotaped so no one can read them.' A couple of situations appear verbatim in her first novel, *Anita and Me*. 'When I cut my finger in the playground, some of the children were amazed that my blood was red. And when the teacher asked, "Why is it the Black Country?" one kid said – not maliciously – "Is it because there are so many darkies there?"'

Comedian Phil Cool does not need to consult a diary to give a vivid description of a significant moment at St Mary's in Chorley, Lancashire. 'I've ended up drawing with my body, really. I describe myself as a stand-up chameleon.' He was always the best at drawing, on paper, that is.

'I remember the head walking past one of my drawings pinned up in the corridor, doing a double-take and then coming into our classroom, where there was an English lesson going on, and asking who had drawn it. He then began to give an art lesson, using cartoon faces.' That sounds like some head teacher. 'He was Bernard Grime: how's that for a name?' (Phil obviously takes names seriously, as he has switched from the Phil Martin he was born with.)

The downside of the school was an eternal love triangle involving Jeannette Flyn, who hated him. 'I was keen on her but she fancied a boy called John McCarthy, who wanted nothing to do with her. I was *a* class clown but *the* best clown was McCarthy.' If it's any consolation to Phil, these days he is probably a better clown than his young rival in love.

Comedian and writer Rhona Cameron was top in English at

her primary school in Musselburgh near Edinburgh. 'I was good at art, although I didn't do any art for a year because a crazy teacher hated me and would say, "Rhona – corner!" as soon as she came in.'

She made up for that in her teens: 'I was going to evening classes and doing naked paintings of my boyfriend and a girl I was sleeping with; the teacher put them away in a high cupboard.' A very high cupboard, one hopes, for the sake of all concerned.

It is hard to say whether the first school attended by cartoonist Michael Heath counts as a kindergarten or an infants' school. Not that it matters either way; he learnt nothing. He was evacuated to Devon at four and a half when the war started.

'The village school didn't do lessons but we were sat down in a room and an old guy – all the young ones were away being shot at – gave us the comic sections of the US newspapers. Then they bombed the poor old village, so that was it: we were sent back to London.' At six, he found himself at Hampstead Hill School with its playground on the roof, not the best situation during the Blitz. The children would sit down in the classroom and the sirens would go off. They were supposed to take cover in the basement but when bombs are exploding you think your house is being flattened and your parents have been killed. 'I ran home through the shrapnel and incendiaries. Then we were sent back to Devon.'

The title of his strip in *The Spectator*, where he is cartoon editor, refers back to this time: 'Battle for Britain', though one shouldn't stress the point too much because (a) it's very contemporary, being all about people losing their iPhones and (b) Michael would laugh and put you in a cartoon.

He was sent to other odd schools: 'No one attempted to teach me anything.' He does remember being sent to the school gym, where the lights were put out and they saw free Ministry of Information films, doubtless invaluable for soldiers and sailors, on subjects such as Gonorrhoea – Just Say No! Then there was one about the removal of a kneecap; he passed out.

Again, he was given American comic sections to look at. He concentrated on drawing, possibly because he thought that drawing was writing. He was sent into an exam room but couldn't do anything. By the time he was twelve, he was keen to be able to read and write. He managed to get hold of a copy of H. G. Wells's collected short stories that he pretended to read, just as his baby daughter was to do with her picture books while making 'blah-blah' sounds.

'My real education was courtesy of Lord Reith. On *Children's Hour* I picked up on all sorts of intelligent stuff: music, plays, *Uncle Mac*, *Toytown* and *Norman and Henry Bones – Boy Detectives*.'

As her father was in the Navy and consequently was steered all over the place, Ann Widdecombe had gone to five schools by the time she was eleven. This rapid movement had its advantages:

> I was at my first school, Bridge Mary Primary in Gosport, Hants., for only a couple of months. I hated it; it was the only school I did not enjoy. There was a horrible girl who used to pinch me surreptitiously. Also, my grandmother, who lived with us, had taught me all my times tables but she told me 'Twice one is two', and at school they said, 'Two ones are two'. This made maths difficult to deal with.

At seven, Bernard Hill went to St Margaret Mary's Primary in Manchester where 'I was bullied and got my lunch nicked … by the bigger girls. Girls round our way were tougher than boys; they still are.'

Christopher Hitchens was an extremely violent man, though only in print and debate. No one was safe: his books included ferocious denunciations of both Henry Kissinger and Mother Teresa. He did not beat about the bush in his account of his education.

'My first school, Inchkeith (near the naval base at Rosyth, Fife, where my father was posted) was so brutal that my parents took me away. It was the rule of the cudgel and they noticed that I flinched every time an adult came near me.'

His next school was also something of a war zone. 'Camdean was a Protestant school with a Catholic school over the road and every lunchtime there was a pogrom.' (The word 'pogrom' has Jewish connotations but we take his point.) 'On my first day I was hit by a slate between the eyes.' The scar he acquired was with him all his life.

When the family moved to Plymouth, he went to a school where a teacher, noticing his high reading age, took trouble with him. Also there were no pitched battles. This was followed by Mount House in Tavistock, a school for sons of naval officers where the dormitories were named after admirals. He found he could cope with being a boarder, though he could have done without quite so many cold baths and runs.

'There was a certain amount of random terror from the mood swings of the headmaster but I was quite good in lessons, particularly English and history, the headmaster's favourite subjects.'

Playwright Stephen Poliakoff had five years of appalling misery at a prep school in Kent that had a similar name to, but no connection with, a famous public school.

'It was an Evelyn Waugh world; the headmaster had lost a leg on D-Day or Dunkirk and you could hear his wooden leg as he walked around the school.' It was a 'harsh, Spartan regime' and some of the teaching was on the malevolent side: 'A slightly

Dickensian ridiculing of children in front of the class at an age when they have very little defence against sarcasm. It has given me a rebellious streak and a suspicion of all forms of authority.'

Tony Robinson went to a small private school with the sort of posh name that sounds as if it prepares boys for Winchester. 'In fact, it wasn't a school of "fag" and "tuck".' It was the sort of school that Baldrick could have gone to or even set up in the first place.

There are things about a school that you learn only after you have left. In the case of 'St Baldrick's' he heard of the ultimate fate of the teacher who terrified him the most. ('She was such a bully, with that cold contempt for children.') The story was that she died penniless because the school had not paid her National Insurance stamps. Her pupils may not have been too upset about this.

It is no surprise that the author of *The Dangerous Book for Boys* was accused of breaking a window at his primary school. Conn Iggulden hadn't done it but the headmistress of Sacred Heart Roman Catholic Primary in Ruislip, Middlesex, snapped, 'I know when little boys are lying.' Meeting her years later on a station platform, he accosted her with, 'You won't remember me but twenty years ago you accused me of breaking a window.'

'I'm sorry,' she replied, 'I don't know who you are.' Having been a teacher himself, he accepts that these things are much stronger in the minds of children than of adults. The headmistress was not, needless to say, his favourite teacher. That was a Mrs Brown. 'I found out twenty-five years later that she'd kept a poem of mine. I was fascinated by words from an early age. I would tell my father stories to send him to sleep.'

Like Michael Heath, Edward de Bono spent the war listening for the sound of enemy bombs, but in his case they were falling on Malta. 'At seven I went as a boarder to St Edward's College, similar to an English public school, a quarter of a mile from the docks. The school was evacuated during the war to a building in Mdina, half a mile from the main fighter base.' This might seem safer from enemy attack only by the difference of between a half and a quarter of a mile. Perhaps three-quarters of a mile might have been a bit smarter? Apparently not: 'Although we could hear the whistle of the bombs, it felt perfectly safe because the Stuka dive-bombers were very accurate.' So as long as the German pilots had completed their bombing homework and dropped their lethal loads at the correct angle, the lads had nothing to worry about. This might have been an early example of the 'Lateral Thinking' that Edward was to champion later – 'Vertical Thinking'.

'I used to come first in nearly every subject,' he says, adding modestly, 'I was from an English-speaking family, which would have helped in essays.' His lowest mark ever was when he was seven: 54 per cent in art. His drawing deserved more, in his opinion. He moved up twice to a higher class and therefore much larger boys: 'I always made friends with the big bully of the class.' One lad who bullied him married his sister – not when they were still at school, obviously. Edward had another way of ingratiating himself: Lateral Escaping.

'At eleven, I made an escape route which went underground into our air-raid shelters, then the shelters of the girls' school next door, and finally the public shelters, coming up in the town half a mile away. It was never discovered.' If the bigger boys wanted to go out drinking, they had to come to him for one of his skeleton keys – an unfortunate term, in view of all that diving-bombing.

Sir Chris Bonington was shipped out of London as the war was starting. Having shinned up tree trunks in a Hampstead Montessori establishment – early training for his Everest ascent – he was sent at five to a boarding school in Kent. This school in turn was shifted further away from any invading tanks and he ended up in Kirkby Lonsdale, Cumbria.

'I was quite happy at Kirkby Lonsdale…' he recalled – and one suspects a 'but' is on the way. It is: '…but, at about the age of seven, I masterminded a Great Escape.' Obviously Steve McQueen cannot be blamed for triggering off this naughtiness, as not only the film but also the original breakout were still in the future. Chris thinks the childish breakout may have had something to do with the fact that his father was then a prisoner of war in Germany. (His parents had split up when he was very young but his father remained in contact, in as much as one can remain in contact with one's son while banged up in Stalag something-or-other.)

In what must have been excellent preparation for his 1970 expedition up the South Face of Annapurna, he and his fellow-escapers gathered up their supplies: 'I remember pinching some bacon rinds, a large malt loaf and a cake that must have been made for a parental visit.' First thing in the morning, they slipped away and managed to put five or six miles between themselves and the prison camp, or school.

'Towards the evening we became worried about wild animals and thought about sleeping up a tree but that proved very difficult.' Presumably these were the wrong sort of trees, not the Montessori-friendly type. Fear of foxes and killer sheep got the better of them. They had turned round and were already heading back to base camp, or school, when the headmistress drove up and took them back in disgrace, which did not happen in the Annapurna expedition.

With the fortunes of war becoming more favourable, he was brought down south after two years and sent to St Christopher's in Letchworth, Hertfordshire. Although it has a good reputation, he found it a shock, being much larger than his Cumbrian hideaway, and there was also a bit of bullying. A great escape, or even a small breakout, would have been feasible, as there would have been fewer wild animals in Hertfordshire, but this time he did not have to start saving the bacon rinds as the bombing was slackening off in London and he returned to his home in Highgate.

At ten he got a place at another private school, the junior section of University College. It was a day school run by what sounds like a magnificent personage. My own prep-school head was called 'Chalky' White, which made him sound agreeably like a character from *The Beano* or *Dandy* but this beak was in a class of his own. 'The headmaster was called Bunny Lake. He carried an old Zulu spear; if he was in a good mood, he would point the butt at you and say "Pax" (peace – he taught us Latin). If he was in a bad mood, or if you were, he would aim the point at you and say "Bellum" (war).'

Those who came through World Bellum II (as I shall now have to think of it) have many different and bizarre memories. Meeting Mr Lake when he was not a happy bunny and armed with a Zulu spear must be as odd as any.

Actor Juliet Stevenson's experience of Maltese education was much worse than Edward de Bono's. She was very happy at her first school, in a tiny Australian village where the headmistress cried when she left. Juliet would have cried too if she'd known what was in store for her when her father's army posting took the family to Malta and Juliet to a small private school where, when she walked in, the boys would jump out at her and take the lunch she had brought.

'I never told anyone because I thought that's what school was: people jumped out from behind doors and ate your lunch.' When her mother found out about the jumping and the stealing, she took her away to the safety of an army school, where she was happy. Unfortunately, every two and a half years her father would be posted somewhere new and this time she found herself in Germany, where the army school was as bad as it could possibly be.

'I was eight and the oldest person in the class was fifteen. They gave crayons to the younger ones and told us to do colouring. It was very aggressive and I would hide in the loos for most of playtime. I think I stopped eating,' she added.

The place was so hopeless that her parents shipped her, at nine, back to England: 'I thought boarding school would be glamorous: *The Famous Five!*' In fact, Hurst Lodge in Sunningdale, Berkshire, was low on Enid Blyton-style smugglers, buried treasure and dogs called Timmy, but what it lacked in glamour it made up for in scholastic rigour, drama, the arts and an inspirational principal, Doris Stainer, who – perhaps a tiny touch of the girls' school novel here? Life imitating art? – had been a ballerina and there was ballet every day. 'This is where I found my feet. Everything was kindled and everything started to ignite.'

So far the sequence of her schools had been good alternating with bad, so she was due for a bad one after she had taken her O levels and, Hurst Lodge having no sixth form, left to take her A levels at a boarding school near Guildford. Fortunately that was good too, so the good/bad sequence was over. 'Golly!' as Timmy the dog would have put it.

Despite the intergalactic technology humming through his science fiction novels, Iain M. Banks praised the very primitive device provided for lessons at North Queensferry Primary in Fife. 'We still had slates – not that paper hadn't been invented.' The teachers used it as a reward system: 'If you were good, you got a wet sponge to wipe it down, because you could be trusted not to throw it and splat someone on the back of the neck.'

Terry Deary's horrible personal history of schooling continued at Fulwell Juniors in Sunderland. With the paper shortage continuing after the war, his school too used slates for something other than nailing to the roof. As with Iain Banks, writing on slates is not something to be complained about but to be praised as 'good educational practice' and there wasn't a lot of *that* in his schools: 'Mistakes in grammar are easily corrected and it is less inhibiting, like a word processor.'

What he did complain about was that when he was seven, children were allowed to read their end-of-term reports, but not take them home. Perhaps it was that paper shortage again. Terry jotted down his marks on the corner of a page of the report and added as a comparison the marks of his cousin, who was in the same class. He then tore off the corner to show his parents.

'The headmistress took me into her room and went on at me for twenty minutes, asking me why I had torn off the corner. Out of bloody-mindedness I refused to tell her. I learnt that teachers are not unbeatable.'

One of them did beat him – but not physically – at the end of a term at Fulwell Juniors in which he came a very creditable third out of fifty-two in the class. Terry still has the report: 'Can do better,' it stated. 'The bastard!' stated Terry, though not to his face.

Until he was eleven, Terry possessed only two books: Enid Blyton's *The Island of Adventure* and *The Ladybird Book of British Birds*, which he loved so much that he stole it from the classroom shelf. At the end of the Eleven Plus exams, the teacher decided to read a book to his class: 'It was John Buchan's *The Thirty-Nine Steps*, which is racist – all the Germans are evil – and adult. Wholly inappropriate. I didn't get my love of children's books from school.'

It is somehow fitting that Andrew Loog Oldham, the first manager of the Rolling Stones, should have had a Bohemian schooling that broke all the rules. 'My mother's boyfriend paid for my education. He rewarded me when I did well at school by taking me to dinner at The Ivy. When I did less well, it was Lyons Corner House.'

He has no memory of the lessons at his boarding school in a leafy part of Oxfordshire. He does remember the general *Brideshead Revisited* ambience and the parents with the shooting-brakes and the required number of dogs. Then the local vicar wrote to his mother that there was something 'awfully wrong' about the school. Further details were provided by a report in the *Daily Express* a year later: 'Four Jailed in School Swindle Ring'.

It turned out that a gang of four used to buy up a school, collect the fees, run up credit in the town and scarper, leaving the school to collapse. They had pulled off this 'St Fagin's' stunt seven times before the police felt their collars, or blazers.

There was more daylight robbery at Andrew's next school, a state primary in 'dirty and depressing buildings' in Swiss Cottage, London. 'On the first day the older boys forced me to steal from the local sweet shop. I got caught.'

Cherie Blair's last year at St Edmund's Catholic Primary, in Crosby at the northern end of Liverpool, was a magical time, thanks to her teacher. 'I knew Mr Smerdon already; his son was the first boy who ever kissed me.' She went back to the school some years later and his presence was still very vivid to her. 'We must have done all the subjects but I can't remember many formal lessons.' What she does remember is his wartime yarns. He was a former fighter pilot and would devote hours to recounting his experiences.

Now that the World War Two generation are too old for the teaching profession, today's children have lost a rich source of distraction. Back in the 1950s, our form had a former tail gunner who could occasionally be sidetracked from past participles to past times.

Clive James missed every second day at the little one-room school in the bush at Jannali, a suburb of Sydney. He would have liked to miss every first day as well, because school took him away from his mother. The word 'the' was introduced to the class on one of his 'off' days, so when it turned up again in a lesson during one of his 'on' days, he read it out as 'ter-*her*' and the whole class fell about laughing.

'I vowed I would be the cause of deliberate laughter rather than derision.' He succeeded brilliantly. (When I met him in his first week as a Cambridge student, he had a show opening in London; its theatre may not have been exactly *in* the West End but it wasn't far to the west of the West End. Later, as *The Observer*'s television critic, there was a lot of derision around but it was being heaped by him on deserving victims like the laughable soap *Dallas*.)

The playground at Jannali was a patch of earth, the bush was a few feet away and one day a bush fire was threatening. While parents poured water over the flames to save the school, Clive's contribution was to pray that the building would be reduced to cinders.

His family moved to Kogarah, closer to the centre of Sydney. 'I started doing very badly' is an odd way of describing his progress: what did he mean by 'started'? He showed most promise at 'quiet time', when you would skip around until exhausted and then lie down.

He showed a more useful promise at about nine, when he moved to Kogarah Intermediate High School and became a star speller, which is a useful ability for a literary critic. It also meant that he racked up the 'early marks'; the opposite of a detention, it means you can go early and in my opinion should be more widely adopted as a general principle in school and work. He was also demonstrating the creativity that would power his poetry: 'I persuaded the other boys that I had been in the war as a secret agent.'

There then followed a more formal enquiry into his abilities, the IQ test: 'I did quite well, in the ninety-eighth percentile, which means you are not a top scientist but quite glib.' This proved accurate on both counts. He moved on and up to a special school for glib young boffins, with the un-poetic name of Hurstville Opportunity 'C'. The competition here was fierce. It certainly was in the fantasy department.

'I developed my story-telling. Previously I had fought Rommel in the Western desert but now I was on Rommel's staff.' On an open day he showed off the expertise he had allegedly gained there by organising an elaborate warfare demonstration in the sand tray with buried explosives. 'I did a Peter-Snow-in-short-pants number but overdid the fireworks and sand was everywhere.'

People generally remember their early disasters and nature writer Richard Mabey seems to have had more disasters than most to remember. This was not necessarily the fault of Rothesay, his pre-prep school in Berkhamsted, Hertfordshire.

'In one classroom there were two teachers and two classes facing in opposite directions. In my first year I once sat in the back row facing in the wrong direction and was subjected to an hour of fractions, bursting into tears at the incomprehensibility of it.'

He was quite timid and began to suffer from indigestion and dizzy spells, his first experience of psychosomatic symptoms. 'In those days, one was diagnosed as "highly strung" – like a harp.'

At Berkhamsted Prep he became more sociable and enjoyed the kind of outdoor life that is to be expected of the nature writer he became. He had a gang and also a brilliant teacher of nature studies, Mrs Benson, who took them on daily walks on the commons.

'I remember first seeing a fly agaric toadstool, the one that's always drawn in children's story-books with elves sitting on it.' It was a very encouraging school. He once drew a picture of the human body 'in wonderful genital detail' and, instead of telling him off, the teacher pinned it on the wall. Incidentally, children and elves should be warned that the above toadstool, though included in his ever-popular *Food for Free*, is indeed free but not a food; he points out that it's poisonous.

Rick Stein and his little chums took a less cerebral interest in Mother Nature. 'I've been there, been a savage!' thought Rick when he read *Lord of the Flies*. (William Golding, its author, lived in Cornwall and used to come to his restaurant in Padstow.) At Wells Court, a private school outside Tewksbury in Gloucestershire, the boys had a wild time: 'We built two-storey houses out of branches and leaves, and in gangs we would raid each other's houses and set them on fire.'

It wasn't like that when he graduated aged ten to Wells House, the Court's bigger sister at Malvern Wells. It was much wilder. The headmaster was very enthusiastic about the open air and let them roam over the Malvern Hills, where they built camps out of corrugated iron filched from farms and set fire to old man's beard (nothing to do with the chins of senior citizens, it's a sort of vine which they would dry and smoke). They wore shorts, naturally. 'At both schools we used to swim naked in the swimming-pools, which seems odd, looking back, but there was no underhand' – or indeed 'under' anything else – 'behaviour.'

The jungle that BBC World Affairs Editor John Simpson had to cope with at an early age was urban rather than rural, in the badlands between the Crispin's School, Penge and his south London home. His father had fallen on hard times but still thought it better for John to go to a private school than the local primary. Unfortunately he lacked the one (old) penny for the bus fare so his son had to walk home.

> The uniform was bright purple and was like the gear worn by pilots designed to be visible when they fell into the sea. You could be spotted by local yobs from a quarter of a mile away. This taught me from an early age to be street smart and, although terrified, I got a kick out of it. I have still had this feeling when talking my way out of trouble from lunatics in Belgrade and Afghanistan.

Of all the boarding schools that Ann Leslie went to as a young child in India, her favourite was St Hilda's, an Anglican foundation in Ooty. She liked the routine. She liked knowing that they would have puffed rice and eggs for breakfast. She had a strong feeling that life in this mini Garden of Eden would not last and that another long train would be carrying her away. There were what she saw as omens.

'I was taking a dog for a walk and a panther got it; later I was bitten by a rabid dog.' The omens were correct and at nine and a half she was shipped off 'home', which meant not where her parents lived in India but to 'exile' in England.

If there is anything worse than going to school, it is not going to school, which is what happened – or didn't happen – to Jean Marsh. 'I'm poorly educated, not because the teaching was rotten but because I was not taught for long enough.' In this she resembled her character Rose in *Upstairs, Downstairs*, the series that she created together with Eileen Atkins; being a maid in the 1920s, Rose would not exactly have been the recipient of an Oxford education. For Jean there were gaps caused by the war, her illness and her family's frequent moves which led to her going to seven or eight different schools.

'My proper education stopped at twelve, otherwise I would certainly have gone to grammar school and perhaps university. I liked the smell of chalk. I had a proprietary feeling towards my desk, or rather half a desk.' There was a good reason why she should treasure what was taken for granted or even disliked by those of us who were force-fed school for longer.

'At home we had lodgers and I always shared a room; there was not much you had to yourself.' She also shared a bed with her older sister. (The writer Hunter Davies can beat that: 'I shared a bed with my brother. I once came back from Durham University and found a lodger in my half of the bed. My mother had sublet it.')

The two Marsh sisters also shared a career: Yvonne as a child starred in *The Little Ballerina* with Margot Fonteyn and Anthony Newley; she has now retired.

'The last thing she did was a TV series called *You Rang, M'Lord?*' explained Jean, adding, with commendable lack of irritation in her voice, 'a spoof of *Upstairs, Downstairs.*'

Sir Peter Blake will always be associated with The Beatles, as he designed the cover of their Sgt Pepper album. His picture of the headmistress of his primary, Maypole School in Dartford Heath, Kent, would have been called an example of Pop Art if Pop Art had been invented in the 1930s. 'I did a drawing of Miss Gaspar chasing me with a cane. In fact she was kindly and I don't think she had a cane and I probably got the idea from a comic.' It's a bit late now but let's take that as an apology to the good Miss Gaspar.

Michael Frayn, playwright and novelist, can bear witness to enormous variations in quality in the bumpy highway of scholastic progress. You are cruising along a smooth surface, come to a junction and find yourself crashing over pot-holes. His academic journey began with an absolutely delightful little private school in Ewell, Surrey.

'I was part of a gang run by a very Amazon-like girl. I wore glasses, so she appointed me as the gang scientist with the task of making explosives.' Well, his play *Copenhagen* did discuss the creation of the atom bomb, so Miss Amazon was smarter than she knew.

He was parted from the delights of the school and the gang at the age of seven when he went for an interview at an 'unspeakable' dump in Sutton with architecture that expressed the philosophy of the place: the front facing the road was brick but all the other walls were of corrugated iron.

'The headmaster, a clergyman, asked me to spell "beautiful". I spelt it wrongly but he let me in just the same.' This was a shame, because there was a lot of bullying and caning; if it had been possible to fail that entrance 'exam', it would have been a good career move. Michael endured the corrugated disaster area until fate rescued him in the cruellest of ways: 'My mother died when I was twelve and my father had to get a housekeeper, which meant he couldn't afford the school fees.' *My Father's Fortune: A Life* is a memoir that has been described as 'beautiful' (spelt correctly, of course). It is a tribute to Tom Frayn's struggle to rescue something from the ruins of a family tragedy.

Having to find a school in the state system they had previously eschewed was, of course, the least of their problems and in fact Kingston Grammar was a perfectly decent place. Canings took place only once or twice a term and the teaching was extremely efficient. Michael stayed there until his National Service, half of which he spent learning Russian. Alan Bennett was on the same course and they used to do little sketches together. This was during the Cold War and the Russians must have been pretty worried.

Tony Hawks. To avoid disappointment, please note the spelling: there is an S on the end. He is a comedian and author of *Round Ireland with a Fridge*. He is occasionally mistaken for the S-less Tony Hawk, the American skateboarder known as 'The Bird', who is in turn presumably mistaken for Tony Hawks and asked about his 1988 No. 4 hit single 'Stutter Rap' with Morris Minor and the Majors.

Tony Hawks, then, enjoyed Goldstone primary in Hove, Sussex. It didn't bother anyone that there were classes of forty pupils or that there was always building work going on. 'One of the boys asked me to join a gang he had organised called the Laughy Gang, who laughed whenever the builders dropped anything.' This group chortling may or may not necessarily have prompted Tony's later career.

It was her smiling that had teachers frowning at Zoë Salmon. One would expect a future Miss Northern Ireland and *Blue Peter* presenter to be squeaky-clean but the teachers at Kilmaine Primary in Bangor, County Down, thought she was too good to be true. 'I was called "The Smiler" by teachers, who thought I was up to something. But I never was; I was just being polite. I was very well-behaved. I was never even asked to leave the room for ten minutes.' Of course, suspicious teachers could retort that she would say that, wouldn't she, thus proving that a kid just can't win.

Actually, Zoë did win: her first award was at the age of ten, for handwriting. (There must be a calligraphy gene in the Salmon DNA; her older sister cleaned up on all the handwriting cups, studied typography and created her own font.) 'I got a C only once in my life – and the devastation of that!' This academic disaster was at secondary school. 'Then Mrs McCracken, our chemistry teacher, said that for the same piece of work I'd got an A for effort: yes!'

Gail Porter is another television presenter who was a goodie-goodie at school. In her case, this is more surprising, in view of the fact that her naked image was to be projected onto the Houses of Parliament as a stunt for a men's magazine and her biography is entitled *Laid Bare*. But she swears that at Brunstane Primary, next to her nursery in Edinburgh, she was quiet, studious, and fearful of upsetting any of the teachers. This may have pleased the teachers but it got up the other kids' noses and they used to call her 'Snobby', as in 'Let's get Snobby to swear.' Fortunately she had some 'snobby' friends.

Colour only became a professional issue for David Harewood when he left RADA, where he had played Chekhov and Ibsen characters. After that, his early reviews were of 'black actor David Harewood'. Race and violence were not issues at St Benedict's Primary in Small Heath, Birmingham, although one of his earliest memories there is of being attacked after bumping into the school's hard man while playing aeroplanes. 'I'd never had a fight before but I remember laying him out flat and I never had any more trouble.'

It was even easier at his next school, Washington Heath. On his first day, a boy said to him, 'Three-thirty – outside!' The lad was so impressed when he turned up that – respect! – there was no fight.

The late Rose Hacker, a wonderful woman who wrote a fortnightly column in the excellent *Camden New Journal*, was three in 1909 when her parents moved into a cottage in Horsley, Surrey, near the railway line. What sets the nerves jangling today is not that she walked to school – the stationmaster's daughter took her by the hand – but that they strolled along the side of the track. Still, she survived to write a book in 1960 for teenagers, *The Opposite Sex*, which sold 250,000 copies, and to give me an interview when she was a lively 101 years old.

'I remember picking big daisies for the teacher and I also remember a rocking horse; if you brought a farthing in your hot little hand, you could have a ride.' NB. A farthing was the smallest value coin but even so quite a drain on a three-year-old's piggybank in the early twentieth century.

Thirty years later (Lord) Melvyn Bragg was astonished by the sight of the rocking-horse in his primary school: 'I was absolutely knocked out by the toys in the first-year classroom.' Mind you, it was in 1938 a brand new school, indeed, it was called The New School. He too had a journey to school that now appears dangerously free-range.

> My mother took me there on the first day. I told her that I didn't want her near the place after that. Here was this four-year-old walking three-quarters of a mile through the back alleys of Wigton, pottering around near the rivers. These days we'd have been reported to the police.

There were twenty-five boys in Stefan Buczacki's class in the village primary school. 'Three or four of us ended up as professors of one sort or another.' Dr Buczacki ended up on *Gardeners' Question Time*. The headmaster of the William Gilbert Endowed School in Duffield, Derby, used to say about his class, 'It's not a bad year.'

As a boy, Olympic runner Chris Brasher had a very bad stutter, which caused a problem of biblical proportions at Oakley Hall, Cirencester. 'First thing every day, there was a quarter of an hour of morning prayers. You had to read one verse.' The poor lad was always trying to calculate, days ahead, when it would be his turn to read his single verse and was always praying – a fitting word, in the circumstances – 'for the shortest verse: "Jesus wept".'

Bombs had a big effect on Barry Norman's education. The film critic went to an 'elementary' school, as primaries were known, in Edgware, north London, until his back garden suffered a direct hit and his grandfather was blasted into the front door, leaving a nose-shaped hole in the glass, though he was unhurt. After that he was moved from his school and indeed London. Taunton seemed a safe bet, until a bomb fell in a garden a few doors away. 'I thought someone had it in for me.'

You must have seen those nostalgic films about growing up in World War Two. Barry certainly has, being a film critic. (His father made some of them, or at least movies about grown-ups at war such as *Dunkirk* and *The Cruel Sea*.) He was living them at the time. Back in London he rather got used to the explosions. He was hit on the nose but that was when his new school, a little prep school named Highwood, tried to interest him in boxing – after that he wasn't interested.

'I used to go on the bus with a friend and we always liked it when a V1 or doodlebug came; the bus would stop and we would go home. You are quite callous as a kid.'

For a writer whose Labrador featured in his books as 'the Dog of Peace', Adrian Mitchell lived a life that was bound up with war. World War Two kept him away from London and his most famous 1960s poem was 'To Whom it May Concern (Tell me Lies about Vietnam)'; this was updated for the present century by the simple expedient of substituting 'Iraq' for 'Vietnam'.

After kindergarten in his north London house, he went to a school 'somewhere in Surrey' where he gave an early demonstration of his wonderful way with words: 'I got engaged to two little girls at the same time. I told one of them that she was my reserve fiancée in case the other was ill.'

The family was on holiday in the West Country when war

broke out. His mother declared, 'We're not going back,' and they jumped out of the train, staying for a year at a farm in Pawlett, Somerset. On the first day at the village school, a ring of boys invited the newcomer to fight a huge lad.

'No thank you,' answered Adrian, but the Pawlett pugilist bopped him on the nose, he cried and that was that. 'It tried to be a good school,' in Adrian's later judgment, 'but there were about fifty in a class.' The over-sized class did not prevent him from having one of those moments of understanding: 'I remember being shown a picture and learning that it was "*an* owl and *a* bear".' At the end of his life his children's books were still teeming with animals.

He also worked his magic on Greek myths, which he first came across at his next school, Monkton Combe near Bath, on a very hot day: 'I was so excited by the story of Perseus rescuing Andromeda that I fainted. Many years later, I wrote a play about Perseus for Japanese children.' To be performed on a cool day, we hope.

This was at the 'pre-prep' part of the school. He found the prep school proper – or, as it turned out, improper – was absolute hell because many classes were left unattended and the big boys tormented the little boys. 'They used to torture us.' He didn't want to tell me more but he does describe it in 'Back to the Playground Blues'.

'I'm never going back; I'd rather be dead,' he told his mother one day, so she sent him to a little boarding school run by a friend in Wiltshire. Sometimes there were classes of four or even one-to-one private tuition. The entire school consisted of only forty boys and two girls – smaller than a single class at the village school.

Diana Melly is a former night-club hostess, model, and the

author of *Take a Girl Like Me*, her account of forty-five years with her sadly departed husband George Melly, singer and writer. She and school suffered from mutual incomprehension. She does remember being sent at the age of about five to the Convent of Marie Auxiliatrice in Finchley, north London. When her mother took her in on the first day, one nun declared, 'She's very small for her age.' The next nun said, 'She's very tall for her age.'

Ideally there should have been a third nun who said, in a Goldilocks sort of way, 'She's just the right height for her age,' but there was nothing ideal about the convent. At weekends Diana was allowed to visit her grandmother, who lived quite near, but only if her neck was clean and she had done a Number Two. Asked 'Have you been?' Diana, under the impression that it was a Number One they were referring to, would reply that indeed she had. The loo bowl would then be examined and the verdict given: 'You're lying.' So no trip to granny.

She ran away once and got lost in Golders Green, where she sat on the pavement in tears. A nice woman took her home and comforted her with milk and biscuits. After she had been taken back to the convent, she felt the nuns had become more agreeable to her, which wouldn't have been difficult.

'I have no memory of a single lesson at school,' she says. Another school at which she can't remember learning anything was housed in a barn in a field near Swaffham, Norfolk. Her aunt was the teacher but otherwise the only thing that stuck in her mind is her father coming into the classroom wearing his RAF uniform. This all took place during the war and he was going overseas. She went up to the front of the class; he gave her a watch and was gone for five years.

It rather seems like a lesson in English sang-froid; nobody actually asked 'Is this au revoir – or goodbye?' but otherwise it could have been an out-take from *The Dambusters* with fewer bouncing bombs.

George Melly, Diana's husband, was one of a wonderful generation of 1950s jazz musicians who turned to writing and cartooning as their day job when the paying public decided to turn down the volume on their kind of music. If you sat around long enough at the premises of the now extinct *Punch* magazine, as I did for some seventeen years, four of these doubly or triply talented folk would amble in. As well as George, our contributors included trumpeter-writer-broadcaster Humphrey Lyttelton, clarinettist-cartoonist Wally ('Trog') Fawkes and saxophonist-writer-broadcaster Benny Green.

Of the four, Benny had the least formal education but was probably the most educated – largely by himself. His schooling began in London in a normal way: 'I had a wonderful elementary education at Clipstone Junior Mixed on the slummy edge of Marylebone. Then, two days before war was declared, the headmaster told us that we were going to be evacuated and might never see our parents again; some kids burst out cheering.'

This evacuation turned out to be a good idea, as Clipstone Junior Mixed took a direct hit. Evacuees were at the mercy of the whims of fate; in the first billet of film director Bryan Forbes, he was put in an actual dog kennel, before ending up with a lovely couple who provided him with the unknown luxuries of books and a bedroom of his own.

Benny had similar variation with his accommodation. He and his friend Max were billeted in the genteel home of a snobbish couple with a maidservant in Moor Park, Herts., until Benny, by now on the roll of Marylebone Grammar, was forwarded to the school's new address in Redruth, Cornwall. He was made much more welcome down there in the home of a kindly bank manager and his wife, who treated him like the son they never had. (He never saw Max again until he was reviewing *Ben Hur* in the 1960s: there, slaving away behind Charlton Heston in the galley-ship, was good old Max in the number two position.)

By the time he caught up with the school, he had missed two months: 'I didn't know what they talked about when they used words like "algebra" and "Latin".' Benny wrote an essay about Cleopatra having a son by Julius Caesar, an intriguing item which he had picked up from his reading of Bernard Shaw, but which enraged the teacher sufficiently to throw his exercise book across the room and snap, 'You're only fit to be a barrow-boy.' It's hard to say what the teacher was fit for but it may not have been teaching.

(Lord) Chris Patten remembers walking to school with his sister at the age of five, a rather frightening journey because he was not able to see his hand in front of his face in the London smog. (Lady) Doreen Lawrence would not have minded having lessons in the middle of a Norfolk field, or in smog, as there would have been fewer lizards. Her extraordinary life, which now sees her as surely the best-loved member of the House of Lords and the campaigning mother of murdered son Stephen, began in Jamaica.

'It was like running a gauntlet,' she says of her walk as a five-year-old to the village school through a forested area. 'At a certain point, out of nowhere among the bushes, would come scuttling big, vivid-green lizards that had a fan round their throats. I would stand riveted to the spot and I would be braying like a donkey with fright.'

Otherwise, school was fine and she did really well, even though pupils had only one reading book for the year, which her grandmother bought for her.

Nine-year-old Darcus Howe was one of the seventy-five out

of 4,000 candidates who got a free place at Queen's Royal College in Trinidad. Now a writer and broadcaster, he could have been expected to excel at essays but what he wrote was so good that it pushed the boundaries of the marking system: 'My teacher used to read my essays out and give me twenty-five *out of twenty*.' To emphasise these over-the-top marks, he would give other boys *minus* five.

Some console themselves that they are 'late developers'. As the years go by, and school is far behind them but intellectual achievements not yet on the horizon, they can always console themselves that they are *very* late developers. I was neither early nor late but a medium developer, peaking at thirteen with an exhibition (admittedly the lowest given, more of a foothill than a peak) and the second-highest mark in Latin O level (annoyingly, the boy with the highest mark gave up Classics and specialised in science).

Both Karren Brady and her teachers peaked early. In other words, the 'First Lady of Football' encountered 'the best teacher in the whole wide world, Mrs Peters,' when she was at her private primary in Southgate, north London.

'I gained confidence from her; it was the only time I was ever top.' After that, both Karren and the standard of her teachers went downhill. Maybe there was a connection.

Challenge Anneka Rice about what she had for lunch on 2 January 1969 and she can look it up. She kept a diary from the age of eight, so you may rest assured that the next few paragraphs at least are perfectly accurate. 'My parents bought me a diary with a lock, which seemed very glamorous. I kept it going until I was about fourteen.'

'I just loved being at Dunrobin' – a great name, suggesting done-robbing or done with being a small, red breasted bird – 'in Limpsfield, Surrey, a most phenomenal private school with a sense of eccentricity, which I think is very important.' It had an atmosphere that guided her on to 'the artistic road', with a love of performance and music. The inspiring Miss Pace – good name for a headmistress – used to invite the girls into her study to play recordings of Joyce Grenfell's monologues, including the one about the teacher losing her grip: 'Oh George, don't put that into your mouth…'

Mrs Swaddling – another great name – doesn't sound the type to lose control. 'There was a piano in every room and singing every day. Mrs Swaddling, with her big bosom, would play songs from *The King and I* and *Salad Days* and, when it came out, *Mary Poppins*, which we thought was very racy.' (Those were innocent days, when *Mary Poppins* counted as 'racy' and, indeed, when people used words like 'racy'.)

Although she has turned her back on the Swinging Sixties and as Jean Cox runs the Abbey Hotel in Penzance, Jean Shrimpton was our first supermodel. She was born in Buckinghamshire in 1942, a very serious era. 'It was wartime and there was an awful uneasy feeling: children pick up on that. There were tanks going past and, as we were near Bomber Command, the buses were always full of servicemen.'

She was just five when she went to St Bernard's Convent in High Wycombe and was terrified about going to school. The bus stop was just outside her house and she kept running back to ask her mother, 'Are you quite sure you'll be there?' – that is, to pick her up from school.

> I was too nervous to go to the lavatory and would usually bring home a wet parcel for my mother. Nuns are quite daunting and make you feel very guilty. With my wish to please, I learnt quite a lot – but really I was relieved to get home to my pony, Ricky.

Her riding could be blamed – or credited – for her next move. Although the school at which she took her O levels wanted her to go on to university, she had discovered boys during her equine activities and preferred to go to London, presumably because there were more of them in the capital.

Christopher Timothy will be forever associated with horses … and cows, sheep, pigs, dogs … and other creatures great and small encountered while playing the saintly James Herriott. Having seen *Annie Get Your Gun*, *Peter Pan* and 'a musical with lots of cannons on stage', he had decided to be an actor by the time he went as a boarder to Kingsland Grange prep school in Shrewsbury.

Some years ago he was asked back to present the end-of-year prizes. 'As I handed over the cup for English, I saw my name among the winners; I'd won it in 1953. There had been a choice of topics and I did "Magic"; I interpreted it as "the magic of show-biz", about which I knew nothing.' In fact, there was a connection.

His father had read law but was sent down from university. He then became a clergyman (later Christopher played Jesus in the York Mystery Plays, which could be said to outrank him) but was defrocked after getting divorced. He then became – what, has it come to this? – the first announcer on *The Goon Show*. Because of the divorce, he was not around much in Christopher's life but remained a living connection to a landmark in the history of comedy.

At his next school, Priory Grammar, Christopher worked at his acting and got to play the Second Gravedigger in *Hamlet*, wearing, as it happened, a ginger wig. The First Gravedigger decided to introduce a line that is largely unknown to Shakespearean scholars: 'Ginger, you're barmy.'

St John's Primary in Camborne, Cornwall, was a very happy school indeed, 'run by nuns, who were very good teachers, actually', according to comedian Rory McGrath. He explains that it was a particularly happy school on St Patrick's Day, because it had a football match: English versus Irish. 'I played in the Irish team, as I had an Irish surname; Polish and Italian children counted as Irish. The Irish always won – and if they weren't winning, the match was played on until they did.'

'Happy' was not the word for Eric Burdon or his school career, which could not go downhill: it began right at the bottom. East Walker Primary in Newcastle was an awful place, stuck between a shipyard to the west and a slaughterhouse to the east: 'Right out of Dickens.' It gave him, he says, his first taste of what the Blues were about – and he should know, being hailed as one of the finest white Blues singers of our time (beginning with The Animals and later the band War).

In a class of fifty, he sat at the back and sketched. To put it in a more positive way, as he does, 'Every class was an art class for me.' One day the class was given the task of drawing a scene from the Bible for homework. In RE they had been taught the story of the genocidal Herod and now had to depict the slaughter of the first-born. We'll leave theologians to debate the spiritual benefits offered to young children of drawing babies being speared, but what put the teacher in a state of shock was how Eric updated the scenario: 'I drew *British* soldiers with fixed bayonets kicking down the door of a farmer's house.' And if you ask why he didn't at least make them SS soldiers, he replies that he and his mates were all fans of the German army because of the graphic appeal of their uniforms in the comic books.

'My brightest memory is of when some horses escaped from the slaughterhouse and came charging towards the school. We started pelting the cops chasing them, because we were rooting for the horses.' The kids must have identified with the equine escape. As Eric was to sing with The Animals: 'We got to get out of this place.'

When he lived in Donaghadee near Belfast, (Lord) Paddy Ashdown's school day began with a walk along the edge of the shore to his primary school. Much of his education consisted of travelling. He was a 'weekly boarder' at eight, which meant a 25-mile journey by two buses twice a weekend and, from eleven, waving goodbye to his parents at 7 a.m. on Belfast docks, reaching his boarding school in Bedford late in the afternoon. It was in primary school, however, that he showed how tough he was: 'We had a dreadful headmistress, a martinet, and on one occasion I locked her in the stationery cupboard and ran away.'

Talking of cupboards … For Glenda Jackson, the rot set in at the age of fourteen when she stopped being such a good and academic pupil at West Kirby County Grammar School for Girls. She blames the hormones kicking in. 'If you infringed the rules, you would get points marked against you and if you got five points you would have to appear before a "house court" consisting of prefects and sixth formers.' It sounds as if she might have been frequently in the dock of this small-scale kangaroo court.

'There was one English teacher who we plagued mercilessly. We would lock someone in a cupboard, usually me, and lose the key. There would be mysterious rappings…'

Martin Burton also misused a lock but it wasn't the one on a classroom cupboard. If his teachers at the School of St Helen and St Katherine in Abingdon, Oxon, didn't call him a clown, then they are fully entitled to now. He is the Zippo of Zippo's Circus and has won the coveted Clown of the Year award many times.

At first all went well at this Church of England convent school, but at the age of six he locked himself in the toilet with Mary Brunton, the local vicar's daughter. 'Although she received no admonishment, I had to sit in the headmistress's study during every break for a year. That really put me off the school.'

Jenni Murray's misdemeanour was trifling by comparison: 'I got into trouble for staring at a woman on a bus. I still stare at people because I find them endlessly fascinating.' This is a useful attribute now for a *Woman's Hour* presenter but was not recommended when she was a pupil in the charge of Mrs Hudson, the very strict headmistress at St Mary's, the girls' section of a Church of England School in Barnsley. Jenni also got into trouble for telling a lie. It was an absolute whopper.

'I wanted a brother – I'm an only child – so I invented one. I told the dinner ladies that my mother had gone into hospital and had a little boy.' She even invented a name for the non-existent sibling. Two names, in fact: 'David Robert'. The teachers were very surprised when her mother turned up at school that evening for the fund-raising 'beetle drive', unaccompanied by any new-born baby.

'All the things that made me what I am – being inquisitive and making up stories (I'll write fiction one day) – they tried to knock out of me!'

Francine Stock, whose presenting jobs have included *Newsnight* and Radio 4's *Front Row*, had an even richer fantasy life than Jenni Murray: 'I was an only child but at school used to talk about my brothers and sisters. When I wiped out my "elder brother" in a dramatic car accident, the teacher said to my mother how sorry she was. My mother was first puzzled, and then embarrassed, and then pretty cross.'

Otherwise Francine was the goody-goody at Tormead Juniors near Guildford, Surrey, who got the gold stars. She was horrified when her friend got the 'black stars' of shame. She thought – and still thinks – that this was a miscarriage of justice. 'I went and removed them from the board but was caught and got them myself.' That makes it two miscarriages of justice. Watch out, Tormead Junior, we're on your case.

Another former goody-goody is Mel Giedroyc, who is 50 per cent of the double act Mel and Sue (and is often solo as 100 per cent of Mel). She had four years of being beaten up in the very tough St Peter's Primary in Ashtead near Leatherhead, in a class that contained two boys destined for borstal and then prison. After that, she tried to be 'hard' too and sat at the back wisecracking.

'My mother is as posh as you like and would come to collect me wearing a head-scarf; I put on this estuary, mockney accent and said I was adopted.'

Fortunately the teachers were good: 'There were hardcore old-school like Mrs Esdale, a Hattie Jacques lookalike with big brooch and scary traffic warden shoes and then there were the woolly, vaguely hippy teachers and some random nuns.' She then moved to the other extreme of the education spectrum, the private Oxford High School for Girls; she remains glad that she experienced both types of school. The contrast could not have been greater.

'I remember the joy of walking into the class – and it was quiet. Everyone listened to the teachers.' At RE, the teacher asked, 'What do you think of when I say "God"?' One girl said, '*The Praying Hands* by Dürer.' Mel thought, 'We're not in St Peter's anymore.' The girl, incidentally, was last heard of as a lesbian flamenco dancer in Venezuela.

At about seven, Shirley Anne Field, who we left as she was being sent to a children's home and thus separated from her loved ones, took to devising and acting out scenes about family life:

father, baby brother, sisters and mother. She called these dramatic interludes 'concerts' and would sometimes sing.

Instead of inventing family events, June Brown did precisely the opposite and concealed a family tragedy: she didn't tell St John's Church of England School in Ipswich when her sister died at the age of eight. 'One teacher, Miss Rae, was rather sarcastic to me and I told my mother. I didn't know for years that my mother went up to the school and said, "Be a bit kind; her sister's died." Miss Rae was kind after that.'

Unlike her *EastEnders* character Dot Cotton, June was taught never to say anything like 'I don't never.' She didn't realise she was clever but she certainly had brains, hence the scholarship to Ipswich High, which was affiliated to the Girls' Public Day School Trust. Unfortunately the snooty head teacher told the girls that brains were nothing to be proud of but one's birth was. So much for scholarship girls.

Triple jumper Jonathan Edwards was a timid lad. Inverteign Junior School in Teignmouth, Devon, had an architectural feature which bothered him: 'It was open-plan and that didn't work for me. I liked the idea of boundaries and I didn't like the fact that the classroom had no walls.' He suggested that there might well be a connection between his feeling about boundaries and his choice of studies: 'There is a real beauty to maths and I liked the certainty of science; you wrote an answer, drew a line under it and that was it.' These subjects, with their definite border between correct and incorrect, appealed more than the less clear-cut world of arts subjects, and made up two of his three A levels.

His degree was in physics: 'It helped me to understand the mechanics of jumping. Testing a theory, revising it, all part of the scientific method.' That was all very helpful when he was engaged in athletics. Now that he has retired, it's different: 'I'm finding life is more open-plan.'

If the same pupil has enormously different experiences of two different schools, it might be just the idiosyncrasies of the child. Or it might be the schools. Take Rosie Boycott. She was to become the first female editor of a national daily paper: two, in fact, *The Independent* and the *Daily Express*. This may be an indication that she would have been born under an Awkward Squad star.

'When I was ten, my parents moved to Shropshire and enrolled me in a school – I've forgotten its name – which I hated so much that I used to hide up an oak tree or make myself sick to avoid going there. After one miserable term, my parents took me out.' She then went to St Mary's near Tenbury Wells, Worcestershire. 'It was a fantastic prep school, the only school I loved.' She was a sports champion and the headmistress liked her. 'I was very good at maths and most things.'

'Very good at maths' would not describe my own exam results but I am very proud to say that my daughter has more than made up for that. She learnt one valuable lesson when she was very young. One day she began counting out loud. Beginning at the beginning, i.e. at 'one', she carried on confidently up to 'ten' and then progressed steadily through the teens. Having picked her way through the twenties, she slowly charted an accurate passage through the thirties: 'Thirty-three, thirty-four.' A sudden thought struck her: 'Wait a minute. When do numbers stop?' Being told they continue forever, she packed in the counting exercise there and then.

Like numbers, schooldays stretch ahead to infinity for a small child. After the first day at primary school comes the second day, second week, second month, second year. Would it not be more agreeable if, instead of traipsing all the way to school every day, they had their classes at home? The same thought sometimes occurs to parents.

CHAPTER 4

HOME SCHOOL RUN

As with kindergartens, parents can set up their own primary schools. This is more elaborate; you're in the territory of curriculum details and assorted bureaucracy – indeed, you can be sure some of the arrangements below would not have survived one of today's dawn swoops by Ofsted.

As was mentioned in *The F**king Fulfords* (their asterisks) on Channel 4, there have been Fulfords in Great Fulford, Devon, since the time of Richard I. Francis Fulford does not pride himself on his academic achievements but he does know that the Lionheart was roaring on the throne from 1189 to 1199.

Francis was initially uneducated at home: 'My parents couldn't be bothered to get up in time to take me to a conventional school,' he explains, and God knows we parents have all felt like that. 'My father didn't come down before nine and my mother would have had to get up at seven to make the breakfast, which wasn't on.' Even less on, naturally, would have been the idea of his father getting up at seven to cook the porridge. There was only one thing for it: 'We had a governess until I was seven: several governesses, completely useless.'

Since he went on to a pre-prep school at seven and then a prep school, the governesses cannot be blamed entirely for the fact that he failed Eton entrance: 'It was my introduction to the word "failure", which would feature quite large in my life.' Nor need the governesses feel too guilty about him failing maths O level three or four times. But he did rather spoil the run of failures by getting three A levels. He admits that they were probably at D grades but he remarks cheekily that, because of today's lax marking standards, they would now count as A grades.

Stately home schooling sounds even better. Cricket commentator Henry Blofeld was brought up by a father with a monocle which fell out in his fury when young 'Blowers' committed a crime, such as not standing up when his mother entered the room. In the gun room of the north Norfolk estate where the Blofelds had landed in about 1520, Mrs Hales, the governess, taught Henry before he was packed off to boarding school at seven. He enjoyed being with his four or five cousins and children of neighbours. How up-to-date was the curriculum provided by the teaching staff of one? 'I was quite good at the Old Testament from an early age,' he claims, which probably answers the question.

Antonia Fraser is the author of the prizewinning *Mary Queen of Scots*, *Marie Antoinette* and other history books which people enjoy reading. Until she was eight, she was taught at home by her mother who, if she had any queries, could always turn to her husband, Lord Longford, an Oxford don and later Cabinet minister. He himself had been taught at home until the age of nine: 'We had a governess. I was very well taught: one-to-one teaching. An old clergyman came in to give me instruction in Latin.'

In view of her present ability to zoom through a text at a supercharged rate, Lady Antonia thinks that her mother accidentally taught her to speed-read. (Her second husband, Harold Pinter, will go down in literary history for quite the reverse, the pauses indicated in his stage directions. Incidentally, having met the great playwright not long before he died, I can confirm that there is another way in which this was a marriage of opposites: Lady Antonia Fraser is not at all surly.)

Lady Longford certainly got her little girl up to speed in general and Antonia gained admission to The Dragon, the high-powered boys' prep school in Oxford that at the time had twenty girls on the books as well. The eight-year-old relished the move from no competition to fierce competition.

'We had the form order every week; more often than not I was number one – at least, that's the way I remember it – so it showed me that girls were just as clever as boys.'

There was one odd absence in the curriculum of this prestigious school with a catchment area packed with Oxford academics. It occurred to her later that she had no memory at all of being taught the subject which was to become her day job: history. This was not a case of amnesia. She checked her old reports and they were full of Latin, Greek, maths and other stand-by subjects of a traditional education – apart from history.

This did not deter her: 'I made history my own thing; I used to walk to the Oxford public library, take out a book and then walk back. Then I would take out another book on the same subject to

get a different angle.' This sounds like the essential modus oper-
andi for a professional historian – apart from the walking; many
Oxford scholars can afford bicycles.

Born in Egypt, Penelope Lively grew up there and did not
darken the doors of any school until the age of twelve, a depri-
vation which does not seem to have hindered her writing skills
in any way, given that her novels have won the Booker and
Whitbread prizes. 'I was educated at home by a sort of nanny-
turned-governess who used a jolly good teaching kit from the
Parents' National Educational Union.' This was not the reason
for her home tuition: 'I think my mother couldn't be bothered
to drive the four miles to a school in Cairo.'

Elizabeth Jane Howard was a pupil from the Home School
of Hard Knocks. She had only two terms of school but this did
not prevent her from enjoying a prolific writing career which
included the massive 'Cazalet' series – and, come to that, from
having a fellow-novelist as a husband (her third, Kingsley Amis).
Her family was musical and gave her all the music she could
devour but never any books, which she had to buy on her sixpence pocket money. 'I started writing at nine because I ran
out of books.'

Lessons began with a Miss Kettle who came round for three
or four years to teach her and a few friends. After two terms of
being terrified at Francis Holland School in Belgravia, she managed to develop a serious case of tonsillitis, after which her she
was taught by her mother's former governess, mornings only.
Shakespeare, Latin and Greek were on the curriculum. A series
of *mauvais* French teachers turned up in the afternoon. She went
to a painting class with a gloomy young man.

When she was sixteen, she went to an establishment in Beaconsfield for a year's course but it was in domestic science and

she didn't count it as school. 'I was so homesick, I kept breaking the pudding basins, so I had to stay an extra term.'

On the face of it, home schooling might seem like authorised truanting. However, Elizabeth Jane Howard does not seem to have suffered from the experience, nor did the other examples of kitchen-table tuition mentioned above. Admittedly, Antonia Fraser had the advantage that both her parents were historians and authors, which put her home statistically in something of a minority. (Her three daughters, incidentally, are also writers.) I was away on the afternoon when my primary school did child psychology but please bear with me when I offer a possible theory about their success, a theory particularly based on her education but also applicable to the others. Could it be that the do-it-yourself element of her home schooling is helpful by showing that you didn't have to be spoon-fed by a teacher? That instead you can pick up material waiting out there? Perhaps children are drawn to the challenge of fruit that is, if not forbidden, at least concealed from the common gaze.

It is a challenge that appeals to some parents. It helps if you have more than one child, otherwise playtime isn't much fun; you need at least two to play 'It'. Another snag is that if their kids do badly, the parents can't blame the teachers.

CHAPTER 5

ELEVEN PLUS
AND MINUS

Before the conversion of (most) grammar and secondary modern schools into comprehensives, the state system operated a major filter, sorting pupils into (alleged) sheep and (apparent) goats. Children were in the position of John , who described it as a make-or-break exam, lifting a child up into one of the comparatively few grammars or casting them down among the majority in the secondary moderns. Before the massive programme of converting grammar schools into comprehensives, the Eleven Plus was the hurdle that everyone tried to jump over.

The sense of failure extended down into the primary schools, or it did for Charlie Whelan, former spin-doctor to Gordon Brown and a man with a brutal turn of phrase. He was in a junior school that consigned him to the band of pupils on which it was deemed a waste to spend too much time as they weren't going to make it anyway: 'You failed before you failed.'

While the emphasis in a secondary modern was on the 'secondary' bit, grammar schools offered a high-powered, free education – among bright kids. My cheeky public school headmaster once told us with a twinkle that we might not have got into a grammar school, as the competition was tougher; by contrast, the fees for our school would keep down the number of potential candidates. (If you wonder that a head should insult his paying customers, you should be aware that he was married to the redoubtable Lady Trumpington, one of the few Leaders of the House of Lords to be a guest on *Have I Got News for You*.)

If our lives had been less financially fortunate, we might have been at a school like that attended by former MP Clare Short, where the Eleven Plus did matter but where, as she puts it, 'Out of forty-four girls in the class, I was the only one that passed the Eleven Plus, which is why I'm against that exam.'

Like Clare, Terry Deary passed but otherwise his experience was precisely the opposite. His class had spent two years doing nothing but test papers: 'Out of the fifty-two in the class, fifty went to grammar school.' He too was not impressed by the whole process: 'Success equals exam success: that's what they tell you. Big lie.'

Warren Mitchell was in a class with a similar success rate. When he described himself to me as a dinosaur, he was not referring to the part he once played of Alf Garnett in the sharp sitcom *Till Death Us Do Part*. (For younger readers, think of *Al Murray, the Pub Landlord* but without the wishy-washy liberal streak.) He meant that he belonged to the Jurassic Age species that can do long multiplication and long division: 'I don't need a calculator.'

This mathematical competence is due to 'a tyrannical teacher' at Bows Road Primary in Palmers Green, north London. 'There are thirty-three of you in the class – and you will all pass the "schol-arship" this year,' stated the tyrant as he prepared the class for the Eleven Plus. 'I have never had a failure!' They were all duly tyrannised and they all passed.

'I sat the Eleven Plus,' says John Humphrys. 'It really did dominate your life: a watershed. If you passed, you got a decent education. If not, you didn't. I did. You got into Cardiff High School by not only passing but by coming top. It was regarded as the best in Cardiff, if not Wales. It was academically brilliant and certainly the most snobbish.'

Wearing his uniform and cap, he was extremely aware that he was the only boy in his area to go to this high-powered school. He was also uneasily aware at school of a scarcity of working-class boys. His father was a French polisher; the other dads were white-collar.

Although mainly in the B stream, he took ten O levels, failing only woodwork. When Cardiff High asked him to go back, he replied, 'Do you really want me to stand up and say how much I hated it?'

The headmaster told John's parents that he ought to stay on, but that didn't happen. Nobody in the family had ever gone to university. And there was something else at the front of John's mind: 'I had the idea of being a glamorous reporter: Clark Kent turning into Superman.'

Glenda Jackson, who made an exit from the stage to enter the House of Commons, was a good pupil at her Church of England primary in Hoylake, Merseyside.

'Taking the Eleven Plus there is a memory that will live with me to my dying day.' The results were posted but on the date when they were due the letter still hadn't reached Glenda's home by the time she left for school. It was a small community in which they all knew one another.

'Have you passed?' adults asked her.

'I don't know,' she would answer. 'The results haven't arrived.' They took this as a 'No,' and she felt an instant change in their attitude to her. When she went home as usual for lunch, the letter had arrived. She had passed.

'The attitude of those adults changed again. I had been made to feel a failure and then a success. I don't know if I felt it then but I am scandalised that a child of eleven should have to go through this.'

'There was something hanging over us that I couldn't quite comprehend: the Eleven Plus.' Tony Hawks passed; kids he was friendly with didn't. He remembers seeing them a month after they had all started at their new schools – and some had turned into little thugs. 'It seemed cruel, to make people fail at eleven.'

'If you failed, you were down the pan,' said Trevor Baylis. He later invented the wind-up radio and received the OBE, so clearly has de-panned himself, but success didn't feel like a possibility at Dormers Wells Secondary Modern in Ealing: 'I got the impression that I was doomed to serve those who had passed.' He was 'old school braces', i.e. secondary modern, while the others were 'old school ties', grammar school, that is.

Gary Lineker took the Eleven Plus and came out thinking, 'That exam was really easy.' There was one question that asked, 'Which is the tallest tree?' This referred to an illustration of three trees whose tops were at the same height – but one of them was in a dip in the ground and so was obviously twice the size of the others. 'How,' he wondered, 'can anyone fail to get that?' (Having once been set an IQ test as part of my son's psychology course and felt my brain rapidly slowing to a remedial mode, I can reply to Gary: quite easily.)

Barbara Dickson speaks for many when she says, 'I wish I'd concentrated, I always enjoyed school really; I liked being around other people. But I just didn't try very hard and I have the attention span of an amoeba.' She may be insulting amoebas here, which for all we know concentrate their razor-sharp intellects on the job in hand, but we take her point. More specifically, she added that she never seemed to do any homework. She had very good parents – 'terribly respectable', she insisted – but they never questioned her when she announced, 'I've finished,' five minutes after starting her homework.

The same was true with her music lessons, which she started at the age of five: 'The problem was that if you didn't practise, the game was up; and the game was up for me every week.'

Her parents had selected Dunfermline High, a grammar school. She sat her Eleven Plus – and failed. 'I was rather knocked back. From the age of ten I'd wanted to be a teacher but now I think I jacked in the whole idea of a decent job.' There was 'nothing down for me', as they say in Liverpool, where her mother hailed from, to signify that there's no hope. She certainly could not support herself by shorthand: despite her school's classes in the subject, all she could do was 'Dear Sir,' and 'Yours faithfully,' with nothing in between. (To be fair, that was better than Shirley Anne Field, who admitted to me that she could only get as far as the 'Dear Sir' bit.) Barbara thought, 'I'm going to have to live on my wits. I just picked up the baton of music and ran with it.' And, it seems, came out ahead of the pack.

Susan Greenfield, a professor, baroness and researcher into

brain physiology, had no idea as a girl why the Eleven Plus was important. Her parents said, 'We'll love you whatever happens,' which suggested there was something important riding on it. 'I knew there was something odd about the exam because we took the tests in the school dining-room and had newly sharpened pencils.' Fortunately this did not put her off and she passed.

Her parents were keen on Godolphin and Latymer in Hamersmith, west London, a direct grant school with its own exam. At the interview she was asked if she knew what a galaxy was. Some would say that it was a collection of stars, others that it was a chocolate bar. Smart Susan said both and got in with a free place.

'Of about thirty-five boys in my class, only one, a pale spidery boy called Williams, passed the Eleven Plus or "the Scholarship",' recalled novelist Barry Unsworth. 'The reason I failed was that I was no good at shapes, which the intelligence test involved. Words, I scored on.' (The Booker Prize judges were to confirm that.)

He still went to Stockton-on-Tees Grammar, where he got As in his A levels: 'You could buy your way in.' Which made a bit of a nonsense of the exam.

'I failed the Eleven Plus miserably,' recalls Eric Burdon. 'I had no idea what was going on during the exam, except that the teacher looked more serious.'

Steve Redgrave's teacher must have been beyond serious: 'My older sisters had all failed the Eleven Plus – and they were a little bit more academic than me.' Steve does not know if his parents even put down a choice of grammar school: 'I knew I was going to a secondary modern. It was written on the wall beforehand and that made it a little bit easier when I didn't pass the Eleven Plus.'

'You failed the Eleven Plus,' her careers teacher said. Constance Briscoe, the barrister jailed for intending to pervert the course of justice in connection with former Cabinet Minister's

Chris Huhne's driving case, was stunned: 'I didn't even remember taking it.'

The writer Hunter Davies definitely did not take the Eleven Plus, as his family had moved to Scotland at the time. 'When I arrived back in England, all my friends, including my best friend Reginald Hill (author of the *Dalziel and Pascoe* novels) were all going to grammar school but I was just sent to Creighton, the secondary modern in Carlisle.'

At sixteen, he had eight or nine O levels and was one of three boys transferred to Carlisle Grammar. 'The other two went on to get PhDs and, last heard of, were professors.' They had presumably failed their Eleven Plus.

> Arriving at the 800-year-old grammar school, with teachers in gowns and forms named 'Six Alpha', I did feel rather inferior. I felt out of it, educationally, until I was eighteen and at Durham University, starting from square one with everyone else. I got a Second. I did no studying but still thought I might get a First; after all, I had spelt my name correctly.

Somehow Brenda Blethyn managed to take the Eleven Plus twice. (Maybe she was disguised the second time? She does a very good Northumbrian accent in *Vera*.) She also failed it twice, yet at fifteen she had clocked up ten CSEs, passing maths with 98 per cent (shame about that 2 per cent – must try harder).

Sue Townsend failed the Eleven Plus. (*The Secret Diary of Adrian Mole, Aged 13¾* has sold 20 million copies worldwide. Just saying.) Not doing any of the maths questions could have been a factor here; the subject was and remained a mystery. 'I don't think I had a conversation with anyone about which secondary school I was going to.'

BBC reporter Sue Lloyd-Roberts was another failure. 'The Eleven Plus was considered a chore not to be treated seriously and the school was far too embarrassed to tell me that I'd failed.' The clue was the pack of leaflets about secondary moderns pushed through the door of her home by the local education authority.

Some of my interviewees can be described as enjoying success despite failing the Eleven Plus. Jason Bradbury is confident that he succeeded *because* he failed. His examination disaster has certainly not prevented him from presenting Channel 5's *The Gadget Show* and writing the *Dot.Robot* series of children's novels.

'I was a bright kid and it seemed like the wrong result when I failed my Eleven Plus, unlike my brothers. They went on to grammar school.' He asks us to imagine the problems *that* started at home. 'But going to Gartree Secondary Modern (now Community School) was the best thing that happened to me.'

There was, for example, Mr Ritson, the English teacher who brought Beatles' lyrics to the boys: 'What does this line in "Eleanor Rigby" mean?' When he was twelve, Jason handed the teacher a play he had written based on *Just William*: 'You are going to direct this, Mr Ritson – starring me!'

Then there was the 'very austere' science teacher, Mr Walker. 'It was like the Stockholm Syndrome, when you fall in love with your captor. He wouldn't let me not do science at O level.' The thought of Mr Walker looking sternly over his shoulder seems to have stayed with Jason over the years. He swears that the science in his books is real and that the robots doing handstands in his school shows really are obeying the children's commands.

He himself seems to have become a kind of Bionic Pupil. The concept of messing around at school was totally alien. He believed the teachers and did exactly what he was told. He would ask himself, 'Why am I here in this lesson for forty-five minutes?' and work out what he would expect to get out of it. The ghost of that Eleven Plus may well have haunted him; he was always aware that there would be a further test waiting at the end of the year.

A lesser lad would have taken the line that this academic malarkey was all a waste anyway and bunking off was more fun. Jason, however, dedicated his life to winning more qualifications than all his brothers. At North Lincolnshire College, he told himself: 'If I get four more O levels, my brothers will never catch me.' He got three A levels and thirteen O levels and CSEs. At Bristol University he achieved a 2.1, by which time his brothers must have been throwing in the towel and yelling, 'All right! You win! Enough!'

Sebastian Coe also has no quarrel with the examiners who marked his Eleven Plus papers. 'I am one of the band of those who failed. The local secondary modern at that stage didn't have a very good reputation but my parents said, "He will go there – and be fine." It was the best thing that happened to me: I was exposed to a greater cross-section of people and issues.' Within a year, Tapton Secondary Modern, Sheffield, was turned into a comprehensive and became an even better school during his time, so that people from all over the city tried to get their children there. (As it had no sixth form, he did his A levels at nearby Abbeydale Grange and can claim to having been educated at a secondary modern, a comprehensive and a grammar school.)

Another plus for Sebastian was his year tutor David Jackson, an athlete who had run for Derbyshire. He also took RE and would tell young Coe: 'If you are a bit low on your mileage this week, this is your chance to catch up.' Sebastian's eight or nine O levels did not, for obvious reasons, include RE.

Nor, incidentally, did that last subject feature among the eight O levels clocked up by fellow athlete Jonathan Edwards, which was more surprising since his father was a vicar and his own faith was so strong that, like Eric Liddell in the *Chariots of Fire* Olympics, he did not compete in races held on the Sabbath, thus missing out on the 1991 World Championships. He has since lost his faith but retains the trophies.

Ideally, this chapter would end with a personal perspective on the Eleven Plus. I would have concluded that passing/failing was in my case deserved/undeserved and had enhanced/destroyed my future prospects.

However, I still do not know if I passed. For those of us educated in the private system, the most crucial exam of the state system scarcely registered on the radar. The big examination was the Common Entrance, taken at twelve or thirteen. That's 'common' as in 'common to most public schools', not as in 'vulgar'. Alternatively, there was the scholarship exam set by an individual school, at which I was pointed. Taking the Eleven Plus therefore was of minor, if any, interest and we did no preparation for it.

The only notice that it was on the way came from a chance remark of my mother, who happened to have heard of a question set in the previous year's IQ test: 'If yesterday was Monday, what's tomorrow?' To this I answered promptly, 'Tuesday,' though was bright enough to realise when corrected that the correct answer was, let me see, I'll just check my notes, 'Wednesday'. The IQ test in my paper included the question, 'If last month was January, what is next month,' so by applying the principle I had learnt I was able to answer snappily 'March' instead of 'February', which would have been my answer. The point of an IQ test is that it is supposed to measure what you are, not what you've learnt, so my answer was bogus and it was just as well that my result, whatever it was, had no bearing on which school I went to.

Whatever the exams we took and whatever our results, they all led inexorably to the next stage. Secondary school. Things were getting even more serious.

CHAPTER 6

ON SECONDARY
THOUGHTS

C hildren entering secondary school could be over halfway through their entire educational careers; they
could leave immediately after taking GCSEs. Alternatively they could progress to A levels and then to
further or higher education.

These new kids will be tougher than when they started at primary school, but so will the bullies. The schools will be bigger,
with numbers running into four figures.

The pupils can start to concentrate on the subjects that could
launch them into their careers. They could go behind the bike

sheds with pupils of the opposite (or indeed same) sex for fags or both.

It doesn't look as if anyone was concentrating on Phil Cool's case. 'I never took the Eleven Plus, for some reason.' That would have been fine if he had been in a comprehensive system but he clearly wasn't, because after enjoying his two primary schools he went to an all-boys Catholic secondary modern.

'I was in 1C, although I knew for a fact that some of the kids in 1B had done academically worse than me. There had been some kind of mix-up but I kept quiet about it.' The reason for keeping his head down was that among the lesser mortals he could shine: 'I was always top of the class in 1C, 2C, 3C … then I was put in a class called 4Y, in which the kids were really brainy and I was always bottom.'

In Phil's opinion, it was not a good school. Take the pottery teacher, for example. The boys used to call him 'Fester' or 'Fink', which does not sound like a vote of confidence. Mr Fester (let's be polite here) used to do religious instruction as well. There is on the face of it nothing wrong with a teacher having two strings to his bow, but there was a snag: 'If you couldn't recite the catechism word for word, you got thrashed.'

Mr Fink (let's see if that sounds more agreeable) also did French in the same room. Three strings to his bow! Was there no end to this man's talents? Unfortunately there was: 'The people in the C stream never did French, just scrubbing clay off the tables.'

Phil seems to have discovered why Fester-Fink remained on the payroll of the school or indeed any organisation at all: 'His knuckles weren't that far from the ground and if any of the teachers were threatened by angry fathers who wanted a fight, they would send for him.' And to give credit where due, Fink-Fester was in a sense inspirational, in that Phil was inspired to write a long poem about him based on the song 'Monster Mash'. He could have called his version 'Fester Thrash', perhaps. 'My poem got round the school and people used to chant it on the bus home.' And the bus home must have been more cheerful than the bus going there, particularly if your day began with a double-pottery lesson.

'At Ampleforth, rugby was second only to religion', recalls Lawrence Dallaglio. It could hardly be *above* religion, of course, this being a boarding school run by the Benedictine Order of monks, but for a future England captain this was as good as it could get. 'All the eye could see was rugby pitches.' The problem for Lawrence Dallaglio was getting in. He had been in the choir of his prep school and had sung at Andrew Lloyd Webber's wedding (well, one of his weddings) and on Tina Turner's 'We Don't Need Another Hero', but that might not cut much ice in Catholic circles.

'I don't think so; that's a little ambitious for your son,' said his prep school headmaster when Mrs Dallaglio suggested Ampleforth, but that only made her more determined and Lawrence went to Yorkshire for an interview.

'You were born on 10 August,' said Father Dominic Milroy. 'What's special about that?'

Lawrence remembered that this is St Lawrence's day.

'What's special about that?' asked Father Dominic.

'He's the head of the Order,' answered Lawrence. He looked at Father Dominic's face. It was a done deal.

Lawrence had a good time: 'I probably had too good a time; I wasn't one for rules.'

He achieved three passes in the last year of O levels and eight passes in the first year of GCSEs. Then came the family tragedy. In his first A level year his sister died in the sinking of the

Marchioness pleasure boat on the Thames and, in shock and trauma, he left the school. It was because she had won a scholarship to a ballet school that his parents could afford his private education. He passed the exams later and went on a course in urban estate management at what was then Kingston Poly, chosen because it was near the Wasps ground. When he joined that rugby club, no one asked, 'How many A levels have you got?'

Although Karren Brady was quite definite that it had been downhill all the way after primary school with the wonderful Mrs Peters, things did pick up again in her A level years. At least the beginning and end of her school career were pleasant experiences. Shame about the bits in between. Unlike her husband, Fulham striker Paul Peschisolido, who remained at the same Canadian school until the age of eighteen, she jumped around between establishments which were not all, as it were, in the Premier League of education.

One of them was a state secondary school whose name has thankfully been deleted from her memory by a kindly amnesia. 'It was very hard-nosed and I was ridiculed because, having gone to private schools where you are taught manners, I said "Please" and "Thank you".' As a supporter of state schools, I wondered if she wasn't going over the top. Then she added, 'To put the school in context: Vinnie Jones went there.' I took her point.

She was then moved to a private school that was no great shakes either. 'It was quite a shock, at thirteen, to go to a boarding school in the middle of bloody nowhere.' St Middle of Bloody Nowhere would be a good name but it was in fact called St Poles, situated in Ware, Hertfordshire. 'My memory is of being cold and hungry.' Her best lesson was cooking: 'Then you could eat!' Games consisted of running out with a hockey stick and running back in again. (Sounds fine to me. I always found the bit in between, where you have to hit the ball, to be the boring part.)

St Poles was poles apart from Aldenham School, Elstree, where she did her four A levels: 'It was like night turning into day. It rekindled my faith in education. I learnt more in those two years than in the previous ten.' The girls lived in a real house with the housemaster and his wife. She even played hockey, just to make up the numbers.

Penelope Lively too has forgotten the name of one of her schools. She was there for only six months, the first she attended after being taught at home. Unfortunately she was at her next school, whose name she can remember, for four excruciatingly unhappy years in Sussex. 'The Downs was rigorously devoted to the improvement of its girls'…' she told me. This sounded very good but what was that final apostrophe about? She went on to finish the sentence: '…girls' lacrosse and netball.'

There must have been some lessons squeezed into the sporting timetable, because she emerged with eight subjects, seven of them being distinctions, in her School Certificate (the predecessor of O levels). These were all *real* subjects like Latin and maths, none of your cooking or needlework nonsense. 'I have never had so great an exam success.' (Her subsequent Third at Oxford, where she had a fine time not doing much Modern History, cannot compare with it.)

The Downs was not up in the air about her marks: 'Her exam results were good,' her report conceded grudgingly, continuing, 'If only we could say the same about her performance on the lacrosse field!' That might have been a helpful point if they gave the Booker Prize for lacrosse instead of for books.

'My father at this point thought that girls as well as boys ought to be sent to university but the school pulled a face and said that its girls went to finishing schools in Switzerland.' He sent her to a crammer in Surrey where they concentrated on cramming girls into Oxbridge – netball was not high on the curriculum.

One senses that The Downs was not staffed by the first wave of feminists. Nor was the newspaper that came up with the patronising headline to celebrate her Carnegie prize for her children's novel. By this time she was married to Professor Jack Lively, so naturally it announced, 'Don's Wife Wins Book Award.'

There was no bullying by older boys at Ecclesbourne School, Duffield, Derby. There weren't any older boys in this excellent new grammar, which had a total of seventy-five split between two classes and taught by a handful of teachers. 'We had to start everything,' says Stefan Buczacki. 'I was the founding editor of the school magazine.'

The headmaster had his heart in the right place but he rather amazed them at the first school assembly by declaring, 'The following will be the school traditions...' Stefan has forgotten what they were but he is certain that the words of the school song were written by the headmaster and his wife: 'all very patriotic and about Derbyshire. The music was virtually unplayable. We had four houses, named after famous Derbyshire people.' (Name four famous Derbyshire men and women! Er...) 'I was a house captain. We had a house feast when we stayed behind and had a plate of sandwiches, but with fewer than twenty of us it felt more like a bungalow feast.'

Jimmy Greaves too was among the first batch of boys through the door and was always in the top year of his sparkling new school. He failed the Eleven Plus – 'I just took one look at the paper' – and went to Kingswood in Hainault, east London, one of the first secondary moderns. 'They were secondary to the grammar schools but Kingswood provided a superb, diverse education.'

'Greavsie' enthuses about the playing fields, which naturally were of consuming interest to the lad who would be the first player to score 100 goals before the age of twenty-one. He joined in all the activities, including a poetry-reading contest that he won, and became head boy.

> After we had suffered two years of school dinners delivered from outside in big tins, the kitchens were opened up and meals became quite bearable, apart from the tapioca. You ate them because you were bloody hungry; school dinners were about the only meal we got, as there was not a lot of food around.
>
> Discipline was strict; you used to get the cane, slipper, ruler or duster thrown at you. As they say, the 1950s were the last days of Victorian Britain.

'I was given some bad advice at the time of the Eleven Plus,' states Gary Rhodes. He had struggled in his first year at junior school, when his work was badly affected by his father leaving home: 'I didn't see him for thirty years.' He was thrilled when he managed to claw his way from the D to the B stream. As often happens, his favourite class was English, with its freedom to invent his own stories. The teaching was good, he felt cared for and he has fond memories.

At the end of his time there, he was faced with three secondary schools: grammar, 'technical' and secondary modern. 'My mother was given the advice that I was a borderline case; I would struggle at a technical school but would shine at a secondary modern.' They plumped for Rainham Boys'. 'This was a bad mistake.'

He does not blame the school. Although vast, with forty-three pupils in one class, it was fairly new, not to say 'quite flash', and had 'heavy' discipline, of which he approves. The trouble lay in his being assured that he would shine in the secondary modern. He rather put his feet up. 'You only did five subjects at O level or CSE. I did two O levels, in English. I was told I might find maths difficult and should do it as a CSE. So I became lazy. I got a B and C in the English O levels and mid-grades in my CSEs.'

'You should go to Chatham Docks as an apprentice,' the careers master advised. But Gary had other fish to fry, not to mention chicken, steak, potatoes, aubergine...

Polar explorer Sir Ranulph Fiennes can boast of his early skills at two sports. He did well enough at boxing to be awarded what Eton called a 'Cap'. If his school had known he participated in the other sport, he would have been de-Capped and thrown out on his ear.

Ranulph is one of a small band of schoolboys for whom going to Eton was a come-down. His full name is triple-barrelled – Twisleton-Wykeham-Fiennes – but wisely he stopped using the first two barrels; if he had to radio for help from a collapsing iceberg, he would be tumbling into the icy water well before he had finished telling air-sea rescue who he was.

'Our family's school was Winchester College; William of Wykeham had built the place and our family was related to him and so got a financial preference there.' The problem was that this cut-price scheme for descendants of the founder depended on a good performance at the entrance exam, which Ranulph failed to pull off. 'That's why I went to Eton, which wasn't particularly difficult, educationally speaking, to get into in those days.'

Now for the other sport. 'Stegophily', as anyone in the Classics Sixth would tell you, derives from Greek and means 'love of roofs' or 'night climbing'. It also meant: 'You will be expelled if caught.' The urban mountaineers would shin up some part of Eton's architecture, taking with them a dustbin that they would sling over a handy spire to proclaim to the world that they had scaled the Etonian peak.

On one occasion they slipped up. This was better than slipping down but still very awkward. Gathering as usual in the early hours, the chaps discovered that the dustbin was not in its place at the bottom of the climb. One of them was sent off to get his 'tailcoat' and the long Etonian jacket was duly hoisted aloft to be left swinging bravely in the breeze at the top of 'Lupton's Tower'.

This was a particularly difficult climb but finally they got down and opened a bottle of cherry brandy (that was forbidden, too). At this point, very late in the day, or rather, early in the morning, it occurred to the owner of the coat that his name might have been sewn in it. None of the others were prepared to schlep all the way up there again so he had to ascend and descend by himself.

A note about that cherry brandy. The night climbers tended also to indulge in skulduggery by day:

> You weren't allowed into Windsor town centre unless you were wearing your tails, which made you conspicuous: you could be spotted in those streets where you weren't allowed at all. We knew some 'civilians' [non-Etonians] in a hotel, where we kept overalls in a stable. You'd re-emerge in a street where there was a shop that sold every cigarette known to mankind. There was also a shop that sold drink.

Cherry brandy, for example. The smugglers would take orders from other boys, add a modest commission and slide back into school looking innocent and sober. 'The art was to bring all the bottles back in the pockets of your tails without them clinking when you passed a master.'

This would hone those skills needed as a spy in, say, occupied France during World War Two but there is not much call for it these days. The night-climbing is an even more extraordinary pastime; Ranulph suffers from vertigo. As therapy, he tried a few years ago to defeat this condition by going on a charity climb up the daunting North Face of the Eiger. The good news was that he raised $3 million for that excellent organisation Marie Curie Cancer Care. The bad news is that it made his vertigo worse.

William Donaldson differed from Ranulph Fiennes in that he did actually get into Winchester. He also differed by being an impresario, a joker, a writer and a self-confessed degenerate sort of fellow. A typical stunt was to write a letter to Esther Rantzen under his pseudonym of 'Henry Root' in which he went over the top in his enthusiasm for her TV show. He received from her office a thank-you-for-your-nice-letter letter and a signed photograph. He then wrote a follow-up beginning, 'You're a fat fraud and your show's a disgrace,' to which the response was, yes, a thank-you and signed photograph.

This shows that 'Willie' had in his work a joking relationship with the truth, down to rebranding himself as Mr Root and several other fictitious characters. In addition, he differed from those who talk themselves up by talking himself down. Both of these were good career moves, but it does mean that you might want to take what follows with the contents of a large saltcellar.

'I was the stupidest boy at Winchester,' for example, though he qualified this by adding, 'Actually, it was between me and the Earl of Whatsit and Somewhere; after one term it was suggested he try Eton.' Like Ranulph Fiennes, Winchester clearly shared the view that Etonians were the intellectual B-listers.

> I was never in trouble for being stupid but the head of the house beat me after one cricket match in which I was fielding at mid-wicket. I had realised that by turning through 180 degrees I could also be cover-point in the cricket match next door. When I caught someone out, the captain in this match twigged that he was fielding in a team of twelve people.

The multi-tasking on the cricket pitch should have been rewarded for keenness, not punished. It was an early example of Willie turning his life through 180 degrees and, as it were, bowling a googly. However, it was odd that he should be playing in one game of cricket, let alone two, as he was an expert in getting out of 'ecca' (i.e. exercise – Winchester has its own official slang, which includes a slang word for the word 'slang').

> You said you were playing squash when in fact you had been up to no good with someone behind the squash courts. I was normally up to no good with someone who is now a judge; much later, when I asked him for money, he must have thought that I was blackmailing him.

That would be a reasonable assumption. Willie was no friend of authority. 'To my credit' – not a phrase he could use all that much – 'I instigated "positive" bullying.' By this he meant that he used to bully the prefects. Together with a friend who was a 'senior inferior' (translated from the Winchester, it means someone just below prefect level) he used to toast them in front of the fire or, by way of variety, tip them up in their beds with their feet in the air.

He got his School Certificate (O levels) but never made it to the sixth form. His account of the rest of his school career was somewhat vague and I gathered that maybe he was not encouraged to come back the following term. 'I did get into Cambridge somehow,' he concluded. Maybe he blackmailed someone.

Willie Donaldson went to the same university as David Starkey but, as with Ranulph Fiennes, the differences between them were considerable. For a start, Dr Starkey, the historian and presenter of history programmes, went to Kendal Grammar. He found the transition from junior school to be quite difficult.

I had what would now be called a nervous breakdown and pulled
out for three or four months. I wore a surgical boot until I was
thirteen, which made me a target for mockery. Fortunately I
was unusually tall for my age and even then had a sharp tongue.

Christopher Hitchens had an equally sharp tongue, though he
was too young to use it much when we coincided briefly at The
Leys, a minor public school in Cambridge; my (very welcome)
last year was his first.

The place must have improved somewhat during his time there,
because he credited it with having 'a civilised atmosphere'. One
thing didn't change, though. 'What I couldn't stand were the sons
of Lancashire businessmen who didn't realise how very privileged
we were.' Yes, I knew them well.

John Hegley was top of the form in his final year at primary
school. To put it another way, as honesty compelled him to do,
'In fact, the boy I sat next to should have been first, and I should
have been second, but I did some copying.'

All right, John Hegley was top-ish of the form in his final
year at primary school. He passed the Eleven Plus but something
went wrong at Luton Boys'. He was down at number sixteen in
his first year.

'You are what you are perceived as: the teachers perceived me
as an under-achiever.' If he had wanted to prove them right, he
could hardly have done better: 'In my second year I was twenty-
eighth out of twenty-nine.'

Yet by the time that O levels were looming up on the horizon, he decided he had to buckle down. 'Why did I do that? I
had discovered the local football team, Luton Town; I had for
it a passion that approached a spiritual goal.' Presumably this
was to go with the non-spiritual sort of goal which they were,

or weren't, scoring on the pitch. Although he realises that football could seem like a distraction, it somehow spurred him on to greater things such as O levels.

Being advised not to take woodwork, he did extra maths in the storage room instead. His best subjects were English and biology and these were two of the three A level subjects which he studied when the Hegley family exchanged Byron Road, Luton, for a home within striking distance of Rodway School, Bristol. He used to wander around the lanes reading Byron (obviously) and John Clare.

In his second year in the sixth form, they went on a biology field trip to study *Sphagnum cuspidatum* and came back talking not so much about the moss in question as about John, saying how funny he was. 'I was Lutonless, yes, but no longer alone. I just knew that I had found my milieu.' You can take the boy out of Luton but…

For Ken Hom, the problem was the weather. And the gangs in Chicago. The chef-to-be started his after-school culinary career at his uncle's restaurant when he was eleven. At twelve he went on to a junior high school which was in such a rough area that on Fridays he had to put on his running shoes to nip past the hoodlums waiting to shake him down for money for the weekend.

Yet it was in a high-class district when compared with his next school, which was located in such a war zone that he was taken away after just a week. His mother's solution was to give a bogus address, that of his uncle in a smarter suburb which put him in the catchment area of a safer high school. The downside was that it was miles from where he actually lived, so it could take two or three hours to plough through the snow between home and school. When it snows in Chicago, it really snows: 'I didn't go to graduation because it snowed so much our door was blocked.'

Joanne Harris had a problem with her French. Although she now writes bestsellers in English – *Coastliners* went to No. 1 – when she went to her first school in Barnsley this was a language she barely spoke. (We'll have no snide remarks about what language they speak in Barnsley, thank you.) French was what they spoke at home and, embarrassingly, the headmaster was a teacher of French (allegedly) who couldn't actually speak it.

It was almost as bad at Wakefield Girls' High, a private school with some very good teachers but again a French teacher who was hopeless. Joanne was *une fille méchante*: 'I made lists of her mistakes and handed them in to her at the end of the lesson.' Finally she was rescued – or perhaps one should say that the teacher was – by a smarter colleague who gave Joanne sixth form work in order to keep her *occupée*.

Being a teacher's pest, Joanne was the kind of girl your daughter would want in her class but not necessarily the kind the teacher would wish for. She set up elaborate practical jokes such as rigging up a cuddly toy behind the blackboard. When she pulled a string, the toy would leap up but when the lovely Latin teacher looked behind her to see what they were laughing at, the offending toy would have disappeared.

More creatively, she and two friends volunteered to clear out the 'book room'. The staff should have smelt a rat. This was a wheeze to escape the rule that said girls had to stay out in the cold during the lunch hour. They were in fact reading and performing plays from dusty old set texts. 'We also wrote stories and devised our own outdoor version of the siege of Troy. I was Achilles and dragged Hector around behind my chariot; her mother never got the grass stains off her dress.'

Having achieved nine or ten O levels, Joanne left Wakefield Girls' High (presumably the French and Latin teachers could live with that) and went to Barnsley Sixth Form College for A levels. She got the top grade in English and French but the lowest grade in German. People often remember their English teacher most fondly out of all the members of staff but Joanne is not one of them. This member of the staff didn't like her (I hate to think what japes Joanne might have pulled on her) and demanded a re-mark – of her *higher* grade papers.

Terry Deary had no more joy with Monkwearmouth Grammar than he had with his primary school. 'I wasn't asked to write a creative English essay until the age of thirteen, which was very late.' He got seventeen and a half out of twenty, top of the class, but no one said this was a talent that should be developed.

What someone in authority did say at the end of the third year was, 'Girls will do history and boys have the option of additional maths or Latin.' Needless to say, there was a dissident voice from, guess who, the Horrible Historian-to-be: 'I wanted to do history and had to stand up to the head, who, in his gown, looked remarkably like Michael Howard in a Dracula cape – a scary guy. I won but he never forgave me.' Nor, we're guessing, was there any forgiveness the other way either.

Terry just managed three A levels, with Es in the two that have since made his name, English and history. 'I'd switched off by then. History consisted of taking down desiccated notes and preparing for exam questions. I was never taught the skills of historical investigation.

'It was all kings, battles – and dates. Dates are easy to test: 1066, tick. 1067, cross. I see *Horrible Histories* as righting the wrongs of centuries of history teaching. That sounds pretentious,' he added quickly. 'I see myself as an entertainer first of all.' So do his readers, in a good way.

'I was convinced that Wharrier [*sic*] Secondary Modern was

filled with warriors – and indeed it was,' said Eric Burdon. 'Your induction on your first day was being thrown over the crossbar of the goal post on the rugger pitch.'

A similar form of new-boy-hurling was described in *Tom Brown's School Days*, although in this case it was an indoor form of torture. At Rugby, the school on which the novel was based, it had died out by the time Chris Brasher was there in the 1940s. This is not to say that the place had been totally modernised; it still had its own language that to outsiders would need subtitles or simultaneous translation. Chris thinks he was 'Holder of the Bigside Bags'. The 'bags' would be for the paper chase and 'Bigside' was the code word for the playing field.

The playing field had something more intriguing to offer in his time at Rugby. One of the headmaster's daughters was a Wren who, when she came home on leave, used to run up to a low wall and jump over it to the playing field to get to the house of the master on the other side whom she was courting.

'We would be there, pacing up and down for the marvellous sight of her skirts going up and of her black stockings and suspenders – the only female flesh we saw.'

We don't know about the flesh but there were somewhat fewer females at St Michael's after an incident that took place during Anneka Rice's time. This small private girls' school in Surrey started out as a missionary school but standards had slipped. And we're not talking about Anneka's organ-playing ('I wasn't very good at it') during 'Dear Lord and Father of Mankind'.

Her diary has run out by this advanced period in her schooldays but this was not a crisis that anyone would forget.

'Some of the girls were mucking around with a lighter and set fire to the curtains in the common room. It was arson and the police were called in because of the potential danger; the whole school could have gone up. The girls who had been in the common room were expelled.' She was saved from expulsion by an accident of timetabling. 'I had been at a music lesson.' When the smoke had cleared, there were only four of them left in the entire A level year. This made team games a bit tricky.

Drayton Manor County Grammar in west London was a marvellous school for rocker and self-proclaimed 'Grumpy Old Man' Rick Wakeman but the nightmare of a journey there could easily have made him a grumpy young boy: 'A one-mile walk, then a bus, then a train, then a half-mile walk.' There were three grammar schools closer but a cousin named Alan Wakeman was already at Drayton Manor and the local education authority may have thought they were brothers and so placed them in the same school.

'There was a detention if you were late.' Talking of detentions, Rick also received one for getting the entire first form drunk by slipping Scotch into their Coca-Cola bottles.

Stockport High School for Girls gave Joan Bakewell a 'cracking' education. In her School Certificate exams she got six distinctions and three credits, as a result of which she was awarded a travelling scholarship. This took her abroad for the first time and, as a bonus, she went out for two years afterwards with one of the fellow-travelling boys.

> Then came a major disappointment. I wanted to do a 'Higher' [A level] in English but wasn't allowed to because I had only got a credit instead of a distinction; I think the English teacher didn't like me. Because of that, I couldn't do English in the sixth form, so I couldn't do English at university, so I couldn't become a writer.

With her four A levels in other subjects, and a degree in economics, she has since then been forced to eke out a precarious existence as one of our most respected broadcasters – and, come to think of it, a writer.

'I was a bookie at school: if somebody had threepence-half-penny at 11-4, I could tell you instantly what their winnings would be.' Despite that skill, Sir Tony Robinson was completely useless at maths. 'English was a doddle, not like working. And history was like football; I couldn't understand why other people didn't like it.'

He has four O levels that should be taken away: 'I cheated.' (He had, after all, played the Artful Dodger in a professional production.) 'I took in a Robert Graves novel in case I finished early in the exams – and in faint pencil there would be written some French vocabulary.'

The school wanted to put him in the Oxbridge set but he panicked, realising what this would mean: 'Latin O level, maths O level and three A levels.' A cunning plan worthy of Baldrick came to him: 'I want to go to drama school.' The Central School of Speech and Drama didn't bother with that A level stuff. Later, playing Baldrick brought him into contact with glittering Oxbridge types like Stephen Fry, so everyone assumed he had been to Cambridge too. And he didn't have to bother with all those university exams either.

Simon Weston, the Welsh Guardsman who suffered 46 per cent burns when his ship was bombed during the Falklands War, recalled that 'Things were fine at Graddfa Secondary Modern, although on my first day I got strangled: a guy picked me up in the corridor. We met again in the Welsh Guards, when the arrangement was, shall we say, slightly altered. He didn't remember me and had no idea why I gave him a thump. Bullies don't prosper!'

Joseph Heller's war was, of course, World War Two, which gave him the material for *Catch-22* and also paid for his fees at New York University via the GI Bill of Rights. By his own account, he was a conscientious student, both at university and at his school before the war. He did well, not very well, but quite well: 'I always got the lowest distinction.' He confessed that he loved going to Abraham Lincoln High: 'I even liked homework; I liked very much having something to do.'

He played truant twice: 'I calculated with remorse afterwards that I hadn't had as good a time at New York's Paramount Theatre as I would have had in classes, the cafeteria and the sweet shop at Lincoln.'

(One of his novels was entitled *Good as Gold*, which could easily describe him at school. As a features editor, I once had the pleasure of choosing an extract from it. The book was fine but not spectacular. It is said that people occasionally told him he had never subsequently written anything as good as his *Catch-22*, to which his retort was, 'No one has.')

Professor Kathy Sykes is one of those television lecturers who make you wish you hadn't dropped physics at school. That's what she nearly did, until persuaded otherwise by a new teacher at her Abingdon comprehensive, Mr Quill. She did well but had to keep quiet about it: 'I got a healthy string of As. I didn't always tell people my exam results and I stopped swimming for the school. You could get your head beaten in for doing well at *everything*.'

At Xaverian College in Rusholme, Manchester, the tradition was that the older boys would stick the heads of the new boys down the toilets. The bullies didn't know it but when Bernard Hill arrived, that tradition was about to be tested. For some reason my street in south London always has a token actor living in it and in the 1980s this was Bernard Hill. He was seen as a radical sort of person, not least because he had played the hard-done-by Yosser ('Gizza Job') Hughes in the gritty television series *Boys from the Blackstuff.* (He has since graduated to more upmarket parts including the captain of the Titanic, the King of Rohan in *The Lord of the Rings* and the Home Secretary in a television play about David Blunkett.) On the first day at the tough Catholic school, it was a case of 'cometh the hour, cometh the new boy'.

'In an instinctive trade unionism, a group of us new boys said, "Why don't we stick together and stop 'em?" It worked, until the second day, that is.' This time the bullies regrouped and picked them off. Bernard was ducked twice. Having lost the Battle of the Bogs, Bernard's boys turned out to have won the War of the Waterboarding. 'We caused such mayhem that this was the last time it happened; we never did it to the next year's new boys.'

Unfortunately this under-age solidarity was no use against another set of bullies: the staff. 'The teachers were a pretty nasty crowd. We got hit a lot and they would pull the hairs at the side of your head, which is very painful.'

It was a grammar school and a real eye-opener to Bernard: 'I had never some across the class system before. Kids came to school in cars! These kids were always prefects and house heads.' Still, they never get to play captains or kings.

Jean Marsh and her sister did not stay anywhere long enough to get their heads beaten in or shoved down loos. Their problem was more serious: the Blitz. They ended up in Mill Lane School, West Hampstead, a quite heavily bombed area of north London.

'The girl who sat next to me was killed. Telling us that she had been killed in a raid the night before, the teacher said a very peculiar thing: "Fortunately, all the family were killed,"' Jean presumed she meant that it was fortunate for the girl that she had died, because otherwise she would have been an orphan.

'I left proper school at twelve and went to Ada Foster's just down the road, a dance and charm school. Jean Simmons and

Shirley Eaton were there. My parents thought that show business would be a way out of the working class.' She was still twelve when she did a play in the West End and at fourteen or fifteen it was decided that she would not go back to Ada Foster's: 'I remember taking my books home. I felt terribly sad. It meant I was an adult.'

We left Andrew Loog Oldham being forced to shoplift and being nicked on his first day at his new junior school. After that, he worked hard, passed his Eleven Plus, and was accepted at Marylebone Grammar, which was very dark with silly little windows. As Benny Green had discovered a decade or so earlier, it was a rough school and it got that much rougher now that Andrew was on the books. Having gone to problem schools, he was grooming himself to be a problem child.

'My mate and I would sneak up on an unsuspecting boy, forcibly steal his wooden pencil box and offer to sell it back for sixpence.' His mother had previously been advised to take her son away from a corrupt school; now she received a letter from another school telling her to take her bent son away from this one too. She put him in a private crammer that specialised in problem kids, one of whom was, by coincidence, Nicholas Mason, later the drummer for Pink Floyd.

'The two gentlemen who ran the school did a wonderful job,' is Andrew's grateful endorsement. 'They took your train and put it back on the track.'

His track led to the sidings at Wellingborough, 'a minor public school providing a life of narrow-mindedness and sport.' The curriculum did not impinge much; he passed English language O level but not literature, as he disapproved of the set books. As for physics, he has a photographic memory but only for what 'the guy' was wearing. The physics teacher, who was also his esteemed housemaster, was so well dressed that even the black gown did not diminish the elegance of the ensemble beneath.

Andrew made the most of his situation in extra-curricular ways: 'There is not much I have done in later life that I didn't have the opportunity to rehearse at school. I learnt the rules of war.' He even formed a band and sang the maudlin ballad 'Tell Laura I Love Her' at a school concert. The loudest sound was that of his knees knocking but hey – it wasn't his singing that was his major contribution to the success of The Rolling Stones.

There is a story that sometime after leaving school he returned in his sky-blue Chevrolet with Keith Richards in the passenger seat and crashed the car into his old school house. That's what people tell him but he has to admit that he has no memory of the event in question. He is more certain about a speech day much later, this time at his son's school: 'He told me to go home, that I was a drugged-up father and my face looked as green as the suit I was wearing.' Kids – don't they say the cutest things?

We left another hero, Benny Green, between the devil (West Country teachers who derided him as a barrow-boy) and the deep blue sea (wartime London). He decided that the Blitz was the better deal, so returned to London and a grammar school for de-evacuees like him. 'Into what was called the North London Emergency Secondary School was tipped all the ragtag and bob-tail, a most wonderful, dissident rabble. It gave me a marvellous streetwise education.' At fourteen he joined a youth club. 'It was the first place where I played the saxophone in public, made a speech and wrote for a magazine, which I later edited.'

At fifteen, another piece of his educational jigsaw slotted into place. On his way to a school first-eleven football match, he was knocked down by a bus. During the six weeks on his back while his knee recovered, Benny devoted himself to a close study of

P. G. Wodehouse, about whom he later wrote a literary biography. As his son Dominic put it, thanks to London Transport he discovered his second vocation: writing.

His grandfather's house was blown up while he was sheltering in the cellar, so failing the School Certificate was really the least of Benny's problems. But fail it he did and, half a century later, this clearly rankled. 'I passed in five subjects, with distinctions in English grammar, English literature and history.' All he could write in the physics exam was 'B. Green: Physics', which was fine as far as it went but the examiner was hoping for more and so awarded nul points. Another zero for our hero was in Latin, in which he was given no credit for the one question he answered, mainly because he got it wrong, writing down 'habere' ('to have') instead of 'habeo' ('I have' – near enough, one would have thought).

'The headmaster had me disqualified from *all* five subjects,' he complained. In fact, it was nothing personal. School Certificate was something of a double-or-quits operation. Unless candidates passed a minimum of six subjects, they had to take them all again. 'I stayed down in the Upper Fifth – but I studied by myself for the London University "matriculation", which was of a marginally higher standard than School Certificate, and I passed it.'

'Did you go to Cambridge, Benny?' I knew perfectly well that I did and he didn't, so I cannot imagine why I should have asked this question. However, I have his answer in front of me: 'Yes, three times and twice to Oxford – to lecture to music societies and jazz clubs.'

In her similarly unorthodox educational career, Rosie Boycott continued the pattern of not liking and liking her schools alternately, with the emphasis on the former. She passed the entrance exam to Cheltenham Ladies' College. This establishment is highly thought of but not by Rosie, at least as far as her own experience is concerned. 'I was put in a class a year ahead of my age; all the other girls had best friends and wrote in italic.' Even her handwriting, which she asserts was fine for a twelve-year-old, was mucked up by the Saturday mornings spent on compulsory calligraphy.

In this intellectual hothouse, a high proportion of girls were bound for Oxbridge but Rosie managed only five O levels: 'They wouldn't let you take an O level if they thought you were going to fail.' She left at sixteen after a year of 'a dunce's course' taken by only three of them. 'Why don't you do a secretarial course? You could probably manage that,' suggested the school.

Instead, she worked at home but not very well, achieving only two A levels at Grade E. She then went to Davies's, the crammer in Victoria which interesting young people in her position sometimes turned to. By 'went' she means 'hardly ever went in, not even for the exams'. But all was not lost: 'I went as a boarder to a crammer in Market Harborough.' That's 'went' as in 'lasted three weeks'. Actually, all was lost.

At the end of this period, she suddenly noticed her parents' car in the drive. Summoned to the head's office, she was accused of smoking dope and causing trouble. 'I now plead guilty as charged,' she told me. (Don't you love that 'now'? Is she implying a 'then' in which she made an indignant speech for the defence?)

There followed a kind of sea change in our heroine's mind: 'I was pissed off with myself and thought, "I can't go on being kicked out of schools."' The schools would also have agreed with this point of view. Her parents certainly did. She went (that's 'went' as in 'actually went') to Shrewsbury Technical College, where the teachers were fantastically encouraging and she was appreciated as an eager beaver.

'My parents found me brilliant lodgings with a retired maths teacher. For over a term before the exams, she would cook dinner and we'd stay up till midnight doing old maths papers. I got two As, with an S in maths.' This meant that university was a possibility. We'll see how she got on later.

Nicola Horlick was another Cheltenham Ladies' dissident. She asserts that she is a very conventional person: 'Running away from school, and going to Frankfurt, were both out of character.' The Frankfurt episode is what drew her to the world's attention in 1997. She was just another Morgan Grenfell fund manager when, after being suspended, she made a highly publicised flight to protest at the company's German HQ. OK, she didn't get her job back but we all knew who she was.

Her early great escape was known only to her school, family and the Cheltenham coppers. Having been one of only six girls among hordes of boys at a Wirral prep where she was always Mary in the Nativity play, she was sent to the Ladies' College as just another boarder in what she saw as a highly regimented academic hothouse.

'The school was suffering from deep paranoia that we were all going to get pregnant. After lessons you were just left in your houses.' They were permanently hungry. On one occasion, they found the deputy housemistress's keys to the back door and nipped out under cover of darkness for fish-and-chips.

'After almost two years, I ran away.' We may well wonder what took her so long. 'Once each term you were allowed out in pairs to go shopping. My plan was to go to my best friend's mother near Banbury. I took a bus towards a most obscure spot and walked towards a hiding-place in a wood.'

This was around the time of what were known as the 'Black Panther' killings and she asked herself, 'What do I do now? What if I get murdered? My parents will never forgive me!' What she did was to take a bus back to Cheltenham and a taxi to the station. Any similarities to a film about British POWs on the lam were strengthened when, five minutes before the train was due to arrive, two SS storm troopers, or rather Cheltenham police constables, turned up but, this not being a movie, she failed to evade her captors and was frogmarched back to the Cheltenham Colditz.

Unsurprisingly, she left. 'I then went to Birkenhead High School, where all the girls seemed completely normal and weren't locked up.'

'A lot of the kids didn't aspire to anything,' according to Bradley Wiggins, who was remembering his contemporaries at his comprehensive, St Augustine's in Kilburn, north London. It was largely an ambition-free zone and no wonder: 'There wasn't really anything to aspire to in that area. Their role models would hang around in the betting shops and the pubs. Signing on with their dad was all there was to aspire to. Everyone wanted to be a footballer – and Arsenal footballers weren't necessarily good role models.'

'I enjoyed my time at Southgate County School,' says Warren Mitchell. 'The Blitz was on; it was exciting and there was not too much bombing around us.' Yes, we'll all agree with that: there is nothing more annoying to a teenager in wartime than too much bombing. A reasonable amount, of course, is fine. Since neither Warren nor his north London school suffered anything as tedious as a direct hit, he was able to clock up nine subjects at 'matric' (O level equivalent) level and 'Inter BSc' (A level equivalent) in an impressive four subjects: maths, applied maths, physics and chemistry. That was on the plus side of the ledger.

There was a minus: 'I was a pretty naughty boy. They used to say, "You'll never get anywhere" – and then I'd come top. This upset the staff.' It would. The grinding of teachers' teeth could probably have been heard by German bomber crews and mistaken for the latest in British anti-aircraft defences.

'The headmaster's report once said that he was unable to congratulate me as he should do in the case of someone who came first, because of … and then there was an asterisk. The asterisk referred to my thirty-one detentions that term.'

Stephen Poliakoff has no scientific abilities at all, but is an artistic cuckoo in a nest of scientists. 'My brother is a chemistry professor. My father invented a bleeper for St Thomas's hospital and, together with my grandfather, he made hearing aids; Churchill was a customer.' A day boy at Westminster, Stephen wrote a drama entitled *Granny*, which was performed as a school play and featured his contemporary Nigel Planer, who was to have a grown-up part – if that's the right word for the gleefully immature series – in *The Young Ones*. *Granny* was then accepted by Hampstead Theatre Club and it would have been directed by Richard Eyre in his pre-National Theatre days had it not been cancelled by a new artistic director. This was an early introduction to the pleasures of show business.

The headmaster of his wonderful prep school thought that Michael Grade would shine at Stowe, which was in those days a middle-ranking public school. Michael, now Lord Grade, the former Chairman of both the BBC and ITV, did shine but it certainly wasn't at Stowe. He found the place to be horrendous: the classes were at the time very big and he felt he was going backwards academically.

'I did learn that anti-Semitism – I am Jewish – was alive and well among public schoolboys. It was a bloody miserable place, freezing cold. The regime was brutal, the usual public school "hang-'em-and-flog-'em".' After a couple of terms, he could stand Stowe no longer. He rang his father to say, 'Get me out of here!'

'Fine,' said dad.

Michael then managed to get into St Dustan's, an independent school in Catford, south-east London: 'Much more egalitarian and meritocratic, the antithesis of Stowe, a wonderful experience and a lot of fun.' Known as 'The Card', he played the fool but not enough to get in the way of his three A levels.

His name lived on at Stowe but not necessarily in a good way. His friend, the writer Reg Gadney, had been a contemporary there. He told Michael later that the school had put a bit of spin on his early departure, which it claimed was because his family could not afford the fees.

'What a joke!' snapped Michael, who was born into a legendary showbiz family. His father Leslie Grade and his uncle (Lord) Bernard Delfont were theatrical agents and another uncle (Lord) Lew Grade was a pioneer of commercial television. (At the age of seventeen, Michael turned up for his first day's work at the Daily Mirror in his uncle's Rolls, not a good career move.)

Finally Stowe changed its tune somewhat: 'Years later they were claiming me as an 'Old Stoic' in their magazine, among the Old Boys Doing Terribly Well – bloody cheek!'

Michael Grade would doubtless like to see a public list of Old Schools Not Doing Terribly Well, for which he would nominate Stowe. Many of his contemporaries who made his life a misery there would presumably beg to differ. It is hard to define exactly what pupils take away from the school (apart from other pupils' games gear, that is). My father used to swear that his school, West Bridgford Grammar in Nottinghamshire, taught you mainly how to live in West Bridgford. (He moved shortly after leaving school.) Yet there is one public reminder of your time at school that remains on the record forever: the exam results it gets you.

CHAPTER 7

ON THE O LEVEL

G CSEs (and, for an older generation, O levels) will become important to employers, colleges and universities. They also point the way to other exams. My academic scores peaked with 92 per cent in Latin, a mark that meant that A level Latin was on the cards. Chemistry O level was below the pass mark, which ruled out, as if I wasn't aware already, that particular subject being suitable at the higher level. Quite apart from what you passed, the selection of subjects rules out some careers. 'What, no physics?' a potential employer may ask. Or 'No languages? This is not the place for you, then.'

'I did Ancient Greek for a laugh because the teacher was insane.' Charlie Higson is, after all, a comedy writer and actor, and the comic potential of a teacher must have seemed as good a reason as any for choosing an O level. Having done O level Greek myself with an eminently sane teacher, I could have told him that it is no joke, as he discovered: 'I was nowhere near getting it.' Despite that, he went on to select the new A level of Classical Civilisation, which is much more interesting as it doesn't involve all those tedious Greek verbs, and achieved a B.

He did not immediately forsake his classical background. At university he formed a punk band with Harry Enfield called, rather unfortunately, The Right-hand Lovers and then another with the nicer name of The Higsons, which had an indie hit single with 'I Don't Want to Live with Monkeys' – released on the Romans in Britain label.

Pippa Funnell, Britain's most successful three-day eventer, began her equine career early. Her mother owned a horse and would plonk young Pippa on its back while she did whatever it is people do around stables. Then Pippa had her own ponies with names like Pepsi, Flighty, Jeremy and the more aristocratic Sir Barnaby.

Wadhurst College, her private school up the road, was not best pleased when she asked if she could have, er, half a day off for eventing competitions. Head of school games, she did not enjoy the academic side of school life. She had the useful ability to study and retain information for a couple of weeks, by which time the exam would be over, and clocked up eight O levels. 'I hated algebra. I didn't like languages either.' She never made it to the French oral, which was a shame, as her predicament would have made an interesting exam question. What is the French for 'Pardon me, Monsieur, but my friends and I felt we needed a cigarette before this test but the cleaners turned up near the loft where we were hiding and we couldn't get out in time'?

Sports broadcaster John Inverdale too had a problem with the

French oral. He got to the test all right but, when asked 'What is the colour of the school blazer?' his reply came out in German; the German oral had been the previous day. Despite examiners on the whole preferring you to get the language right, he did end up with a good overall grade in his French O level.

John Peel had trouble with his maths, managing to get the O level only on his second attempt. This may explain why he and his (perhaps more numerate) wife Sheila disagreed over precisely how many O levels he actually achieved. She said the total was five but he claimed a grand total of six. He added that he was the proud possessor of a certificate crediting him with what he referred to as 'Divinity'. But how could he have passed the O level in religious knowledge? After all, 'as a way of entertaining the examiner' he wrote some of his answers in the style of Damon Runyon – Goys and Dolls, as it were. If he did actually pass, he must have entertained the examiner enormously well.

He must have succeeded when channelling another witty writer, this time in an essay competition on the subject of 'What can the individual do to promote international goodwill?' because he won a prize for his thoughts. He livened up the sombre theme by drawing on the style of the great humorist 'Beachcomber' from the *Daily Express*, creator of Mr Justice Cocklecarrot and the Huntingtonshire Cabmen. What A levels did he take, or at least start? 'It would probably have been history and geography.' He left halfway through the course because, having started his school career by being placed in a class of younger boys, he would have been nineteen before taking the A level exams and the army wanted him for his National Service. In a sense, he failed that too, as the reference it gave him two years later was, 'At no time during his service has this man adjusted to military life.' He was rather flattered by this unsolicited testimonial.

Piers Morgan showed lots of early promise when he went to Chailey Comprehensive near Lewes, Sussex. In fact, he was thought to be so far ahead in French that he could take the O level at fourteen. He got a D, so retook it at fifteen and got a B. Being on a roll, he had one more go and hit the jackpot, an A. This in turn led to his taking it at A level but unfortunately he was past his prime now and was awarded only an O level grade: 'So I got four O level passes in French.' Altogether, he clocked thirteen O levels if you include these multiple results in French.

As with the old O levels, the taking of GCSEs coincides with the end of the period of compulsory schooling that began when you were five. Kids don't have to run away from truanting officials any more. They – or their parents – are positively choosing that they are in a school. Those who choose otherwise are happy too: they are off.

CHAPTER 8

ON THE A LEVEL

A levels are a liberating time. You can switch to another school or sixth form college. You specialise in the subjects you like or, to put it another way, you drop the ones you don't. The stakes are higher, though: if you fail one GCSE, that may be a mere ninth of the total but losing an A level means you're down by a third and limping heavily in the university entrance marathon.

To fit in with the timetable, Rick Wakeman's third A level after music and English would have to be British constitution. 'You'll waltz through it,' promised his teacher, Mr Crowe, using a very happy turn of phrase to reassure a musician. 'But,' he added, 'you mustn't write anything opinionated.'

It was the wrong word. (Opinionated? *Moi*?) 'That was like a red rag to a bull. Knowing it was going to be marked by extremely left-wing examiners, I wrote from a point of view to the right of Genghis Khan. Yes, they did fail me.' He has regretted it ever since and his ambition is to re-sit the exam or do it as an Open University course: second time lucky, we hope.

Phill Jupitus made a bad career move merely in his choice of A levels. Moving to a new school, Palmer's College in Grays, Essex, he asked himself 'What A levels will be useful in getting ahead?' This, he soon realised, was a stupid idea.

Although he had failed geography O level, he decided to do the subject as an A level. This was not what a brilliant panellist on *QI* like him would in retrospect call a 'Quite Intelligent' wheeze and it is no surprise that he soon felt he had better drop down a gear from A level and take geography at O level again; this time he got a B.

His other A level was economics. At least, it was for a time, until this too he downgraded to an O level; it is a subject heavily dependent on maths, at which he had not excelled at O level. 'My friend and I were slackers but borrowed the exercise books of our girlfriends who had done the economics course in the previous year. We were the only two people to pass.'

His heart clearly wasn't in any of this: 'I only stayed at the sixth form college because of my girlfriend.' Thanks to a great teacher at school, he had taken and passed his O level English language early. Next year, although passing O level art, he somehow failed English literature O level, despite actually performing in one of the exam's set plays, a disaster he puts down to a mistake by an examiner exhausted on a Friday afternoon after a hard week's marking.

'Had I played to my strengths and done art and English

literature A levels, I would have gone to university: I have a great sense of loss. I have no idea where I would have ended up – but I wouldn't have appeared in *Hairspray*!' As it is, he feels his university time was when he left his civil service job and went on the road with Billy Bragg. The surprising part of his saga is that with his exam record he was seen as employable at all by the civil service. Thank heavens for Professor Bragg.

Chris Bonington too has severe doubts about a set of marks – with, it must be said, somewhat more justification than Phill Jupitus. Having done well in his O levels, Chris Bonington went into the history sixth and won the history prize; he had London University in his sights. However, when he was in Scotland – climbing, of course – just after taking his A levels, he picked up a letter from his mother at the youth hostel where he was staying. It must be one of the most puzzling results ever received by a candidate. 'In one of my papers I got 0 per cent – in English, which I enjoyed.' How does one get nought, zero, zilch in an exam? Today there would be an appeal or even questions in Parliament. In 1952 there was nothing for it but give up any attempt at university and graduate in the University of Life, as well as the School of Hard Rocks.

When he was fifteen Mike Newell had, for the only time in his life, the sudden realisation of having a new talent. Surprisingly, it was not that he had it in him to direct a film about a boy wizard based on a yet unwritten children's book nor that he would be the director of a massive box office success on the theme of several weddings and a funeral.

The moment came in the school corps when they handed him a rifle: 'Point it there and see what happens,' they said.

'At my first attempt I qualified as First Class and that was only a single point off the Marksman or Sniper grade.' He never really built on this moment of success at St Albans School, so he missed out on gainful sniping employment in Bosnia or Ukraine. Instead, he made the most of the more academic offerings of this direct grant school where his contemporaries included Stephen Hawking.

'With the exception of one supervisor at Cambridge, I feel I was better taught – more engaged – here than at university. The first A level term felt like riding a motorbike: you were freer than before and – I think I was probably in love – I felt very alive.'

He was a very easy rider. The A levels he was studying were English, history and French. At the time, Oxbridge allowed candidates to take the scholarship exam two terms before their A levels, as a way of snaffling the young talent before anyone else could grab the winners. Mike took the scholarship exam in his fourth term in the sixth form merely as practice for a serious attempt after A levels. 'To everyone's amazement I got an exhibition in English and history.'

With those two subjects wrapped up, all he had to do was achieve his French A level. This left plenty of time for the school play. And maybe a bit of sniping.

Rick Stein is a man who has given us a wonderful demonstration not just of cookery but of the fact that there are second chances in education. After his O levels, he began to listen to rock'n'roll. He used to meet a 'maid' or Uppingham school waitress in a barn down the road. These were not the values of a public school chap. He worked hard at not working for his three A levels and, having duly failed them, he went to a crammer in Brighton where he took just two, achieving only E grades. Planning a career as a hotel manager, he spent six months as a chef in the Great Western Hotel, Paddington.

Having created his own mini-disasters, he was suddenly faced with a real tragedy: 'My father died; he committed suicide. Every-thing came to a crisis with me and at nineteen I went to Australia, where I did all kinds of labouring jobs. I worked in an abattoir and as a clerk in a naval dockyard.' Being on his own, he read a great deal and realised that, after all, he had not given academe a chance. When he applied to Oxford, academe gave *him* a chance. He is a chef again but now he is a master chef. He owns the joint – and the vegetables, starters, pudding...

Moazzam Begg may well have been accused of real sniping. The people who locked him up in Guantanamo Bay must have had *something* in mind but presumably it wouldn't stand up in court, because he was not charged with anything. He would have liked to make use of all that free time, which the Americans had given him, by studying; his studies in England had been trun-cated. Some of his O levels taken at Moseley Secondary School, a Birmingham grammar school that had just gone comprehen-sive, only just reached the pass mark.

'The reason was that I had started getting involved with gangs to fight racism; my brother got terribly beaten up outside the school by skinheads and neo-Nazis and he remained in hospi-tal for a couple of weeks.' This atmosphere was not conducive to study and he left school to work for his father's estate agency.

> Two or three years later I took an A level in law at Solihull Col-lege. This was because of constant nagging from my father, who said I had a good mind for an argument and thought law would be a good place to channel it. I got a B and then went to the Uni-versity of Birmingham for a law degree. I did that for two years.

In Guantanamo he asked the Americans if it was possible to study but they said, 'No, the most we can get you is Dickens and the Brontës.' The only other offer was mind-numbing Danielle Steel books.

If he had been convicted, he would have been able to study, but he could not be convicted because he had not been charged. (I wonder if the authorities at Guantanamo Bay are given any sort of legal training? There's a course at Birmingham University, I gather.) He was approached by British agents anxious to pick his brains. Instead of offering study materials, they brought him what can only be described as a sweetener: a Mars Bar 'all the way from England'. He refused to take it; 'I don't like Mars Bars.' After his release, he has been locked up again, this time in the UK, and suddenly released again. This time, no one seems to have tried to bribe him with Mars Bars.

One doesn't want to make light of his time in Guantanamo Bay. And one doesn't want to insult a world-famous public school. But it was a friend of mine who, having been at one of the tougher houses at Eton some decades ago, said that Old Etonians were ideally suited to surviving in a prison-of-war camp, as they had experienced years of an oppressive regime. One doesn't want to push the parallel too far – but it does bring us to the thorny topic of boarding schools.

CHAPTER 9

BOARDER COUNTRY

Roger Lloyd Pack was homesick at first. He asked himself the obvious question occurring to any youngsters finding themselves in internal exile: 'Why am I being punished by being sent away?' Then he adapted happily to the laid-back atmosphere of Bedales, the co-educational boarding school in Hampshire. Even after half a decade in less congenial single-sex establishments, many former boarders declare they were not bothered by boarding. Asking how they felt about it is like asking about their attitude to the grass on the rugby ground or the quality of the water in the school taps.

'Boarding' means 'private'. There are some state boarding schools but they are few and far between: the State Boarding Schools

Association lists only eight in the whole of the north of England; parents still have to pay for the boarding element, which is quoted as being around an annual ten grand.

Boarding used to mean 'tough'. Some of the more Spartan memories below, though vivid, relate to conditions no longer existing, like the light from a recently collapsed star. At least, we hope so.

The dormitories that I have been in recently look like teenager's bedrooms that you share with a few friends. The dormitories of the 1950s looked like what might be expected in Borstals; bleak rows of bedsteads and perhaps, instead of heating, a form of 'colding' obtained by keeping the windows open so that frost could form nicely on the inside. This might have made a man of you but these days the schools tend to be co-ed and females have probably decided that it doesn't make a woman of you.

Jonathan Dimbleby declares he was short and timid. I don't know about short but it is hard to think of any of the broadcasting Dimbleby family ever being timid. At prep school, he nearly drowned in the swimming pool when he panicked during a competition; fortunately the games master fished him out.

Going to Charterhouse in Godalming, Surrey, therefore, was not ideal: 'I wasn't to get over my homesickness until the age of fifteen or sixteen.' This public school is near the A3 and Richard, his father, used to say to him, 'I'll hoot when I'm driving past.' That was a mixed blessing for Jonathan: 'I would lie awake at night and hear a car hoot – and then another five minutes later – and wonder which was him.' It seems an odd way to communicate with your son but at least Richard gave a hoot for him.

Corin Redgrave too was aware of people zooming past in the outside world. After a year of being taught with his sister Vanessa and Alec Guinness's son in a vicarage, the transition to Wells House in the Malvern Hills was like being evicted from the

Garden of Eden. 'The headmaster was the Devil incarnate' as far as young Corin was concerned. 'He had a definite penchant for corporal punishment. He would make these terrible, swooping descents and announce someone had done something awful. He encouraged boys to be informers and vigilantes.'

The Satanic atmosphere inside the school gave Corin an ambivalent feeling about the beautiful countryside that surrounded it, as well as a sense of loss. 'If you lay in the dormitory thinking of home, you'd hear a steam engine going to Paddington and think of all the happy people on that train.' Fortunately, after four terms of this diabolical dump Corin was no longer listening to the London train; he was on it.

Novelist Wilbur Smith was over 1,000 miles and two and a half days by 'Puffing Billy' train away from home. After ten days at Cordwalles, his new school in South Africa, he decided, 'This is fine; now I've done boarding school.' Naturally he asked the headmaster, 'Is it okay if I go home now?' Apparently it wasn't.

> I hated the boarding school. To me it was a huge building like the Houses of Parliament but in fact it was a grotty little school. We had chamber-pots under the bed that we had to take out in the morning with whatever we had deposited in them. Ball sports – hitting or kicking balls – were thought to be the mark of a man and if you had no interest in them you were considered a slacker. But I had my books.

And now other people have *his* books.

'I was the first person in this country to wear disposable nappies,' claimed Antony Worrall Thompson. He had the full theatrical upbringing: he was born in Stratford-on-Avon, where his parents were in *Romeo and Juliet*, his godfather was Richard

Burton (his father's understudy) and he was taken on tour with his mother in the first production of *Brigadoon*.

> I went to a boarding nursery school in Brighton where theatrical types dropped their kids. At the age of five, I wandered down to the beach in my sleep and was put in the coal-hole as a punishment. It didn't work. I climbed out through the manhole and ran away for four days with a tramp.

He was starting as he meant to go on. When the teacher at Milner Court, the prep school of King's, Canterbury, threw the duster at him, he used to throw it back. On the first day at King's School itself, a policy decision was made: 'We're going to break this boy's spirit,' which instantly made him a hero to the other lads. 'With some other boys, I pushed a teacher's car into the swimming-pool.'

As both the dazzling 'host and hostess' of the Alternative Miss World competition, the eccentric (his word) artist Andrew Logan sounds as if he was even less cut out for a boarder at a boy's school. And so it proved when he was sent at eleven to Lord Williams's School in Thame, Oxfordshire, dating back to 1575. Its old boys include one Simon Mayne, described simply as a 'regicide', a job for which there is less call these days on account of a scarcity of kings to kill. It turned out that another killer had been housed there.

> Boarding was a shock to the system: uniforms, trunks – and the horrible ghost of a master who had murdered the matron one 25th of November! The older boys used to re-enact this story every year. You'd hear a scream and a thud and something being pulled up the stairs to the dormitory. Then the 'ghost' – it must have been

one boy sitting on another's shoulders – would attack the weakest,
which included me, with a wet flannel that felt like blood.

Spooky happenings aside, Andrew didn't really mix in but sat on
the sidelines reading about Greek myths, an interest which led to
his later sculptures such as the flying horse Pegasus. He also did
some swimming and cross-country running. His sister remembers him tackling someone at rugby and then saying, 'Oh, I'm
so sorry – did I hurt you?'

As well as the bogus ghost, he also experienced something
closer to the Holy Ghost. 'We had prayers in the dorm. I don't
know if there was actually thunder and lightning but one night,
when the net curtains were blowing in the wind, I felt "the spirit
descending" on me. That's when I wanted to be a vicar.' The call of
the vicarage lasted until he took up window-cleaning in his spare
time. He was up a ladder when his brother walked past with an
architectural student who asked him, 'Why don't you become
an architect?' So he did.

The radical comedian and activist Mark Thomas is an equally
improbable product of boarding school, which he thinks of as
'the medieval transvestite monk period of my life', thanks to the
uniform of yellow socks, breeches and tunic which he wore at
Christ's Hospital in Horsham, Sussex. 'I hated the discipline, the
regimentation.' Yet he was not complaining: 'It makes me an outsider, which from my point of view is fine.' Also, the school drama
was great and they used to put on *Hancock's Half Hour* revues.

Al Murray also made the most of the dramatic possibilities of
his school. 'By the sixth form, boarding was fantastic; you had
so much time in the evenings.' He would commandeer the excellent theatre at Bedford School for two full hours of rehearsal. He
took charge of the house play and he too used a *Hancock's Half*

Hour script, in his case the one in which Tony has a reunion with all his school chums.

'Being a show-off I played the Hancock part, but being tall and thin I did it like John Cleese. Fortunately it was a completely indestructible script – and short.'

Ann Widdecombe had whooping cough with complications, which wiped out the whole of one Christmas term, and she was still ill when she took the Eleven Plus in January 'with predictable dire results'. She recovered sufficiently to take and pass the entrance exam to La Sainte Union du Sacre Coeur in Bath.

'I loved the school and loved boarding. It was terribly strict even by my standards. You were in serious trouble if you did not wear little white gloves when you went outside in the summer.'

Sue Lloyd-Roberts, who also failed the Eleven Plus, begs to differ:

> I'm so against the idea of boarding school: those long winter evenings with the wind lashing against the windows of your House, cold draughty corridors and no one to cuddle. The number of tears shed in the dormitories. One spent so long obeying quite senseless rules; there was, for example, the Marble Corridor that you were not allowed to go down.

But she admits that in the long run Cheltenham Ladies' College may have been a useful training for a reporter: 'I now specialise in sneaking across frontiers where journalists are not allowed. This could be one's rather belated rebellion.' And she is aware that, being a late developer, she did gain an enormous amount from the highly academic private school to which her father sent her – an odd decision for a man whose only aspiration for her was that she should marry a grouse moor.

There is one aspect of boarding schools about which Sue does not complain. This is because Cheltenham Ladies would have been too lady-like to indulge in it. Boys' schools, both boarding and day, did cling to corporal punishment until prevented by law, and some of their pupils still bear the scars.

CHAPTER 10

THE CANED MUTINY

If a policeman saw you parked on a double-yellow line, made you bend over and walloped you so hard with a stick or strap that the blood came, your first thought would be that sharia law had been imposed. Your first action would be to get your lawyer on the case. Yet corporal punishment was still a legal punishment in state schools until 1987, after my youngest child had started at her primary (which did not, of course, use it). It was not outlawed in private schools until 1999 in England and Wales, followed by Scotland in 2000, with Northern Ireland fighting what can only be called a rearguard action in 2003.

In my own school it was dying out in the late 1950s. There was a belief that prefects could cane younger boys but, since they offered the option of doing their washing-up instead, the theory was never tested. In other schools it was a lot more prevalent. Some of those on the receiving end have put it, if you'll forgive the expression, behind them. It made more of an impression on some of my other interviewees. And their bottoms.

Simon Callow was, at five years old, a boarder at Elmcroft in Goring-on-Thames which was run, he gathered later when the information meant something, by a man who had been one of Mosley's Fascists. This dubious pedagogue had still not been fully reformed, exorcised or whatever it is he needed to make him fit for polite company:

'He wore shorts and sandals all the year round and was addicted to corporal punishment in its most savage manifestations – and to undressing himself at the same time.' Fortunately Simon's mother was always on hand to save him from being walloped by a half-naked Nazi, as she was the school secretary and lived on the premises.

By coincidence, Simon's favourite English tutor at Queen's University, Belfast, a man whose flamboyance and wit made him his role model, was also of the jackbooted persuasion.

'One day he said he belonged to the British Union of Fascists and invited me to join. I hadn't knowingly met any anti-Semites before. I happened not to know many Jews either. I had moved mainly in Catholic circles.'

Gary Lineker describes his headmaster at Caldecote Juniors, Leicester, as being pretty fierce: 'He was German, straight out of the Gestapo.' That is not a politically correct thought for Gary to utter or for me to report but neither is what the head did to Gary a couple of times: he caned him – 'and one of those times I was entirely innocent.' And the other time? 'Cheekiness.' But even that didn't merit a cheek being caned.

Rick Stein had a brother at Winchester but he was appalled when he had a look round: 'They were still washing in bowls filled with water from jugs.' He then went to Uppingham, which was like jumping out of the frying pan into the hot ring of an Aga. His outdoor life at prep school had been enjoyably savage but this was like a *Lord of the Flies* theme park. 'There was always the fear of the older boys. They had almost the power of life and death; there was the strange business of beating younger boys.'

Wilbur Smith spelt out the 'strange business' as carried out in Michaelhouse, his school in South Africa situated in the foothills of the Drakensburg mountains where the winters were Arctic. He took beating as normal; you went to boarding school – and you got beaten.

> You would be beaten for the heinous crime of being late for roll-call or touching the cutlery on the table before grace. The beaters took it seriously; the prefects would discuss the relative merits of the Malacca cane versus the bamboo cane and they used to practise on a cushion. They used to chalk the cane: four 'shots' on the same line did more damage than if spread out a bit. You said, 'Thank you,' and then you would rush down to the lavatory and your mates would admire your bruise.

At Westminster Under School Oliver James had a teacher with the name of a nice creature in *The Wind in the Willows* but the mentality of the stoats and weasels: 'Mr Badger, the maths master, would take your sideburns and twist them while asking, "What is a hypotenuse?" By the end I was beaten every week for various infringements.' Oliver described himself as being in 'the bottom three' of the class.

Barry Hines went to a junior school in Hoyland Common, a

mining village a few miles from Barnsley. His description of the head is as graphic as anything in his novel *A Kestrel for a Knave*, on which the film *Kes* was based.

> Mr Blackledge, the headmaster, had some fingers blown off during the war and your eyes were always drawn to his hand. For corporal punishment, he would crouch down and his hand would go behind your bare legs (we wore short trousers) and the thought of the gammy hand at the back of my legs, like something out of a horror film, was worse than the actual punishment.

Ken Bruce, the amiable Radio 2 broadcaster, could have taken the Eleven Plus route to a Glasgow grammar school but was sent at nine to a fee-paying 'exam factory'. He once got the belt for failing an exam – history, he thinks.

'I got 20 per cent. The teacher felt I hadn't even bothered. Two of us were called up to the front for the "Lochgelly", named after the place where the belt was made.' The teachers used to keep these weapons in the voluminous arms of their gowns or over their shoulders, so that they could whip them out like quick-on-the-draw cowboys. 'The belts were half-an-inch wide and two inches thick and had either two or three tongues.'

Eric Burdon's secondary school arranged for a much larger audience to watch the weekly whipping. Every Friday, children from a Catholic school came to use his school's woodwork facilities. 'Our teachers chose that day for physical punishment, whipping our buttocks in front of the Catholic kids to make us hurt even more as we had a street war going on with them.'

'There was an incident with a stink bomb in a waste paper basket.' James Naughtie's father was the headmaster of a village school in what is now Aberdeenshire (his mother was the head of a school in the neighbouring parish) and had to administer the tawse or strap. 'It couldn't have been pleasant for him.' The pupil whose hand he was strapping was that of James.

Austin Healey has the distinction not only of playing rugby for England but of being the last boy caned at St Anselm's College, Birkenhead, before corporal punishment was made illegal. The teacher administering it was, by an almost spooky coincidence, the father of the Saracens and England player Ben Johnston with whom he was to tour South Africa in 2000.

'I got three swipes from the leather strap, which hurt like hell, but I smiled through the pain to wind Mr Johnston up.'

When Raymond Briggs was at Wimbledon Park Elementary during the war, the school had such a large playground that part was fenced off so that the older boys could help to Dig for Victory:

> The only time I got caned was for jumping over the fence to get my ball back. It was one single whack from the headmaster and after-wards I was in such a nervous state that I had the curious feeling of my feet not touching the ground. It was as if I was walking, not on air, which suggests elation, but on mud.

Young Raymond looked in the mirror and saw a red stripe on his bottom: 'I hoped my mother wouldn't notice.'

Fellow cartoonist and illustrator Michael Heath did not get off so lightly. Having escaped bombing raids during the war, he failed to avoid direct hits from a more sadistic enemy, his teachers.

It has to be said that Michael is the most hard-hearted fellow I know. Never mind his brilliantly satirical cartoons; there is a story about him going to see *E.T.* and, at the sad bit at the end which reduced the cinema to tears, there came a sound of derisive laughter. That was him.

So, when I say that my heart goes out to my old colleague, it must be about something pretty serious. It was in Brighton, 'a church school just off the sea front called St … Something's. If you didn't learn, they hit you with straps, rulers, anything they could lay their hands on.' The good news is that he was taken away from St Sadistica's but the bad news is that he was then sent to a secondary modern with a staffing policy of employing 'men who hit you with a leather thong, apart from one of them, with a steel plate in his head, who threw chairs.' It was a case of a Darwinian survival of the hitters. 'We did appalling things to the kind ones who didn't hit us, made them cry.'

The war was not much help to Jean Marsh's brief education, either. It was a pity that when she and her sister Yvonne did end up at a school in north London, they were still in trouble.

'Why aren't you working?' the teacher demanded one day.

'I've done all the maths problems,' Jean replied.

'You're lying. Come to the front,' was the response of the teacher, who was preparing to hit Jean's knuckles with a ruler. The girl was reluctant to put out her hand – apart from the pain, she had a slightly deformed thumb that had been injured during the war – but she did so.

Since the girls' parents never laid a finger on their daughters, Yvonne spoke up defiantly: 'You're not allowed to hit us!' She then led Jean from the classroom. The sisters went back later and Jean never discovered how the adults resolved the matter.

It took decades but finally it was the law that sorted it out for all teachers for all time. No teacher is allowed to hit any child.

CHAPTER 11

PET TEACHERS

Every morning I used to pass a car with a sticker on its rear window declaring, 'If You Can Read This, Thank a Teacher.' Since it was parked outside a school on a busy, narrow road, I would be trapped behind it on my bike as I waited for a gap in the traffic. I had plenty of time to emend the sticker to read: 'If You Can't Get Past, Blame a Teacher.'

I didn't, though, as the original was a very good slogan. However grumpily my interviewees might refer to school and staff, they would generally pay ungrudging tribute to at least one teacher who would have come up with something special.

Alone among Wilbur Smith's bad teachers in a unpleasant South African prep school, his English teacher stands out as a good guy.

He praised Wilbur's work and put forward one of his essays for the form prize. He was the teacher who made Wilbur think he could do something other people couldn't. This is very helpful if you end up as a novelist; you don't want to worry that all you are capable of is copying bits out of other people's books.

It is often the English teacher who gets the good report from former pupils. Writing essays encourages self-expression in a way that sterner subjects such as chemistry do not. To my mind there's nothing wrong with chemistry, except that it's the only O level I failed. I blame the teacher – a lovely man but hopeless with those of us who were less scientifically minded and tended to apply the Bunsen burner to our jackets instead of the test-tube.

Will Hutton has been, among other things, the editor of *The Observer* and economics editor of *Newsnight*, so if he says Chislehurst and Sidcup Grammar was a good school, that's what it was. He also gives high marks to the teaching skills of his maths teacher, 'Sexy Nexy', as Miss Necks was known. His chief memory of her is nothing to do with her skill at imparting figures, though.

> She was rather vain and didn't like to wear glasses. We once attached
> a fishing line to the board duster and whenever she went for it,
> we moved it three feet. This went on for ten to fifteen minutes. We
> were sent to the headmaster but it was worth it.

Bertie Brown taught maths, history and a bit of art to Eric Burdon. At least, he did when he wasn't distracted by a question designed to get him off the subject, such as 'Did the Japanese have twin 30-calibre machine guns on their fighters?' And off he would go into the technical details. He had been a pilot in the war against Japan and had the big RAF handlebar moustache to prove it.

Eric received the strap from him twice. On his last day at school he stole the strap from Mr Brown's desk and threw it out of the window. The teacher was not fazed, telling the class, 'I don't know who took it – BURDON!'

Eric had no hard feelings:

> I loved the guy. He took a special interest in me, I discovered later. I guess he had a word with the powers-that-be at Newcastle College of Art and Industrial Design, because I was entered for an experimental scheme in which we failures at Eleven Plus were given a special art exam. At fifteen, my life changed radically.

Agreed, there was a lot of mucking around at art college but Eric ended up with two impressive-sounding diplomas. He also began going to jazz clubs in the evening. His father was not pleased with this distraction, so Eric took him along one night.

'He said I could carry on going to the clubs, so long as I did my homework – and didn't tell my mother.'

'My dad spent a lot of time in prison; we were friends rather than father and son,' says Ashley Walters, alias Asher D, who himself spent a short time in a young offenders' institution; the So Solid Crew rapper was convicted of illegal possession of a firearm. He has since appeared at the National Theatre, the Royal Court and on television. It was his mother ('very strict, a feared parent') who put him at four into the Sylvia Young Theatre School. He featured in adverts and *Oliver!* at the Palladium. Sylvia Young was for weekends and on weekdays it was St George's Primary in Camberwell, south-east London.

'Mr Quarless became like a father to me and a lot of the other black boys; he was my first black teacher at St George's.' Ashley saw him as being distinguished and well spoken – plus he drove a Range Rover. There was no skiving off work, though. 'Thirty sums – then you can have that story,' he would say. The rest of the school became jealous of his class being so close to him.

There seems to have been some tension in the staff room, too.

> We would go out to the playground when everyone else was in their classrooms. One day another teacher followed us out into the playground and they squared up in front of us. Then Mr Quarless just laughed. He stood his ground but didn't retaliate.

This was just as well. It wouldn't do to have teachers going for each other hammer-and-tongues so that the kids had to step in, break up the fight and send Sirs to get a detention from the head.

At thirteen in Bedford Upper School, Al Murray had 'the full *Dead Poets Society* experience'. English teacher Mike Morrison and bandmaster Kevin Street, for whom Al walloped the drums, were the real-life equivalent of John Keating, the idealistic English teacher played in the film by the much missed Robin Williams. They turned the key in Al's creative ignition: 'Without them I wouldn't be doing what I'm now doing. I'd be a lawyer or something: a terrible lawyer.' Al Murray, the Pub Lawyer.

In addition, Al will never forget the words of the headmaster, a tremendous teacher, at his primary school in Stewkley near Leighton Buzzard, Bedfordshire: 'A friend is a friend to the end.' This is not a moral commandment but, as Al explains, 'a mnemonic to show that it is 'i' before 'e' ('e' at the end).' In the days before spellcheck, that was valuable info. It still is.

Similarly, it was a spelling breakthrough that provided Christine Ohuruogu, Britain's first 400-metres female Olympic champion, with one of her chief memories of primary school. Linguistics was the subject in which she would get a 2.1 at University College London. She experienced the linguistic light bulb flashing on at an early age: 'In my second year in juniors I remember notic-ing the word "altogether" was quite long – but quite easy as it is based on three different words.'

Let's see: 'all', 'to' and 'gether'. 'Gether'? (Consults Oxford Dictionary.) This is a variant of 'gather'. Gold stars all round, I think.

Andrew Logan escaped from his ghost-ridden boarding school when the fees went up and did his O levels at Burford Grammar. A levels – geography, English and history – were the happiest time. There were only three of them taking her subject, so the geography mistress could squeeze them into her little bubble car for expeditions around the countryside. 'She'd point at something and we'd end up in the ditch.'

His memories of a teacher he admired later are far less joy-ful. Andrew had an excellent six years at the Oxford School of Architecture: 'I was in seventh heaven. I always enjoyed being taught by Mr Townsend, who did plumbing. Sadly, Mr Townsend went up on the roof and jumped over the edge. For anyone else, plumbing is awful: human waste. But he made it sound, I sup-pose, glamorous.'

Baroness Brenda Dean, the first woman to lead a major union and a voice for sanity in the Wapping dispute between the Mur-doch empire and the newspaper printers, is indebted to two particular teachers during her mainly happy school career. (The unhappy bit was early on, when her cat Snowy, who used to accompany her to and from St Andrew's Church of England pri-mary in Eccles, one day wasn't waiting for her when she came out. An un-neutered tom and thus a nuisance, he had been poisoned.)

'There was one teacher, George Booth, who everybody was scared of. When I realised he was shouting at the boys and not at me, I changed my mind about him. He was really supportive when he saw you were trying.'

His support was much appreciated when the Eleven Plus exam result came through; he refused to accept that she had failed. As there wasn't much he could do about it at that stage, he came to the family's house and promised that he could get her into the grammar school at thirteen by helping with extra homework.

'My parents were all for it. My father, who was a signalman, hadn't been able to go to grammar school because his parents couldn't afford the uniform and he was determined this wasn't going to happen to his children. He always worked with me on my homework.'

When the window of opportunity for thirteen-year-olds opened, Mr Booth put her name down for the Stretford High School for Girls exam and this time she made it. Here Brenda met her second crucial teacher, Mrs Hughes, who told her young charges, 'You've arrived as gels' – she had been to a public school – 'and we'll turn you into young women. You won't be wilting violets.'

Novelist and broadcaster Sarah Dunant was also able to make use of educational opportunities denied to her parents. 'My father, who was very intelligent, had left school at fourteen and I always felt that one of the best things I could do for him was to achieve what he had been denied.'

Her primary school in Shepherds Bush, west London, was the launch pad for this ambition. 'My central memories of Flora Gardens are of a vast number of corridors – and of the headmistress, Miss Heron.' (Kids may not notice but sometimes teachers have the greatest names. You can just imagine Miss Heron standing on one leg in the corridor, tall and slender, occasionally taking off to catch a recalcitrant child in her beak.)

'Miss Heron made you aware that there was a big game at stake here and you had to play it. My post-war generation was taught by women with such dedication and commitment that it really does not surprise me that we grew up to become feminists.'

There was one crucial moment in which Miss Heron helped young Sarah become a player in the game. At the time of her birth, Sarah's parents were living in a bed-sit opposite Godolphin and Latymer Grammar and the family set its sights on her going there.

'During my Eleven Plus, when I was showing a tendency to write too much for too long, I remember Miss Heron standing over me and looking up at the clock and looking down at me. I went on to the next question.' And got into Godolphin and Latymer.

In 1991 Helen Sharman became the highest of high-flyers when she joined the Soviet space station Mir as the first Briton in space. This more than made up for early humiliations at Grenoside Juniors in Sheffield.

'I was very anxious to please and my biggest memory is the devastation I felt when I had forgotten my handkerchief; you had to line up and show it to your teacher.' Much worse was an unforgivable and unforgettable remark made when she had spilt her milk and couldn't find a mop. She heard her teacher sneer, 'She is a dumb one, that Helen.' Helen remembered that when she disproved any suggestion of dumbness by getting her O levels, her A levels, her degree…

For her last five years at secondary school, Helen had a wonderful, enthusiastic teacher called Mr Wilson who would greet a stupid mistake with the cry – a friendly one, it seems – of 'Oh, you potato-cake!'

Much later, she found herself in the Mir space station preparing films for exposure outside. She realised that she had inserted them into their frames the wrong way round.

'Sharman, you potato-cake!' she exclaimed. Sergei, her engineer, would have flicked through his English-Russian phrasebook in vain. I'm guessing there, but he certainly did not understand what it meant. Nor, in fact, did she. She believed it to be something people buy in Sheffield fish-and-chip shops but, at a height of 250 miles and a speed of 1,800 mph, it wasn't a theory she could check at the time.

John Simpson's father had fallen on hard times. Falling on better times, he sent John to Dulwich Prep in south London. One master there was so terrifying that people used to call him 'Satan'. Fortunately the staff room had at least one member who sounded a devil of a lot more fun. 'There was Captain Fleming, who had a wooden leg and a funny eye. He used to make gunpowder and guns; he would invite you to his home and fire them off.'

Released from the prison of his diabolical prep school, Corin Redgrave went cheerfully to Eaton College, so called not to fool gullible foreign parents that it was Eton College but because it was in classy Eaton Square. He then moved geographically downmarket but academically upmarket to Westminster School; it was a decade since he had been at the school during its evacuation to its Herefordshire base during the war.

'There were two or three outstanding teachers. Stephen Lushington taught English and directed the school play. He had acted with my mother [the actress Rachel Kempson] at Oxford.' Lushington is credited with showing sympathy for children whose alleged laziness was in fact undiagnosed dyslexia. He died in 2013, three years after Corin.

'I was taught Classics by Theodore Zinn, a wonderful teacher. His classes were a babble of argument; occasionally, when it went too far, he would cry, which would subdue everyone.' He told Corin that he should not underestimate himself: he could get a university scholarship, not just a place. Yes, Corin won a scholarship to King's, Cambridge.

The third teacher taught a subject that is on the curriculum of few schools: 'I started fencing at Westminster with the greatest of all sabre-teachers, Bela Imregi, and I fenced for Cambridge.' Bela was a fiery character who made enemies easily – and if there's one person you want to avoid, it's a cross Hungarian waving a sword. 'You could tell from the ceilings of his house that he lived there because they were scored with cuts where a sabre had slashed slightly too high.'

Corin reckons that he himself was good enough to beat anyone in England – but not all the time. 'I had to make a choice between acting and fencing; and I chose acting.'

Strangely, his father Michael Redgrave came to Cambridge to see him in only one production, a Restoration comedy, but he was generous about the performance: 'He said I'd taught him a lot.'

'The first teacher for whom I had a massive amount of respect was Peter Headeach, my Latin master,' said John Inverdale. It is perhaps to be expected of a future sports broadcaster that the illicit reading matter with which he was caught at the back of the class at West Hill Park prep school in Tichfield, Hampshire, should be *Sporting Life*, the horse-racing paper.

John explained that it was the day of the champion hurdles at Cheltenham: 'The Queen Mother's got a horse called Escalus.' Mr Headeach could have replied that he didn't see what this had to do with anything and dished out a detention. Instead he remarked that it sounded like the Greek dramatist Aeschylus and therefore he would go down to the bookmakers and put some money on it. This was not what you could exactly call a hot tip from the horse's mouth but good old Escalus came in a good third.

John likes to think that the Latin beak bought them all

chocolates with the winnings. He does know that he stirred himself to work much harder in Latin: 'I owed him one.'

Piers Morgan's final school was Lewes Priory Sixth Form College. 'I was probably most fond of Mr Freeman, who taught history A level. He was cruel but fair. "Your boy is a buffoon," was his entire report to my parents one year. He probably thinks subsequent events have borne him out.'

Sally Magnusson, journalist, broadcaster and daughter of Magnus, has fond memories of Miss Patterson, her form teacher at Laurel Bank, the private school in Glasgow where she went when she was nine. 'Batty Patty', as she was affectionately known, once told her, 'If you don't stop frowning, you'll get a line across the bridge of your nose when it's too late to do anything about it.'

'Now, sure enough, there it is,' says Sally. 'Every time I look in the mirror, I remember Batty Patty and wish I'd paid more attention to her.'

'You're a wonderful asset to the school but nothing you've achieved here will count afterwards,' said Father Damian to George Alagiah. The wise words from the headmaster of St John's College in Portsmouth, a school run by the Catholic De La Salle Brothers, were addressed to the future BBC newscaster whose A level results were not up to scratch for the university of his choice. Father Damian added, 'I want to see that light burn.' He handed over the keys to the sixth form block so that George could do extra study there at weekends.

'That two-minute talk in the corridor – not a rebuke – turned my life around,' said George. He re-did two of his A levels with better results and had a great time at Durham University. It occurs to me that possibly the head said this to all the boys but, if it worked every time, who's counting?

Barry Norman remembered with gratitude an outburst from

one of his form teachers, though the event that he described to me terrified him at the time. As the class was reading quietly, the master was writing end-of-term reports. It was presumably when he had reached his account of Barry's progress, or lack of it, that he erupted. Imagine one of those 1950s black-and-white films in which Richard Attenborough finally loses it.

'Suddenly he got up from his desk, which was on a dais, came down and grabbed hold of me. He said what an idle little swine I was, that I was wasting my parents' money and his time, and that if I didn't pull my socks up I would be asked to leave.' Needless to say, Barry's report that term was an absolute stinker.

These home truths did the trick. Next term B. Norman moved up from near the bottom to near the top of the form: 'He was my English teacher and I had to start paying attention. He certainly instilled a love of English into me and I realised how marvellous Shakespeare and Dickens were if you worked at them.'

The school was confident that Barry could get into Cambridge. Barry was confident that, as this would mean staying on another year, he would move up from being goalkeeper of the school's second eleven to goalie for the first team. However, he decided that he had already cost his parents quite enough in school fees, so he left and got a job on the local paper. I like to imagine the closing credits of a 1950s film, as the Richard Attenborough character pats our young hero on the back and walks with him to the school gates.

That episode tends to support Sue Townsend's theory that the good English teachers are eccentric and the brilliant ones are slightly mad. The author of the Adrian Mole books certainly had highly engaging English lessons at her primary school. 'I came under the influence of Mr Moles (I didn't make the connection when choosing Adrian's name) who taught me to love English comic writing.' She and her primary school class were devoted to him, with good reason. Mr Moles, aged thirty-five and a half (I'm guessing), read them *The Wind in the Willows* and *Winnie the Pooh*. 'He made himself cry big tears of laughter. He used to slide down his desk laughing.'

Her English teacher at secondary school was the complete opposite, apart from the fact that she was very good too. 'Miss Morris loved William Blake, Shakespeare, Milton, Oscar Wilde and, eccentrically, Peter Ustinov.' The class had to learn a poem a week and write two 'compositions', which is how she referred to essays.

'I used to break my neck to get to her classes on time. First of all she would examine our fingernails and we would file in. She would give us tips on grooming.' Miss Morris was the complete romantic, though passionless herself, and seemed to want to live vicariously through her girls. Doesn't Miss Jean Brodie spring to mind here? 'No, Miss Jean Brodie was a Fascist – though she too liked fingernails to be clean.'

Miss Morris even went to Holland with the school Passion Play. Sue had the lead part, i.e. Jesus. This was not because she was particularly saintly but because she was the tallest. She hung from a cross for twenty minutes with her arms up. It was agony.

'Susan, you're so brave,' said one of the teachers. Decades later, Sue was still ashamed of her purple-prose reply: 'It's nothing to the pain he suffered.' She didn't believe in God but continued to believe in Jesus: 'I just think he was wrong about his father.'

She managed to leave school at the age of fourteen, which gave her more time to read. She went back at sixteen to take her exams but her education petered out. 'I fell in love with my first husband instead.' Miss Morris would probably have approved.

Phill Jupitus would not say that he had an up-and-down

education. It was mainly down. The nadir was four miserable years at Woolverstone Hall, a local authority boarding school near Ipswich. It was known as 'the poor man's Eton' – wrong on both counts, as it was for the sons of well-to-do grocers and did not lead to a place in the Cabinet.

There was corporal punishment and there was Saturday morning detention, where Phill usually found himself. 'The guy who taught history destroyed my enthusiasm, I fell behind in French.' He failed both at O level.

There was one consolation: 'Phil Taylor was the reason I got English language O level a year early. He used to make us write and perform poetry and I wouldn't have become a performance poet without Phil. He was wrong in one way: when he saw I was incredibly unhappy, he said I would look back fondly at the school.'

'My English teacher was the key person, which often happens with writers,' says Bel Mooney, who is one, a writer that is, not to mention journalist and broadcaster. 'Mr Boulding was a plump, unprepossessing, sweet, deaf old man. I adored him and he adored me.' No one from her small grammar school in Liverpool had ever gone to Oxford but Mr Boulding's daughter had been an undergraduate at St Hilda's and Bel attempted to go there too.

'I tried and failed – and was heart-broken. I wasn't a good interviewee and was terribly nervous. Mr Boulding was very upset and wrote to St Hilda's to protest.'

His protest was unsuccessful and Bel went to University College London. At the end of her second year she refused to take her end-of-year exams on the grounds that she disapproved of the whole principle – 'a very 1968 thing' – but this was merely the excuse; she hadn't done any work. Her professor arranged for her to take them all by herself in July, which she did, feeling rather foolish.

In the third year she worked hard for her Finals (there was no question of any boycotting now) and hoped for an Upper Second. To her very great pleasure, she achieved a First. 'Great!' she thought. And then she said to herself, 'Stuff you, St Hilda's!'

As Deputy Editor of *The Observer*, Antony Howard would take the first edition home on a Saturday evening and read it through carefully. The subeditors would be expecting the call he always made with corrections to be incorporated for subsequent editions. It is no surprise, then, to learn that John Carleton, one of his teachers at Westminster School, declared that young Howard was good at English. Anthony came up with a mischievous suggestion to his friend Rodney Barker, who always got beta double-minus for his essays, 'I'll copy out your essay and write my name on it – and you copy out mine.'

The essays came back marked, as usual, 'Howard – good as always' and 'Barker – no improvement.' This proved to Antony that John Carleton did not even read the essays. He was still correct about Antony's talents, though.

'Tosher' Oliver, a teacher at a primary school in Stockton-on-Tees, could spot that Barry Unsworth was a winner. He was right: a Booker winner. Barry's *Sacred Hunger* shared the prize in 1992 with Michael Ondaatje's *The English Patient*. 'He said that one day I would see my name in lights,' Barry remembered. 'I had a gift for composition and I used to get my stories up on the wall for all the parents to see. I saw the way forward was to get as many gold stars as possible.'

In her Stockport Church of England primary, Joan Bakewell was also convinced of the gold standard. Yellow stars meant quite good and gold equalled very good. 'When I got a page of gold stars for sums and letters, I knew I was on my way.'

'You'll be a writer one day,' Mrs Crabtree, Margaret Forster's primary school teacher, used to tell her as she handed back her compositions. This was perceptive and prophetic – *Georgy Girl* was published scarcely two decades later – but it rather threw young Margaret, who believed that authors had one crucial thing in common: they were all dead.

She came from a non-bookish family and went to Ashley Street Infants, one of the poorest schools in Carlisle, with forty-six pupils per class. She was a bookish child stimulated, indeed over-stimulated by school: 'My arm used to ache from having it bolt upright all the time: what a pain!'

So eager was she to learn that she had to be taken down to Ashley Street on Saturdays and Sundays to prove that she wasn't missing anything: look, dear, the doors are locked, it's closed.

At St Anne's, Blackburn, Josephine Cox won the prize for a story written about someone you knew. 'One day the whole world will read Josephine's stories,' Miss Jackson announced to the assembly, as she handed over a pencil and writing case. Top marks to Miss Jackson. Josephine's sagas regularly reach No. 1 in both hardback and paperback, while she is in the top three of most borrowed in libraries.

Her own life has elements of a saga – and not a Joanna Trollope-style Aga saga but, in view of her road sweeper father's habit of drinking away his wages, a lager saga. One of ten children, she left school at fourteen, marrying at sixteen.

The Sunday school she went to at four was actually named the Blackburn Ragged School, part of the Ragged School network which Charles Dickens had supported and which still existed in the mid-'40s – the 1940s. 'You had to go there and sing hymns and then you'd get fed. I carried on going until I was about nine.'

Teased and tormented because she was so scruffy, she truanted a lot. 'The only time I went to school was when Miss Jackson was teaching English or history, when I would sit at the front.'

Josephine did, though, have a significant life outside the curriculum. 'On Fridays, after school, I used to charge the other kids a penny each to sit on the rubble in the street while I told them stories.' This was a very professional operation on her part.

All week she would be thinking, 'What stories shall I tell?' Then she would do her research, which consisted of going to her grandad's, sitting on his knee and listening to his magical tales. These were the yarns she would tell her paying customers (issues of copyright did not detain her unduly) plus any new adventures she had made up. The pennies went to her mother for the gas meter. Her fictions were literally keeping the family warm.

She left school at fourteen to work in a vinegar-bottling factory, married at sixteen and had two children. In her mid-thirties she went to evening classes after working in a plastic factory all day. 'It felt wonderful; I'd ask for extra assignments.' She got three A levels at A grades and went to Bletchley College to train as a teacher. And she began to write.

Harry Rhodes of Ilkley Church of England Junior School can go down in gardening history as the teacher who put the green into Alan Titchmarsh's fingers. 'He was a keen cactus-grower and the first plants I ever bought were his cacti, costing sixpence at the school bring-and-buy sales,' said Alan. 'I would take them home and leave them on the loo window. They thrived on neglect – and I gave them a lot of neglect.'

'I had a series of fantastic maths teachers.' Sir Andrew Dilnot, Warden of Nuffield College, Oxford, received a great education from Olchfa Comprehensive in Swansea. 'Dai Jenkins was mesmerising, inspirational, fabulous. He was demanding, too.

He would throw the board duster about and, during one lesson in my fourth year, when I had finished all my work and packed my bag to go home, he put the wastepaper basket on my head – upside down.' But in a good way, it seems.

Andrew has kept the old exercise books with Mr Jenkins's marks in red ink: '3/10 – oaf!'

The upside-down wastepaper basket was an unorthodox teaching aid but it seems to have done the trick: Andrew is also Chairman of the UK Statistics Authority and co-author of *The Tiger that Isn't: Seeing Through a World of Numbers*. He presented *More or Less*, a Radio 4 programme about numerical beauty. Among people who can count, he counts.

Multiplying, though, is another matter, or at least it was for him: 'I didn't know my multiplication tables until my children were learning them. I now know that nine eights are seventy-two but until my early thirties I would work it out: ten eights equals eighty, take away one eight, equals seventy-two.' (Personally, I still do that, as my children never taught me any better. But that's OK too. As Andrew put it, 'This is a reminder that there is more than one way to skin a cat.')

He knows who to turn to for a second opinion when figures don't add up. 'Now my wife,' he continued, 'she teaches at Oxford Brookes. She's a *proper* mathematician.' And he's not? 'With *really good* mathematicians,' he continued, 'the clarity of their insight into this almost abstract world is striking. I'm quite good with numbers but that's different.'

He found out that economics was his subject and at Oxford did PPE: politics, philosophy and economics. He nearly achieved a First and it wasn't economics that pulled him back but the gamma-double-minus, a new one on me, in Political Institutions. His tutor John Kay was furious: 'If you took someone off the streets and got them to do a paper on Political Institutions, you'd expect them to do better that that!'

It is a pity that all these super-hero teachers could not, through a coincidence of time and place, have ended up at the same school, where they could together have up-ended wastepaper baskets, dished out cacti, spotted best-selling writers, set off explosions, waved swords and silently urged pupils to get a move on during exams. Parents would have flocked into the catchment area of their school and children would have fought to be in their classes. But it would, of course, have been most unfair to all the other schools for miles around.

CHAPTER 12

TEACHERS WITH CATHOLIC TASTES

hold no brief for Catholicism but it is a fact that Catholic schools are almost the only faith schools mentioned by my interviewees – both in favour and otherwise. By contrast, the words 'Church of England' cropped up only if this happened to be part of the title of the school. I knew that two of the people I interviewed had been to one particular Methodist foundation only because I happened to have been there myself. Like me, they would probably be pushed to explain the key tenets of Methodism, despite being dragooned into the school chapel twice a day.

Most schools are not faith schools and of those that are, the majority are not Catholic. Catholicism punches, or prays, above its weight. The Pope looms larger than the Archbishop of Canterbury or Richard Dawkins. A man who described himself as 'King of the Witches' once told me that, in the absence of a local primary run by a coven, he would send his daughter to a Catholic school as being the closest to his line of spirituality.

People talk of being 'lapsed Catholics'; they still feel Catholics even if they're not Catholics any more. Anglicans who lose their faith in Christianity rarely describe themselves as lapsed Anglicans and fewer Methodists as lapsed Methodists. Is there perhaps something in the atmosphere? Some extra vibrancy?

Anyway, here are some who have enjoyed, or survived, the Catholic classrooms.

'Like all girls I wanted to be a nun.' Cristina Odone never in fact made it to a nunnery but she did the next best thing, which was to edit *The Catholic Herald*. Her reason for being a nun was that the ones in the convent where she went to school in Rome looked so happy. 'They were calm, serene and never needed to raise a hand or voice. The nuns walked in the garden between the flowers and palm trees – in silence. The teaching was excellent and we were as quiet as church mice.'

Living as she did with a very noisy family in a noisy city, she had never 'heard' silence and found it pretty miraculous. (She is portrayed in the film *Lorenzo's Oil*, which is based on her half-brother's medical condition.) She referred to Santa Giovanna Elisabetta as 'this bog-standard convent' but her years there, from six until ten, were the happiest of her life.

It was a shock to be lifted from here to Washington, DC where her father got a job in the World Bank. After three years of 'show and tell' at a state school, she was restored to a Catholic establishment, Marymount Junior. She had 'a lovely, lovely time', which was just as well – her parents were in the throes of a divorce and Marymount offered a refuge from their strops and rows.

The National Cathedral School for Girls, where she was sent at fourteen, was not a refuge. 'My misery started. It was high fee-paying and Ted Kennedy's children went here – Kara Kennedy was in my class. There were high standards. American tough is really, really tough. There were constant tests and my homework took three or four hours.' She wasn't a cool chick and she didn't have a house that could be turned into party land.

Whether or not Cristina Odone is correct about all girls wanting to be nuns, that wish certainly applied to Karen Armstrong. Until it stopped applying.

'I haven't been a Catholic since 1974. I used to consider myself profoundly irreligious; now I would say that I am a religious person but can't see any of the major religions as superior to the others. I'm a freelance.' Theology aside, she is also a freelance writer and broadcaster.

Her parents were Catholic, though not particularly devout; they went to church on Sundays because it was a mortal sin not to. It took an hour to get their daughter from the depths of Worcestershire to the Convent of the Holy Child Jesus in Edgbaston, Birmingham. The only school she went to, it was fee-paying and run by the order of nuns she later joined. At noon the bell would ring for them to kneel down for the prayer known as the Angelus.

'As a school, it was not bad, not terrific.' She learnt to read very quickly but maths threw her. She was hopeless – hopeless squared – at it. 'It was a school which ruled by naming and shaming and I think I was frightened off maths. They couldn't cope with that.'

At the beginning of her second year in the sixth form, Karen decided to enter a convent. Her parents were horrified but their daughter Karen was now Sister Mary Martha.

Since she was going to be a teacher, she was sent to a crammer for two years and then to St Anne's, Oxford. It was difficult to argue with tutors about Milton at Oxford and then return to the convent and not argue with the Reverend Mother. 'I broke down at the end of my first year and left the convent in the following January, on the day I heard I'd won a university prize.'

It was still difficult: 'I didn't know who the politicians were and I hadn't heard of Vietnam.' (This was by now the late '60s.) The social side of university threw her; friendships had been discouraged in the order. As for anything else, she says: 'Larkin wrote that sexual intercourse began in 1963; I had entered the convent in 1962.'

Fortunately the academic side was brilliant and she was awarded a 'Congratulatory First' which is like the normal First but more so. Unfortunately her thesis on Tennyson went down the pan: 'After four years I finished it but the examiner wrote about four lines saying it wasn't a suitable subject for a thesis.' One would have thought that this could have been mentioned in the first place. 'The faculty told him he had failed as an examiner.'

A complete shambles, it was enough to drive anyone to religion but not, as it turned out, Karen Armstrong.

Cherie Blair (as she was not yet named) was very aware, from her mother and grandmother, that she should go to a good school and 'good' meant not just 'good' but 'Catholic', and Seafield Grammar was the good school for Catholic girls. It was indeed a good school with a lot of emphasis on developing morally.

'My social life revolved round the Young Christian Students, the best chance a good Catholic girl had of meeting a good Catholic boy from St Mary's, the school which faced ours across Liverpool Road. We would discuss the Second Vatican Council.' In case Protestant readers are confusing this with the First or Third, it should be stated that this is the ground-breaking and modernising Council which reached out to non-Catholics and replaced the Mass in Latin with a text in languages people actually spoke. Talking of boyfriends, it was the mother of her young man who said, 'You're good at debating and drama. Have you ever thought about becoming a lawyer?'

Cherie went to the LSE, where they taught law as a social science, with labour law and human rights law; they saw the subject in terms of its impact on political and economic life. 'This was the kind of work I saw myself doing.' She later co-founded the radical barristers' chambers Matrix.

'I did my Bar Finals at Lincoln's Inn, coming top. ("Blair, A." was nestling in the Third Class section.)'

Constance Briscoe is another lawyer with a Catholic schooling. At Sacred Heart Secondary Modern in Camberwell, they were taught that there was a space in Heaven for good Catholics – and there was this huge fence around Heaven to stop Church of England people going in. Otherwise, the teaching was pretty good.

'I found the atmosphere unsympathetic at St Joseph's in Hebburn, the first co-educational Catholic grammar in the North East,' said David Almond, winner of the Whitbread Children's Award and author of *Skellig*, the novel, play and TV drama. 'It was very regimented with a lot of corporal punishment – for girls too. One of the first things I saw was a teacher going down a line of children who were queuing for lunch with a strap to keep them in order.'

The author of poetry collections which include *My Dog is a Carrot* and *Beyond our Kennel*, John Hegley has been described as 'barking' by *The Independent* – in a very good way. He sings funny songs to the strains of a small guitar. One therefore imagines that he would have a sarky take on his Catholic primary, particularly when one is aware that he hails from Luton, not an especially Papist sort of place, one would have thought.

Yet one would be completely wrong: 'I went a year early to St Joseph's. I would say that my first school was happy. There was a sense of the sacred: I was an altar server and felt at home with the Christian aspect.'

He is now equally at home with Buddhism, to judge by his performance at a Free Tibet charity event at which he conducted a straw poll on what the Dalai Lama should call his dog.

Chris Patten found Our Lady of the Visitation in Ealing, west London, a very good traditional Catholic primary, where you learnt to read and write pretty early. He then won a free place at St Benedict's, the local Catholic direct grant school, and was extremely happy.

He has been the Governor of Hong Kong and Chairman of the BBC Trust. 'Life has been extremely kind to me.' This has meant, he laughed, that he is totally unable to write a 'misery memoir', which he feels is most unfair. Is there, he wonders, someone he can sue for loss of literary royalties?

'My mother is Church of England but her Christianity was fluid, depending on what was the best school,' declares Gina Yashere, the comedian known for her appearance with Lenny Henry in the UK and with Jay Leno in the USA. The best primary school must have been Our Lady of the Assumption, a Catholic primary in Bethnal Green, east London, because that was where she went at first. Yet if that was the best school, one wonders what the others were like. Certainly Gina did not take to it: 'The nuns used to hit us. I got the biggest whack on my thighs when I was in the toilets and said I didn't like a particular teacher – who was standing there when I came out of the cubicle.' That can't have made the little girl change her mind about the teacher.

When Gina was eight her mother became fluid again, sending her to the non-denominational Stroud Green Primary in north London: 'No nuns, just hymns in assembly.' More fluidity at the secondary school stage, when the school chosen was again Catholic, St David's and St Katherine's in nearby Crouch End. 'I did enjoy D & K.' This was just as well. 'My mother would have killed me if I'd bunked off.' Finally, mum became fluid once again and Gina went to the sixth form at Camden School for Girls, a comprehensive praised for many qualities but not for its hymns, of any denomination.

Jenni Murray was keen to go to school when she was only four and the local Catholic convent in Barnsley was happy to let her in at this early age. 'As we weren't Catholic, I was not allowed to cross into the chapel of the convent, where there were beautiful nuns, bells and smells; sometimes you could see through a crack in the heavy doors.' She never did get to see more, as she left for a Church of England school at seven, but at her secondary school she got to play a Mother Superior in a drama about a group of nuns who adopt a foundling, so the Catholic years were not wasted.

Like Jenni Murray, Francine Stock had a brief foray into a Catholic school before changing channel to a Church of England establishment. Francine's mother was a lapsed Catholic. Extremely lapsed: 'She was thrown out of her convent for starting a relic business, selling locks of St Cecilia's hair.' Since St Cecilia, if she existed, had met her saintly end some seventeen centuries ago, the odds were against her hair surviving in pristine condition and thus heavily against anyone handing over snips of them for a few quid.

Francine seems to have taken her Catholicism rather more seriously during the two years that her family spent in Australia:

'I went to Mandeville Hall, part of the Loreto Convent in Melbourne, which had beautiful, magical grounds. I built a small altar in my bedroom at home. A very fine fluorescent rosary was the must-have item one term. One afternoon we had to admire a replica of a nail that had stuck in Christ's hands or feet.' She didn't say who had certified it as being a genuine replica of an authentic nail. Let's hope it wasn't her mother.

Richard Griffiths, the much-loved actor who died in 2013, appeared in the most famous of recent films set in a school – the *Harry Potter* series – and the best known of recent plays set in a grammar school – *The History Boys*. Let's hope that in a small way this is some consolation for the shortcomings of his own time in the classroom. His father had a similar pattern: schools that were well below par, with a brief, final burst of quality.

'My parents were deaf and dumb,' he recalled. 'My father had only two years of education.' After six wasted years with a bunch of charlatans interested only in collecting the fees, Thomas Griffiths went at thirteen to a school for the deaf where, from scratch, they taught him to read and write.

With the father's unfortunate history, it is no wonder that his boy had problems too. 'My education was a bizarre and shabby thing,' declared Richard. 'I went to a variety of not very good Catholic schools.' To say that St Cuthbert's Primary in Stockton-on-Tees was 'not very good' is a charitable way of putting it. 'Anyone who hadn't been to Mass was beaten. On my third week I said I had been to church. It took them three weeks to make me a liar: I can't forgive them.'

Fortunately his family moved to a house five miles away and he went to St Joseph's Primary in Norton-on-Tees, a more pleasant and positive place to be. Less fortunately, he failed the Eleven Plus and went to St Bede's, a Catholic secondary modern. It was an impoverished institution that, with its tiny quadrangle and mean Dickensian building, felt like Dotheby's Hall. On the credit side, it was run by the De La Salle Brothers, the teaching order which he describes as 'marvellous'.

Whether they got the best out of him seems a moot point. 'The Northern Counties School Certificates that I got really equipped you to be a tradesman.' It was the under-manager at a Littlewoods store, where Richard was at eighteen in charge of the fruit-'n'-veg department, pointed out something that may have escaped the school: 'You have to get O levels to get on in the world.'

The teenager therefore went to Stockton and Billingham Technical College. 'When I went to my first class in art, the teacher put me in for the O and A level exams in November (this was in September) and in six weeks I got straight As.'

Austin Healey went to St Anselm's College in Birkenhead and was involved in a fight pretty much every day. This does not seem to have bothered him unduly, because he described it as a great school that launched his rugby career.

'The teachers in the early years were priests, which didn't seem strange when I first went there, as I had never been to secondary school before.' Despite being one of the few non-Catholics, he generally came top in RE, which was one of his favourite subjects.

'My girlfriend had to go to Heswall RC church every Sunday; we'd stand at the back by the spare hymn books, snogging through the service.'

'My parents had a deal.' Audrey Niffenegger, the author of *The Time Traveller's Wife*, would go to a Catholic elementary school near Chicago and then to public high school, which is completely secular with no religion allowed, so that you can't even put up a Nativity scene at Christmas. If she herself were blessed – or cursed – with the time travelling gene, she would like to go back to a first school with a lot less religion and a lot more foreign languages.

To be fair, St Joan of Arc Elementary School in Skokie near Chicago was very good on the basics. 'I can spell very well and I can "diagram" (you lay a sentence out on a series of lines and certain types of words go in certain places).'

It was her mother who was the Catholic. 'My father got to stay at home and read the comics when we went to church; I said I wanted to go to the "Church of Comics".'

After India, the Presentation Convent in Matlock, Derbyshire, was the most ghastly culture shock for young Ann Leslie. There were fewer panthers but there were few other advantages.

'This bloody school in the Peak District was so cold and damp that I had permanent chilblains. It was so Catholic: there were endless Masses and confessions.'

However, there was one nun who was an absolutely brilliant teacher. She realised that Ann was a swot and gave her private lessons. 'There was nothing to do apart from bloody praying, so I would read. I don't think I would have been even halfway educated if I had been happy.'

The little swot did her O levels early, at a youthful fourteen and a half, and moved to the Convent of the Holy Child in Mayfield, Sussex. This was more like it!

She had a room to herself instead of just a bed in a dormitory. Thanks to the swottishness, she was ahead of the curve scholastically and got A levels in English, history and French, followed by an exhibition to Cambridge, which she turned down because she accepted an Oxford scholarship.

This school was more upper-class and ancient Catholic families sent their girls here. Latin-American diplomats sent their children here too, all of them looking like Brazilian super-model Gisele Bündchen.

'Every now and then these gorgeous parakeets would go into a huddle and sob and scream: their parents would have written to say that they were now in an arranged marriage with the man who owned the other half of Chile.'

Anxious to please, Jean Shrimpton was always in the top five at St Bernard's, Slough, but hated studying. 'About half of the teachers were nuns. It's quite strange for children to see these black figures and their flapping crucifixes. All those starving Christ figures on the Cross – and then I became a model at a time when everyone was very skinny.'

The girls used to give money for babies in Africa. When they had saved the then substantial sum of half a crown – twelve and a half pence – they were allowed to name an African baby. 'Talk about politically incorrect! It wasn't racist but it was terribly condescending and naïve.' Personally, I think Bernard is a nice name for a boy and Bernadette for a girl.

It could be that, as far as the experience provided by the above schools was concerned, their Catholicism had nothing to do with the price of fish on Fridays. If Catholic schools differ from, for example, secular comprehensives, this might be down to the element of selection that creeps in with any religious foundation: the head of a faith school can always improve the intake of pupils by declaring that the parents of a poorer, less academic child are not sufficiently Catholic/Anglican/Jewish. And until there are RE exams for mummies and daddies, who can prove the heads wrong?

Be that as it may, many of my interesting achievers mentioned their Catholic upbringing, if only to say they hated it. Certainly corporal punishment at the hands, or straps, of a nun and priest seems cruelly inappropriate. Despite all that, it could be said that these children still benefitted from a Catholic schooling, on the grounds that what doesn't kill you makes you stronger.

CHAPTER 13

ALL THE SCHOOL'S
A STAGE

My children's primary school plays always had a cast of thousands, so every child got to tread the boards and entrance their parents. The kids who entranced other people's parents as well as their own then had the chance to take it further, on to secondary school stages and university theatres, where most of them would make their last bows and put away their stage make-up.

At one of his early schools – Charlie Higson's family moved around a lot – he and his two brothers (the oldest was head boy) were known as 'Higson Major', 'Higson Minor' and 'Higson

Min'. Charlie was 'min', as in 'minimus'. It all sounds like the making of a *Fast Show* sketch ('Just a min, Min!' 'Anything major, Major?'). Charlie appeared in Sheridan's *The Critic*, in which he played a woman and had just the one line: 'But see here your stern father comes.' (If it's any consolation, that is two whole words longer that Jeremy Paxman's line in his school's production of *Under Milk Wood*: 'I am Evans the Death.') Charlie enjoyed all his schools, especially this one, because of the dressing up in dramas.

Stubbington House near Fareham in Hampshire, Sir Richard Eyre's 'idyllic' preparatory school where he went at seven, offered something that the National Theatre never did when he was its director: a play was written specially for him. 'There was a very, very good English teacher, Major Maxfield, who had a tin leg. A very romantic figure, he had lost a leg in the Commandos. He wrote a play for me to appear in. It was about a Pools winner and called *Penny Wise, Pound Foolish*.'

Sir Peter Hall, an earlier director of the National Theatre, had a toy theatre as a child. 'My puppets did what they were told but *only* what they were told.' He may or may not have been thinking that this was a sharp contrast to some of the actors in the various companies that he has run over the years.

Roger Lloyd Pack also began his theatrical career in a small way: 'I did shows at home in a glove-puppet theatre and recited Shakespeare speeches while the puppets acted them out. I was always drawn to the blank verse.'

He was also drawn by the lure of being in the spotlight, which doesn't really happen when you are upstaged by your own thumb, so he was very pleased by the excellent little theatre at Beadales, his boarding school. He later regretted not making use of the art, music, basket-weaving and other opportunities on offer but, with his father being an actor, the stage seemed like the family business and he thought: 'This is magic and what I want to do.'

For Paddington Bear's creator, Michael Bond, school during the war – or at any time – had little attraction and, worse, it interfered with his main occupation: 'At home, I made a marionette theatre with big revolving stages. I never actually put on a show because the theatre was up in the attic and, during an evening performance, the light would have shone through the gaps in the tiles.' The theatre of war was now interfering with the theatre of puppets; enemy planes would have homed in on Michael's miniature floodlights.

'That left matinees but no one wanted to come in the daytime.' Also, his mother didn't like heights. Fortunately his main pleasure lay in the building of his minuscule stage, not its programming. (If he still possesses his marionette stage, a play I'd happily commission him to write, and climb up attic stairs to see, would be his adaptation of 'The Bear Who Loved Me' which begins with Paddington growling, 'The name's Bond, Michael Bond.')

'I was pretty naughty at Francis Holland Church of England School for Girls in Regent's Park, London,' admits Sue Lloyd-Roberts, 'but I made an awfully good Angel Gabriel – and did it for three years running, which was quite unprecedented,' Since then, her special reports for the BBC have continued to put her on the side of the angels.

St Machan's, a Catholic primary school in Lennoxtown, just outside Glasgow, gave Alex Ferns an enjoyable introduction to the world of show business. His drama course at the University of Cape Town led to the career that saw him playing Trevor Morgan in *EastEnders*, who has the accolade of being Britain's most hated soap villain. But it was dressing up in a rabbit outfit at St Machan's which was his first step, or hop, onto the stage.

Then came the primary school equivalent of those showbiz legends in which fortune lifts the unknown member of the chorus line into the starring role. At nine he hadn't even landed a part on stage but was just a triangle player in a production of *The Pilgrim's Progress*. (Like John Bunyan, you may not have realised there actually *was* a triangle player or indeed an orchestra in *The Pilgrim's Progress*.) Suddenly the boy playing the Pilgrim went walkabout and the part was up for grabs. It was Alex who grabbed it and began his own pilgrimage towards the professional footlights.

'My first stage appearance was at the mixed kindergarten attached to Streatham House Girls' School in Crosby, Liverpool,' recalled Nigel Rees, presenter of Radio 4's *Quote... Unquote*. 'We had to go on stage to admire the baby Jesus – just as two of the girls playing angels were having a fight.' The un-angelic angels did not put him off a showbiz career at Merchant Taylors', his grammar school. He was so successful as the hero of *She Stoops to Conquer*, who is afflicted with a stammer in the presence of upper-class women, that two elderly ladies in the audience were heard to tut-tut sympathetically: 'Oh poor boy – they shouldn't let him on the stage.'

David Harewood's big impression on his audience in a school production was made when he was thirteen or fourteen. In a show about famous historical figures, he did the Martin Luther King 'I Have a Dream' speech. 'Some black women in the audience were clapping and crying and whooping. This was probably the first time that I was aware of the power of the theatre.' It obviously made an impression on him, too. Two years after leaving drama school, he had a nervous breakdown and 'heard voices': the voice he heard in his head was that of Martin Luther King.

It is no wonder that the young Jenny Agutter seemed such a

seasoned pro in the 1968 television and 1970 film versions of *The Railway Children*. Her acting career went back a decade, beginning with *Alice in Wonderland* at the army school in Singapore where she went at the age of three. She had to say, 'I'm late, I'm late, for a very important date.' There may have been a certain tension in her voice: she was ruled out from playing the lead role because her hair wasn't long enough for Alice.

At eight she went to a small ballet school in Camberley that did not push the girls into professional parts but did not turn opportunities away either. Walt Disney were making a film about the Royal Danish Ballet but wanted someone who spoke English, not Danish. Although the school told her parents she was not expected to land the part, they included her anyway among the five girls who were to have a screen test. She did in fact get it and was surprised to learn what it entailed: she thought she was auditioning for the role of a Great Dane, not a little Dane.

Perrier-Award-winning Simon Fanshawe cut his theatrical teeth on *Alice in Wonderland*, though at a very different venue: 'At Miss Kempsmith's nursery in Stirling I "gave" – as actors say – my Dormouse in the Mad Hatter's Tea Party. I got stuffed into the pot,' he added. With that in his CV, he was confident enough to take to the stage in his first school, a friendly establishment in Salisbury, playing a Thunderbolt in *The Thwarting of Baron Bolligrew*. He returned to Lewis Carroll as the Red Queen – 'very characteristic,' he laughs, having been the presenter of *The Trouble with Gay Men* on BBC3.

Griff Rhys Jones is in danger of being typecast as an animal: Toad in both Terry Jones's film of *Toad of Toad Hall* and in the National Theatre production of *The Wind in the Willows*. Right at the start of his school showbiz career, at Conifers, a select private school in Midhurst, Sussex, he was the Little White Bull in the play of the song by Tommy Steele. The back half of a papier-mâché bull, to be precise. This did limit the amount of facial expressions he could bring to the part but the backs of his knees must have showed promise.

On the face of it, the role that young Mike Newell landed in *The Broken Statue* does not sound as if the director had much faith in him: 'I took the part of the statue.' Actually, it was a speaking part. He was by no means a spear-carrier in this production at Lyndale, a little private school in St Andrews: 'I had a little bow and arrow, like Eros in Piccadilly Circus.'

'One winter, a student died every week for eight weeks.' This was no ordinary school that Julie Fernandez attended between the ages of twelve and eighteen. She went from a day school for the disabled, where at eleven she was learning 'five plus three equals eight,' to what she describes as the top boarding school for the disabled, where she took her A levels and was filmed in the BBC soap *Eldorado* – in the same week. She went on to appear as Brenda in the series that will go down as a comedy classic, *The Office*.

Her parents were told that Julie, born prematurely with brittle bone disease, would not live longer than two years; in fact, her life has been saved by a drug which increases bone density. Her mother, aware that the teaching was 'terrible' at her day school, found out about Lord Mayor Treloar School and College in Alton, Hampshire. This cost a minimum of £45,000 a year but her mother came up with a powerful cost benefit analysis to impress the local authority. Assuming her daughter lived to the age of fifty, it would be cheaper to pay the fees so that she could work and pay taxes, than for her to be unemployable and live on benefits. (Since Julie not only works for her living and went on to create the Disability Foundation, she has certainly given society in general value for its money.)

'She pushed and pushed and eventually she cracked it.' Julie found herself in the school with its own little hospital and its own driving instructor with adapted vehicles. 'Those who were academically capable were pushed heavily; those who were not were taught how to cope in life.'

There was a main school play: '*Bugsy Malone*, *West Side Story* – big stuff!' She and her contemporaries became the first disabled students to take drama GCSE. Then the BBC contacted the school to say that they were looking for a young woman to play a wheelchair user in *Eldorado* and soon she was flying to Spain for the filming.

'During my A levels, I spent Monday and Tuesday filming, flew back on Wednesday, exam on Thursday; yes, it was hectic. I got both A levels, in English and German. Poor grades, mind you, but I got them.' She did not last long in *Eldorado* because no one did. Instead of being as long-running as *EastEnders*, it soon went west.

At Adrian Mitchell's Wiltshire boarding school, run by a friend of his mother, there was a brilliant teacher named Michael Bell, who taught them to love history, T. S. Eliot plays and Britten records. 'He gave me *Animal Farm*; later I did the lyrics for Peter Hall's production at the National.'

One day Mr Bell asked them to write an essay on the theme of *The Brains Trust*, which was the name of a radio programme on which big issues were discussed by, as the name suggests, people with trusty brains. Adrian interpreted his brief very broadly and instead wrote not an essay but a play entitled *The Animal Brains Trust*. He was then sent shopping in the village. When he came back, they acted out his play for him in what must be one the fastest turnarounds ever from script to stage. 'My first play!' Even more gratifying to the child playwright, it was put on at the end of term for the parents. This time he was in it. 'I was Commander Kangaroo, who fights a duel with Professor Toad.' Something tells me he probably won it.

His next big production was when he went to Dauntsey's, a civilised public school near Devizes. Chosen at fifteen to devise the script for the school play, he asked a boy who wrote puppet plays to join him in creating a drama for full-sized, or at least teenager-sized, performers without strings attached.

'To win the house play competition you had to have lots of deaths and we won every year. One year they banned our play because of some mild sexual innuendo; we wrote another overnight and won.'

Rory McGrath had a non-speaking role in the dramatisation of *Rumpelstiltskin* at St John's Primary in Camborne, Cornwall. It was meant to be a speaking role: 'I had one line but was too nervous to say it.' It is hard to think of Rory, whose gift of the gab is today well to the fore in *QI* and other TV shows, as being tongue-tied for long and he would surely have been delivering his lines, or line, perfectly well at his next gig, a Nativity play in which he was well up the cast-list as Joseph.

Another year he was the frankincense king, which was not a coveted part: 'Everybody wanted to be the gold king, because we knew what gold was.' (An interesting point. Do we adults know what frankincense is? Or how myrrh is made, mined, grown or however it turns up? Fingers on buzzers: it ought to come up on *QI* any week now.)

Over at St Andrew's Church of England Primary in Woodhall Spa, Lincolnshire, it was the Easter play that gave young Jason Bradbury his big, if dubious, break: 'I played Judas and was hanged in silhouette. It was only a paper cut-out of a body but even then I was aware that it could have a profound psychological effect!'

There is a convincing theological argument that Judas, far from being a baddie who betrayed Jesus for thirty pieces of silver, was in fact part of the divine plan that led to the highly beneficial crucifixion. Even so, one wonders if St Andrew's Primary knew what it was playing at. Fortunately Jason declares the school gave him 'hugely happy days and a wholesome and healthy experience', so we'll say no more about it. This time. There were no spiritual scars and, as I said earlier, he has gone on to become the enthusiastic presenter of Channel 5's *The Gadget Show* and the author of the *Dot.Robot* children's series.

Before that he studied at 'the best drama course in the country' at Bristol University, in which he and David Walliams worked hard at their double-act. 'We were part of a group who set up a comedy club called David Icke and the Orphans of Jesus.' He seems to have got Judas out of his system by now. Other Orphans included wacky broadcaster Dominik Diamond and Simon Pegg, who was the new Scotty (as in 'Beam me up, Scotty') in the recent reincarnation of the *Star Trek* film.

Among the shows with fewer laughs – or intentional ones, anyway – was 'an overly arty interpretation of Kafka's *The Trial* and a lot of experimental theatre, one production involving the use of rancid fish in a jail cell.'

Tragically, one of the students at lectures was Sarah Kane, author of *Blasted*, who was to write a drama about suicide and then kill herself. She had a play put on at the Royal Court a mere two years after graduating and was dead at twenty-eight.

Playwright Arnold Wesker was evacuated during the war and shifted around the country like a human package in a game of pass-the-parcel. He settled down for a time with an aunt and cousins in Barnstable, where he had a regal part in his school's end-of-term show. 'I recall the wonderful sensation when I rose to my feet with a crown on my head and said, "The beggar maid shall be my queen!"' Is there not an echo of this in his searing dramas *The Kitchen* and *Roots*? (No, probably not.)

Tony Robinson was always good at acting. When his parents saw an ad for the Artful Dodger in the original production of *Oliver!* he went for the audition and got the part.

> I became a marketable commodity. One day I would be carrying a plate of oranges on to a rugby field for Judy Garland and Dirk Bogarde in the film of *I Could Go On Singing* and the next day I would be reading Isaac Asimov in class behind my French textbook.

Joan Bakewell had a tart-ish part in *Point of Departure* by Jean Anouilh, Peter Hall's first Cambridge production. Karl [later Professor] Miller wrote in his review, 'She plays a tart like the Virgin Mary.' She carried on with the student acting but didn't win any gold stars.

During her joint drama degree at Hull University, Jenni Murray saw Vanessa Redgrave on one of their trips to the theatre. Did this legendary star of stage and screen inspire her to take up a career in the theatre? No, it was more of an aversion therapy: 'That was when I decided I could never be an actress. You had to be that good.' However, when fate closed the curtains on one career, it kindly opened them on another. 'Fortunately, this coincided with my first day in the radio studio in the new Gulbenkian building. It felt like coming home and I have felt completely at ease in radio studios ever since.'

At his second primary school, Moorland Road in Cardiff, John Humphrys wondered why he, and not one of the little girls in his drama class, was cast as Boadicea. He had no complaints: 'Wonderful, as I was dragged around in a cart and ordered people

around.' Sounds like excellent training for *Today*, without the
cart. Or the cross-dressing.

The greatest masculine role a little boy can play is Prince
Charming – and John Walker, one-third of the Walker Brothers,
got to play it in California.

> The very first thing that I can recall about Grant School in Redon-
> dor Beach, way south of Los Angeles, was the class play, *Snow
> White and the Seven Dwarfs*. I was Prince Charming. I was sup-
> posed to kiss Snow White on the hand but I was crazy about the
> girl and kissed her on the cheek.

Scholars of pantomime might point out that is usually Cinder-
ella who is kissed by Prince Charming but maybe the school did
a bit of re-writing. Anyway, there was an epilogue off stage to
the drama on it. 'Three weeks later she came down with measles
and so did I right after.' John later switched to the music business, where there are fewer germs.

On the stage of Wood End Infants in Northolt, Middlesex,
Rick Wakeman had a round of applause for his performance at
the school concert but he also had a critic. 'I was supposed to play
two sonatas by Clementi but after playing the first I launched
into "Side Saddle".' This was a number one hit for Russ Conway
in 1959 and its plinketty-plunketty pub-type piano sound was
highly addictive. Muzio Clementi was an Italian composer who
influenced Beethoven, so the difference was not hard to spot.

The head decided that 'Side Saddle' was not apposite for the
concert. 'After the applause,' says Rick, 'I was hoisted up by
the collar, taken to the front of the stage for my bow and escorted
off.' His consolation came years later: 'I produced the last record-
ing Russ did of "Side Saddle".'

The charm of that particular tune is that it sounds as if anyone could bang it out on any piano. Music making of some sort remains accessible, even when school music lessons are far behind, in the shape of joining local choirs or – assuming that karaoke counts as music – belting out the power ballads of our teens. Long after the final whistle has blown on our last match on the school playing field, we can carry on sporting activities of one sort or another, even if it is only some gentle running, swimming on holiday or kicking a football around with work mates. But it's not like music and sport; school is our one chance to utter – or forget – our lines on stage. There is a large number of flourishing amdram societies with an interesting choice of plays but these are for the more committed and competent. Children should make the most of their theatrical moments in the spotlight; it could be their one chance to star, or carry a spear. After that, it is curtains for acting.

CHAPTER 14

MATHS IS ALL GREEK AND LATIN TO DYSLEXIC PEOPLE

I t might be the cogs in the brain not engaging or it might be the teacher not being engaging enough. Either way, there are some subjects that don't work for some pupils. With me it was geography, which consisted largely of figures for jute exports from, er, Jutland? Then there was something about the area known as 'the Garden of England', though I never got to pick any apples there.

Dyslexia can cast its veil of confusion over most subjects. With maths, it can be a problem with teaching or it can be a kind of dyslexia in which the figures have a life of their own, dancing around before the eye can catch them.

Problems with Latin do not require brain scans; it is just an odd language to be studying. My father started me off on the bus to school one morning: 'Mensa, mensa, mensam,' he said, meaning 'table'. For me this was the beginning of a relationship with (non-mathematical) tables and the Latin language lasting a decade but I can see why some people's brains fail to grapple with it. Ancient Greek is an even odder subject; people who fall at the hurdle of Latin may be thankful that they would not have had that bygone language inflicted upon them too.

Here, then, are accounts from some of some of education's walking wounded.

Mr Parsons was actress Josie Lawrence's favourite teacher but even he could not make her feel at home with maths. This led to a slap round the face – administered by her. She used to mime during the mass recitation of the times tables and usually got a red line through her long division. 'Eventually I slapped Mr Parsons round the face and ran out of school.'

The teachers were very good about it, merely pointing out that she couldn't carry on running away from school, 'otherwise my mummy and daddy would go to prison'. Thankfully, it never came to this and she passed the Eleven Plus to Rowley Regis Grammar, a school on the top of a hill and visible from her street. (This may or may not have been a cheering sight for her.) Still no change in her mathematical abilities, though there was an improvement in that at this school she didn't hit the maths teacher.

'I would always be ninety-fourth in the school exam; there were ninety-four in the school.' Her father used to help her, a somewhat thankless task. One day she came home, threw her books on the sofa and snapped, 'You got them all bloody wrong!'

Of her seven O levels, none of them was maths. 'Instead, I did "Computer Mode 3", which was for real "divs". I spent most of my time colouring flow charts.'

Siân Phillips won a scholarship to grammar school, with 100 per cent in English and 0 per cent in arithmetic. When she was taking her O levels, the teacher said, 'Just go into the maths exam, write your name and then sit in a field to revise something else.'

Tamsin Greig (*Green Wing*, *Black Books* and Debbie in *The Archers*) was carried away by her success at Camden School for Girls, north London, in getting maths at O level. She went on to take it at A level but found herself in difficulties: 'It was like being in a foreign country: the maths teacher was a sweet, encouraging young guy, like a policeman in a foreign country who points a lot and you don't understand what he's pointing at. I remember one night trying to work out a calculus problem, going to bed, waking up, going to my desk and writing out the correct answer. In the morning I had no memory of it and couldn't even understand my answer.' She got an A in English and also in French. She did pass her maths but her grade was rather lower down the alphabet.

'Maths was a struggle.' Gail Porter needed a private tutor. She asked unanswerable questions such as 'Why do you need to know the angle of that ladder leaning against the wall? I'm going to hire someone if I need a ladder!' As she said, they had called her 'snobby' at primary school purely because she didn't muck about in class and they would certainly say it again if they knew that this was her attitude at secondary school. They would say it yet again if they heard her talking about her Highers (Scottish equivalent of A level). 'My father thought that accountancy would be useful. I don't know what for; I get someone to do my accounts now.'

Harry Secombe was completely useless at maths, though he claimed, 'I had a nodding acquaintance with long division.' At the Lower Fifth end of term exam his housemaster held up his paper between finger and thumb as if there was something nasty in it.

'Stand up, Secombe,' he commanded. 'You are making history here: no marks at all.' In the geometry section Harry wrote down that he knew only about Pythagoras's Theorem – eating humble Pythagoras, as it were – but unfortunately the paper was about much more obscure topics.

The letter offering Jeremy Paxman an exhibition at St Catharine's, Cambridge had a sting in the tail. There was an addition in ink at the bottom: 'You understand, of course, that this is subject to your getting Elementary Maths O level.' Maths had become a joke to him after his five or six failed attempts: 'The average age of people I was sitting it with got younger and younger. Now that I had got a place, I passed it at once.' This was just as well, because, after staying on for an extra term of Oxbridge entrance, he kept getting expelled, then being allowed back for an exam, then being booted out again.

Although a historical novelist, Sarah Dunant had a similar problem with Latin, which used to be compulsory for entrance to Cambridge. She just scraped through the General Classics O level by learning by heart great chunks of Caesar's *Gallic Wars*.

So did Jonathan James-Moore, a future 'Head of Jokes' for BBC Radio. Like Jeremy Paxman with maths, he kept doing retakes while successive years of younger boys came to the Latin lessons, passed the exam and moved on. To avoid the humiliation of a wrong answer in front of the sprogs, the deal was that the master would ask him questions only if he indicated by an agreed sign that he knew the answer.

Like an actor, Jonathan learnt the English translation of Julius

Caesar's text and used odd bits of Latin purely as 'cues' to prompt him as to which chunks of the 'script' to write out in the exam. Finally this technique worked but, when he came out of the exam, he realised that his memory had been only too good; not realising at what point the Latin passage stopped, he had 'translated' paragraphs that weren't there on the question paper. This rather gave the game away but the examiners must have been glad to see the back of him.

England Rugby player Austin Healey got three A levels at his Jesuit private school but Latin was not one of them. He did not even take it at GCSE: 'Brother O'Sullivan sent me out of the class *before* the lesson.' This was to save time, as Austin was bound to get up to something during it.

Marcelle d'Argy Smith, former *Cosmopolitan* editor and author of *The Lover's Guide*, was often first in her class at Westcliff High, Essex – until the results for maths, at which she was terrible, were added in.

'During my first term of algebra, I asked for extra tuition but didn't get it.' Realising that she was going to fail O level maths, she did German in two terms, which would make up for it. 'I was so stressed when taking my O levels that my bottom broke out in boils and I took the exams sitting on a rubber cushion.' Well, many do take the view that maths is a pain in the ... never mind.

Back in the days when M People's Shovell was still schoolboy Andrew Lovell, he joined a boys' grammar, the name of which he preferred not to utter, in the last year before it went comprehensive. He hated the formal assembly with masters in gowns and classes lining up for inspection by prefects to check that you had the correct buttons on your blazer, in case you had overnight snipped off the official ones and sown on a slightly unofficial set. And then there were detentions – and the slipper.

'I remember a maths teacher who wanted you to write the question at the top of the page, the rough working-out in the margin, the actual working-out in the centre and the answer at the bottom. If you got that layout wrong, you got the slipper.'

What with the teacher's anal layout, and Andrew's worries about maths, he would go into the lesson in a fearful state anyway – 'even before the slipper'.

Richard O'Brien, creator of *The Rocky Horror Show* and master of ceremonies in *The Crystal Maze*, was a very awkward learner and was punished by a strap across his hands. He couldn't 'read' a clock and couldn't tell the time until he was eleven.

When his second son went to school, Richard was told that he could be dyslexic: 'He gets his "Bs" and "Ds" muddled up.' So did Richard. 'The more they described his dyslexia, the more I realised that it applied to me. The freedom I felt in the ensuing weeks was marvellous.'

At Newbury Park Primary, Essex, darts player and commentator Bobby George was good at metalwork and woodwork but no good at reading.

'In my day I was called thick but now it would be called dyslexia. Spelling was like looking out of a window on a sunny day; to me, it was jet black out there.'

The headmistress at Burford School, a new primary practically next door to Steve Redgrave's home in Marlow, picked up the signs that he had dyslexia. The word didn't impinge at the time but at Great Marlow secondary school it meant that his schedule featured extra English instead of French. As he says now, 'If you're struggling with your own language, you're going to be struggling even more with someone else's.'

When his first child started to learn the alphabet, she brought home some letters cut out of wood. 'When I picked up a lower-case letter "a" my wife pointed out that I was holding it the wrong way round – but it seemed pretty normal to me.'

Windlesham prep school was exceptionally good, according to Duncan Goodhew, but it became obvious that something was not quite right with the seven-year-old. 'In an English lesson I was asked to go to the front and read. Sadly, I stumbled over the first couple of words; there were little giggles from the class. Pretty soon I was Duncan the Dunce.'

This was before dyslexia was a word on everyone's lips. 'As a fellow dyslexic put it later, the written word is like a weapon used against you. The advantage of dyslexia to me was that I looked for something positive in my life – and I found swimming: I was good at something!'

For a young boy to turn a disabling minus into a powerful plus is enormously impressive. Yet fate had another minus in store; could he turn this too into another plus? He was ten when the blow, or rather Duncan, fell.

> A teacher set up an assault course that had what we called a 'Big Dipper': a rope went up to the fork of a tree, then angled down towards the ground. I grabbed this rope but my wrists weren't strong enough and I fell eighteen feet, banging my upper lip on the root of the tree.

It sounds as if ''Elf and Safety' as a concept had yet to meet the otherwise excellent prep school. First it was a matter of swollen lips and black eyes. Then Duncan noticed bald patches expanding to become one large bald patch at the top of his head, leaving a fringe round the front and sides. He must have looked like a monk whose barber had overdone it. This was put down to damage from the fall.

'Being bald and dyslexic, my deck of cards was not very good.' Astonishingly, he pulled out an ace, declaring: 'I was *meant* to be a swimmer; look, I'm even more streamlined!' Unlike the teacher whose bright idea the assault course was, he certainly deserved a medal. He got one, gold for the 100m breaststroke at the 1980 Moscow Olympics.

It may not be much consolation to those who have suffered in the past but at least teachers today will be aware of, and on the lookout for, dyslexia. We can also avoid previous problems of our own making; no one is punished any more for being left-handed. Latin is not a stumbling-block, since it is no longer compulsory. Maths, though, looks like being with us for the foreseeable future. Calculators help, of course. A cartoon by Tony Holland commemorated their arrival when they first reached schools: an exasperated teacher asks a pupil, 'If I have three calculators, and I give you two, how many do I have left?'

CHAPTER 15

SORRY YOU'VE GOT TO GO

t is no great surprise that it should have happened to Jennifer 'Fat Lady' Paterson, the extrovert cook clad in motorcycle leathers. Another of the usual suspects is Beryl Bainbridge, who had a fairly wild life, one way or another, as colourful as her novels; the episode which changed the course of her life was the school's loss rather than hers. But that nice gardening guru Monty Don being asked to leave? Who would have thought it? Clare Balding – surely not? Susannah York – tell me it's not true. But, as they relate, it was. They were all asked to take the walk of shame out through the school gates.

It is not everyone who is provided with under-five education and of those only a few are expelled – and for only a tiny fraction of this category is 'attempting mass murder' the reason for the expulsion. James Lovelock is a man in a thousand or indeed million: one of the world's leading environmentalists, he invented the Electron Capture Detector that senses the presence of polluting CFCs. While working in NASA to design instruments for detecting life on Mars (as one does) he came up with a theory about life on earth, the Gaia Hypothesis, which looks at the 'biosphere' as a single self-regulating unit.

All this was in the future on that day in the 1920s when a teacher at a nursery school in Letchworth was showing James's class some poisonous plants. 'When she left the room, I tried to induce the girls in the classroom next door to eat the deadly nightshade. I was sent home and never went back.'

His family then moved to Brixton, London, where he attended an excellent Church of England school. Deadly nightshade was thin on the ground here. And, he adds, 'I was too happy to want to go in for poisoning.' We can only hope that, now in his nineties, the eminent scientist remains a happy bunny.

When his father was a commando based at Aldershot, Monty Don went to Quidhampton, a little private school in Basingstoke. 'I was the naughtiest boy they had ever had. If you got three "black marks" a term you were beaten; I contrived to get eight in my first term. I was asked to leave.'

He managed to stay the course at a Berkshire prep school improbably named Bigshotte and left at the appropriate time but there was trouble ahead.

'I hated Malvern College from the first five minutes. I was very unpopular, mainly because, after I keeled over with hepatitis, it was on my account that the whole school had to have a very painful hepatitis injection. I was teased a lot about my name: Monty – short for Montagu.' (That does not surprise me. My name too is abbreviated and I felt pretty embarrassed when opening our phone conversation with 'Hello Monty – this is Jonty.')

He lasted seven terms. 'For the second time, I was in the situation that, though I was not being expelled, they made it quite clear that they were not going to have me back. My parents were furious.'

He was sent to The Vyne, which his parents thought was still a grammar school but had in fact gone comprehensive. Then, after a year … he wasn't expelled. Unfortunately, he still had to leave, as the local authority switched to a new system in which A levels were taught instead at a sixth form college, so he was on the move again. This college was co-educational and he didn't do any work (he seems to be making a connection between the two) so he failed all his A levels. In his A level English, he failed to manage even the O level grade, which is quite an achievement – one of his few achievements to date. He did not look at all like someone who was going to make it to university and then have two interesting careers.

Just before her fourteenth birthday, which fell about six years after she started at Merchant Taylors' girls' public school in Crosby, Beryl Bainbridge was caught in possession of a rude rhyme. This was a disaster, both at school – and home.

Unlike Beryl the Peril, her parents were quite prim. Aspiring to propel her up the educational ladder, they sent her to elocution lessons. They didn't let her play with 'not-nice' girls, which meant that she did not go out to play at all.

Decades later, she could still remember how the dirty ditty ended: 'Pull down her protection and plug in the main connection.' At the time she thought it rather good and still did when she told me about it. The piece of paper with the offending words was being passed round the school and when it was her turn to have it, she added illustrations and put it in her gymslip. Where her mother discovered it.

Horrified, she sneaked on her daughter to the headmistress. 'I was put on probation for the term,' said Beryl. 'I was sent to Coventry at home and my brother wasn't allowed to speak to me.'

> Miss Williamson, the maths teacher, was instrumental in getting me expelled. She was terrible: short hair, a suit and very cross. She wouldn't have me in her class and I had to go out to the corridor. Miss Peck, the English teacher, spoke up for me but I was expelled.

Fourteen was a difficult age for finding a new school, particularly if you had been thrown out on your ear from the old one. As Beryl had won some awards for acting, her parents chose a Hertfordshire ballet school which also offered drama, known then as 'Cone-Ripman' after the two ladies who ran it, now as Tring Park School for the Performing Arts.

It was quite a leap, geographical and social, from Liverpool to this house in the south. 'For the first six weeks I was enormously unpopular, until I did my "dares", which were to have a bath at two in the morning and to alter my regulation pyjamas.' Not very daring, you may think, but that did it.

There were two snags about the school. One was the expense. The other was that her parents rowed whenever they visited the school and she was worried about leaving her mother alone with her father. 'I left at fifteen; the first my parents knew about it was when my blankets were sent home.'

With the door slammed on a conventional sixth form and university education, she was in her fifties before she knew about, for

SORRY YOU'VE GOT TO GO

example, translations: 'I always thought Proust wrote in English.' Until she started researching for her historical novels, she also didn't realise that 'bibliography' at the end of a book means a list of other books where you can look things up. 'I always thought it was something to do with the Bible.' (It is, in a way. According to my conventional sixth form education, both are derived from the Greek word for 'book'.)

'Because of tensions at home, I went to Wispers, a boarding school in Sussex,' said Susannah York. Susannah, whose first leading roles were in *The Greengage Summer* and *Tom Jones*, created tensions at school too, in the shape of 'being out of bounds, and swimming after midnight. There was also a long history of midnight feasts.' And therefore a short history of Susannah at Wispers. 'Virtually expelled' was how she put it.

'I don't think I got expelled,' says Clare Balding, 'but they weren't overly keen to hang on to me.' She concedes that she did get into quite a lot of trouble at the fee-paying school in Inhurst, which is near Basingstoke and in the village next to hers. To put it another way, 'I was very enthusiastic and inquisitive, and rather questioning of teachers.'

The good news about her time at Downe House, a private girls' boarding school near Thatchem, Berkshire, is that she was not *expelled*. The bad news is, 'I got *suspended* for shoplifting from the local village shop. There was a lot of it going on and I was trying to keep in with the in-crowd and prove my hardness.' She was suspended for only four days, by which time the end of term was upon them.

However awful it was at the time, everything worked out in the long run: 'I ended up as head of the house and head girl.' It helped that she was moved to a different house and formed a new circle of friends who were less light-fingered in shops.

Sadly, both of the stars of the BBC2 mobile cookery programme accurately entitled *Two Fat Ladies* have gone to the Great Kitchen in the Sky. One of them had a double-barrelled, unhyphenated surname and eleven Christian names – Clarissa Theresa Philomena Aileen Mary (only halfway though, sorry) Josephine Agnes Elsie Trilby Louise Esmerelda Dickson Wright – but I shan't mention her again, partly for reasons of space and partly because she, being a star pupil, doesn't fit into this section on expellees from schools. I refer to her only because the other fat lady did, the more modestly named Jennifer Paterson, who paid tribute to the academic skills of her fellow-cook which led to her being Britain's youngest barrister.

By contrast, declared Jennifer, 'The only thing *I* ever passed, apart from the motorbike test, was the Royal Academy of Art exam which we took every year; it was still life and life drawing, which was usually of one of the girls – not naked but dressed in a vest and bloomers.' To give due credit to Jennifer, she passed the motorbike test twice, as she discovered years later that she had been given the wrong licence, the one for cars and articulated lorries. To get insurance for the motorcycle and sidecar combination that she drove in the television series, she had to take the test again. (Immediately after getting it, she hit a camera.)

Her lack of qualifications was largely due to her premature departure from the tiny boarding school she went to at seven, the Convent of the Assumption in Ramsgate, Kent. Here the sixty girls studied Latin, French and the useful art of 'illumination', which she describes as 'those big capital letters with gold rubbed in and a picture inside'. This would be very useful for anyone going for a job in a medieval monastery, a position for which the convent girls wouldn't be applying. Also on the syllabus was 'deportment', which she described as 'how to come through a door properly', which is a lot better than coming through a door improperly.

'I was expelled at fifteen.' She admitted to being rowdy. She questioned things and would not conform. She was an exhibitionist: 'They used to put my table in the middle of the refectory with a screen round it and I would climb over the top, which would cause screams.'

Finally Reverend Mother Rita of the Resurrection (the poor woman could not pronounce her 'Rs' and it will not have helped that the school was based in Wamsgate) ran out of patience with her pop-up pupil.

'She had a wooden arm with its hand covered by chamois leather; she used to take your hand, put it on top of her wooden hand, and pat it.' The saintly lady asked 'Chick-a-biddy-bee', her pet name for Jennifer, to join her on a little walk, trapped her in a chamois leather grip and said, 'I'm afraid we've decided you'd do better somewhere else.' To put it another way, if she were somewhere else, *they* would do better.

If you are going to make your way in the world, you may be the sort of person who gets up the noses of people in authority. They may decide you are a teacher's pest rather than teacher's pet. It is a pity that matters escalate and expulsion is seen as the only solution for pupils who clearly have a lot to offer. For the lucky ones, it can come to be a kind of badge of honour, almost worthy of being put on the CV.

CHAPTER 16

UNIVERSITY
ENTRANCE AND
HOW TO FAIL IT

There are many different doors to university entrance.
When one closes, well, another may slam shut too.
And the next one. But finally those who try enough
doorknockers may hear the unbolting of bolts and
the creaking of hinges. The good news is that, despite disas-
trous mistakes, some losers turn out to be winners. Another
piece of good fortune is that sometimes, having picked themselves up from the floor, they end up better placed than they

would have been if they hadn't been knocked down in the first place.

Terry Jones, for example. There is no question of him being the Messiah but he was certainly a naughty boy when he took his A levels. The future director of *Monty Python's Life of Brian* achieved an A-starred grade in Naughty Boyish Studies when he looked at the English question paper: 'I misread the rubric.'

A 'rubric' is so keen to make life difficult that even the word itself is difficult. It means the instructions for choosing which parts of the question paper to answer – and 'none at all, so can I go now' is not an option. Like a secret agent opening sealed instructions while parachuting down into hostile terrain, the candidate turns over the paper to read at the top something like 'Answer THREE questions from Section 1 or ONE question from Section 3. Failing that, attempt FIVE questions from Section 7 or SEVEN questions from Section 5.'

The rubric at the top of Terry's paper was not quite as tricky as that but even so he failed to read it properly: 'I did four questions in a section requiring only two – and two in a section requiring four.' Those of us who have done the same will agree that it seems unfair to be penalised for this honest mistake but that is the Examiner's Law: there are no marks for doing those extra two questions in the first section and, however well you answer the two questions in the second section, the fact that you have done only 50 per cent limits your maximum marks here to a measly 50 per cent.

English was Young Jones's best subject – and indeed still is, now that he is Somewhat Older Jones. As well as his comedy career, he has developed a highly intriguing line on the life (not to mention mysterious death) and works of Geoffrey Chaucer. However, he had shot himself in the foot in this particular A level. His history result was not brilliant either and he failed French.

'I was turned down by Exeter, Bristol and Manchester,' he recalls. However, this failure turned out to be a stroke of luck. Back in the early 1960s, Oxbridge colleges used to set their own exams that were independent of A levels and Terry took this route to a university education. Having failed at what were then seen as 'B-list' universities, he had a shot at the 'A-list'. This time he must have read the rubric properly, because he achieved a place at St Edmund Hall, Oxford. The rest is history – or, in his case, English. The lesson is that it is always worth having another go. Or to say to yourself, as Monty Python scripts would soon be telling us, 'And now for something completely different.'

At the same time Michael Palin, who did read history at Oxford, was also having problems with university entrance. He ruined his chances of doing the subject he originally chose, English, by declaring at his interview that Graham Greene was his favourite author. It turned out that Graham Greene was born four years too late for the period covered by the English course. Palin was accepted, but not to read English.

Possibly the most colourful – literally – boob at a university interview was made by the late Eddie George, known when Governor of the Bank of England as 'Steady Eddie'. He placed himself on extremely wobbly ground during his interview at Clare College, Cambridge, where he was sent as a promising sixteen-year-old to try his luck.

In view of his ultimate career as the husband, in a manner of speaking, of the Old Lady of Threadneedle Street, he might well have been ready for a tricky question on supply-side economics. In fact, what the Master of the college asked him was, 'Do you like cricket?'

Did he like cricket! Boy George (as he was never known) leapt to his feet, grabbed a bottle of ink from the antique desk of his interviewer and proudly demonstrated how he gripped the ball when bowling a leg-break. Unfortunately the lid was loose.

It is a shame that there wasn't on hand a BBC Test Match commentator to describe the result: 'And he comes in, bowls and – yes – the lid on the bottle is loose! There's blue ink far and wide, so an umpire's signalling a no-ball.' For Eddie it was a case of no admission to Clare but he got a place at another college the following year. During this interview he didn't open the bowling or, if he did, he checked the top of the ink bottle first.

The ink-splattered Clare academic had only his own obsession with sport to blame but he was by no means alone. At his medical school interview a friend of mine was disconcerted to be asked, since he did not even possess a pair of rugger boots, what position he played in the scrum. (I was disconcerted too; in the event of going under the knife, it would be good to know that the surgeon wielding it had been chosen for his brain not his brawn.)

By contrast, King's, next door to Clare, was a temple of aestheticism, not athleticism. It was not the place to go if you preferred exercising the body to exercising the mind but this was precisely how another sixteen-year-old blotted his copybook beyond the absorbent powers of the most effective blotting-paper.

Bamber Gascoigne had won a scholarship from his prep school to Eton but, once in the 'College', the house that consisted entirely of scholars, he soon discovered he was no longer the leader of the intellectual pack. At breakfast one morning he observed two brainboxes playing chess *without a board or pieces, merely calling out the moves.* He decided that all this intellectual business was, as we say these days, above his pay grade: 'I was very anti-intellectual for three years.'

Anyone seeing this lad in those days, devoted to sport but to little else, would have needed psychic powers to spot that here was a potential presenter of *University Challenge* and also *Observer* drama critic. And certainly university entrance was initially to be extremely challenging.

He too was sixteen when he had his first interview at Cambridge. His father happened to be at a dinner where he met the head of King's. The 'Provost' (the obscure term, which sounds like the academic wing of the Provisional IRA, in fact means head of college) told Mr Gascoigne to send his boy along for an interview with the Dean.

'What are your interests?' was the first question put to Bamber. That sounded easy enough. It was hard to give the wrong answer but he managed it: 'Shooting and fishing.' He had never seen a face fall quite as fast as that of the worthy Dean, so he added, quickly and untruthfully, 'And reading of course.'

The elderly academic perked up like a flower in a long drought receiving a bucketful of water: 'What are you reading at the moment?'

This was more impossible than anything Gascoigne was later, as a quizmaster, to throw at competing teams. He was not reading anything, not having had his nose in a book for some three years. However, he remembered having seen his grandmother engrossed in a ripping World War Two yarn about convoys crossing the Atlantic. Not exactly Jane Austen but it would have to do.

'*The Cruel Sea*,' he answered. This nautical bestseller was not much mentioned in a college that gave house-room for decades to one of the great British novelists of the twentieth century. Long after he had written *A Passage to India* and his other classic novels, E. M. Forster was still living in King's without having to do anything much, on the grounds that his presence was enough.

'What do you think of it?' asked the surprised interviewer.

'It's about convoys crossing the Atlantic,' was the best Bamber could come up with. Hence the letter that the Provost wrote to Mr Gascoigne: 'The boy is not university material.'

So that could have been that. Gascoigne Junior could have ended up presenting a show entitled 'Non-University Challenge' on local radio. Fortunately he saw the whole episode as a wake-up call and returned to Eton determined to concentrate on study instead of sport. His subsequent intellectual flowering was thanks to the encouragement of Andrew Sinclair, a fellow Etonian whose books were to include *My Friend Judas*, arguably the best Cambridge novel. Pointed in the right direction, Bamber won not just a place but a scholarship in modern languages. It wasn't at King's, though. And he still hasn't read *The Cruel Sea*.

These Oxbridge entrants who shot themselves so effectively in the foot were lucky to be around in the happy times when money was not a factor in university entrance. If your parents couldn't afford the cash, the state could. A grant of some sort automatically followed a place – at least, it did for respectably academic subjects. Toyah Willcox was unlucky, not because she is younger (which she is) but because of her subject. She was applying not to a university but to Birmingham's Old Rep drama school, for which the grant was 'discretionary', meaning 'not if we can help it'.

As might be expected of someone who was to become an actor, presenter and 'First Lady of Punk', she leapt over the initial hurdle, i.e. her audition at the Birmingham Theatre. Unfortunately, council grants were not automatically bestowed on would-be students of the theatrical profession. It is hard to believe but she remembers it only too well: she had to do another audition, this time for a local bureaucrat. The customary showbiz thumbs-down, 'We'll let you know,' would have been kinder than the way he actually put it.

'I think the man from the council wrote, "Not attractive and has a lisp".' Yet despite her stinker of a review from the bureaucrat, she still managed to acquire the cash for the drama school, by working backstage at the theatre both mornings and evenings. She has not forgotten or forgiven the early slight.

'If I ever meet that man again,' she snarls, 'I shall push him down the stairs.' She could always claim this was part of her second audition, for a method acting course on playing very angry people.

After all these hit-and-miss, not to mention miss-and-hit examples, it is heartening to be able to end this chapter with the success story of a school with a teacher who suddenly upped their game.

Until two years before economist Sir Andrew Dilnot went to Olchfa Comprehensive in Swansea, nobody from that school had gone on to Oxford or Cambridge. Then the deputy head declared, 'My children are good enough!' In Andrew's year, fifteen pupils achieved places at Oxford or Cambridge. Andrew himself went on to be appointed Principal of St Hugh's College and is now Warden of Nuffield College, one of the few Oxford heads to be educated at a comprehensive. Yes, those children were good enough.

CHAPTER 17

TO GREATER DEGREES

There is no getting away from the fact that higher education has a much higher profile than further education. There is likewise no getting away from the fact that Oxford and Cambridge are disproportionately represented in terms of Parliament, the heights of the civil service, the judiciary and broadsheet newspapers. The two universities are disproportionately represented in this book.

You could say that the kind of people who are bound to end up as public figures will gravitate towards Oxbridge. Or you could say that Oxbridge (the term 'Camford' never caught on) gives a leg-up to people who might not have made it otherwise. Both views contain a lot of truth. Yet once you are there, it is not always a doddle to get your hands on those glittering prizes.

There was a disaster in store for Michael Palin and Terry Jones before they were to form their lengthy comic partnership, initially as a duo, then as a sextet with Monty Python and finally as solo acts. The first time that they were under the same roof was in their first year at Oxford when Michael was in a terribly serious play, translated from the terribly serious German, in which he had to speak terribly seriously while gazing down into a well. Terry was in the audience.

The idea was that Michael, instead of walking across the stage to deliver his momentous lines, would wait for the well to swing round to him on a 'revolve'. Unfortunately, an over-enthusiastic stagehand sent the well spinning past Michael before he could get out so much as the first syllable. Sprinting off in pursuit of the accelerating item of scenery might have detracted from the seriousness of the drama, so he waited patiently for it to screech to a halt and reverse back to him. Thereupon the stagehand began overcompensating like mad, and again the revolve whipped the well rapidly past the expectant actor in the opposite direction before he could open his mouth, so the stagehand then went into reverse gear and ... 'My funniest evening ever in a theatre,' recalled Terry.

Michael decided that it was great to have an audience laughing at you, even if it wasn't supposed to be, and later got together with Terry to form a comedy twosome named, imaginatively, 'Palin and Jones'.

It is true that the art critic and broadcaster Andrew Graham-Dixon got a Double First at Oxford – apart from the word 'at'. 'Occasionally at' would be more accurate. 'I had a very sociable university life but the people I socialised with weren't at Oxford, they were at Bristol, because my girlfriend (now my wife) was reading philosophy there.' Also, he disliked Christ Church, his college, and the snobbish rugger-buggers – 'boring, thick, ugly people'– it contained. By contrast, the teaching was absolutely fantastic and he read for between twelve and fifteen hours a day.

So his week would start on the Monday with his tutorial in Oxford, after which he drove to Bristol and went to the library. On Thursday he drove back to Oxford, popped in for another tutorial and then turned the car round for the trip back to Bristol and the weekend. He claims that at the end of his time at Oxford, he knew only four people. Having finished the last exam of his Finals, he went into his college 'buttery' for a drink but they wouldn't serve him.

'Only for college members, sir.'

Juliet Stevenson had a place at Bristol University for a joint degree in drama and English but woke up one day thinking, 'What on earth am I doing – reading when I want to act? Why be nudged off the direct path?' That may sound a dramatic way of putting it but if one can't be dramatic when planning a career in drama, when can one be?

She had acted before, not least in a play put on by a boys' public school, presumably chosen because it enabled the lads to cast her in a harem scene calling for a girl in bra and knickers. Yet being a professional actress felt as remote as being an astronaut and when the RADA audition came up she was confident only that she wouldn't get in. 'My name wasn't on the list read out afterwards, so I got my coat and left.'

She was going down the street when someone ran after her to say, 'That was the list of people who've *not* got in.' This is what you call a happy ending.

Raymond Briggs's interview for the Wimbledon School of Art

did not go well: 'I said I wanted to be a cartoonist and he went absolutely ape.' The frightening principal was a devotee of High Art and, specifically, the Italian Renaissance. Despite his fury at the idea of Raymond's Low Art, the principal did let him in, which was fortunate, as it provided four years of a terrific grounding in old-fashioned, academic painting. 'I think in fact he let in anyone who wanted to come. Several people in my intake should never have been allowed into an art school. One girl used to draw baa-lambs all the time.'

Siân Phillips had a similarly fraught conversation with her tutor at the University of Wales in Cardiff. The back door of the university was opposite the front door of BBC Wales, so it was handy for her to pop in as a newsreader and member of the repertory company. Her tutor told her: 'If you give up the BBC, you've got a good chance of a First. If you don't, a 2.1.' In fact, she had food poisoning and threw up in her best paper. 'I got a 2.1.'

Sebastian Coe enjoyed Loughborough University but found the necessary multi-tasking made it the hardest time of his life so far. 'I was training three times a day and in the British team at eighteen. One of my tutors used to laugh that I was the only one of his students handing in assignments on British Airways notepaper, scribbled during a flight back from an international competition.'

Growing up in Northern Ireland, the former *Blue Peter* presenter Zoë Salmon used to drive past Queen's University in Belfast. 'The most beautiful building, it screamed education and brilliance. I was impressed by the fact it was on every £5 note; it was where the clever people went and it was on my doorstep.' She was undoubtedly one of the clever people. She had notched up ten GCSEs, mostly As, plus a silver teapot for having the school's highest marks in home economics. Having watched *LA Law*, she decided to read law and went to Queen's when she was eighteen.

Arguably the cleverest career move came at the end of her gap year, which she took after her first year at university. She went in for and won the title of Miss Northern Ireland and swanned around the catwalks of the world. Instead of doing more of the same, she then returned to university and the security of a career. She got a 2.1. Although she longer works as a solicitor, she has not forgotten her legal training: 'When I'm in a shop for a refund, I'm always reminding people of the 1974 Sale of Goods Act.'

Like her fellow *Blue Peter* presenter Zoë, Konnie Huq got a 2.1. She was at Robinson College, Cambridge, a comparatively new institution built in such a way that students can bang on each other's windows, even on the high storeys, thanks to the balconies that they can walk over. Its architecture makes it ideal for 'Assassin', a game played during Rag Week, for which she was the college co-ordinator. This sounds like a good way of channelling one's paranoia: 'You were given the name of someone in the college who you would spy on and shoot with a water pistol.' This also sounds like excellent training for *Blue Peter*. Or, on second thoughts, perhaps not. Don't try this at home, kids: all those balconies.

Writer and broadcaster Simon Fanshawe was given a place at Oriel College, Oxford but decided that his second choice of university, Sussex, seemed more engaging: 'It was an irrational decision but the right one: I was born to be in Brighton.'

He got a 2.2: 'I was far too engaged with politics. Like everyone else, I was briefly a Maoist. I was in the CPB(ML)' – this stands for Communist Party of Britain (Marxist-Leninist) and should not be confused with the Communist Party of *Great* Britain, as if you would – 'because I was in love with the man who ran it and then fairly quickly moved into the "Broad Left".'

He was later appointed to the governing body of the university, which he accepts is the most extreme example of poacher turned gamekeeper, or possibly gamekeeper turned poacher: 'When I went to the Vice-Chancellor's office after being appointed, I told him that the last time I'd been there was when we'd been occupying university buildings, probably to end global tyranny and injustice.' Still a little way to go, I fear. Perhaps Simon should be occupying his own office.

'In my early teens I wanted to be a writer and I wrote my first novel at sixteen: 140,000 words. It will never see the light of day,' promised Iain Banks. He put 'writer' on his passport instead of student because he believed, 'I'm going to be twenty-six when this runs out and I'm not going to be a student then, I'm going to be a writer.' In fact, the passport *did* run out before the ambition was fulfilled.

'I thought university would give me time to write' and it did: the 400,000 words of his second novel were banged out during his first year. Comparing his weekly diary at Stirling University with a physics student showed that the hard-working scientist had thirty-five hours of lectures and practicals, while he himself had five, occasionally rising to a still far from arduous nine.

What he liked about Stirling was its continuous assessment; exams made him nervous and he was fed up with feeling sick on a morning when he had to take one.

This paragraph is for the benefit of budding authors: 'I chose my courses with writing in mind: English, because if you are going to write it, you might as well study it; philosophy, because you have to have a theme and purpose; and psychology, to understand your characters.' It all sounds very clever but here are the fruits of this scheme: 'This was total nonsense and had no bearing on my actual writing.' So, apologies to budding writers.

Al Murray had as the head of his college 'a brilliant man, a history star' named Brian Worden. When Antonia Fraser wrote a book, this was the reviewer who would be wheeled out to savage it. His student Al was more of a history planet or minor asteroid: he got a 2.2. Al had *heard* of the 'Rump Parliament' of 1648, while Professor Worden could name the Rumpled Parliamentarians in it. But Al's time was not wasted.

'In my act, I do rather wear my history degree on my sleeve; there's a lot of history – often *wrong* history. My un-vocational degree has actually come in handy.'

In his last days at Oxford, he noticed that Stewart Lee, who had been in the year above, was going round quite successfully in comedy circles. He thought: 'I'm *much* funnier than him; I might as well have a go.' These days, Stewart is still a year older and still a friend but Al is convinced that he himself remains much funnier.

Alastair Campbell is now a walking alcohol-free zone but at university Tony Blair's spin-doctor-to-be used to knock back the sauce with some enthusiasm. 'I got into far too many scrapes. Well, scraps.' Long afterwards, someone came up to him at a Burnley v. Birmingham match to say, 'You don't remember me, do you? You thumped me at Cambridge because I insulted your football team.' The thumpee turned out to be a Labour councillor, so they agreed on politics if not on soccer.

Alastair assured me that the last time he had hit anyone – mind you, we were speaking some time ago – was when Michael White of *The Guardian* made a cruel joke about Robert Maxwell, Alastair's then boss at the *Daily Mirror* who had just drowned in mysterious circumstances. Alastair is not happy about the episode: 'It was a terrible punch, quite hopeless.'

After leaving No. 10 and publishing his diaries, he gave a talk in Cambridge. The only person from his past who turned up was Millie, the barmaid from college, who stood up to say, 'I've loved watching your career and I'm proud to have known you – but I'm amazed that you're still alive.'

Oxford was amazingly glamorous. Ann Leslie wasn't, not in her opinion anyway, but she was always in the slipstream of glamorous people like Paul Foot and Richard Ingrams, the *Private Eye* stars in waiting. 'This was a good preparation for being a foreign correspondent, a life spent in the slipstream of great world events.' She herself did no journalism but her boyfriend, now husband, wrote for the magazine *Isis*. (Michael had a girlfriend but Ann, with that forcefulness which gets her across frontier posts without documentation signed by the right warlord, persuaded him to dispose of her.)

Alan Coren, who was later my editor on *Punch*, said that he was always trying to get off with her at Oxford but not only was he unsuccessful, she didn't even notice. A man who she did notice was a big, shambling guy who used to amble into her room to show off his poetry, which she would jeer about to her friends afterwards. This was Stanley Johnson, father of Boris and, despite the sneering, he won the prestigious Newdigate prize for poetry.

'I used to wonder how Stanley had got into Oxford,' said Ann. 'But never underestimate a Johnson! As they say of Hungarians, they go into the revolving door behind you – and get out in front.'

Richard Whiteley and I lived on the same college corridor in Cambridge and shared our first flat in London, but it was only after he became a public figure that I discovered a hidden part of his private life. I interviewed him when *Countdown*, the daily Channel 4 show that he presented, made him the person with the most appearances on terrestrial television and, sadly, I helped with the biography written after his death in 2005.

'I still remember my first English lecture,' he told me. So do I. It was the same lecture, at noon on our first Friday, but it feels like a different occasion. 'It was given by the great C. S. Lewis.' Correct. 'He was the author of the Narnia children's books.' Correct, though he wouldn't have mentioned them. 'His lecture was deep and philosophical.' Well, in a sense, but, to be specific, it was on the Middle English poem 'Sir Gawain and the Green Knight' and we all used the edition edited by Lewis's chum and Middle Earth creator J. R. R. Tolkien. Some of the finer points of the lecture might have passed Richard by, as he was immediately distracted.

'At that first lecture, I also remember sliding into a spare seat next to a girl with the most beautiful, wistful, gorgeous and dreamy face I had ever seen. She became the only reason I turned up for lectures, although I never dared to sit next to her again.' He gave clues in his autobiography that led directly to Helen Drabble, the beautiful sister of the novelists Margaret Drabble and A. S. Byatt.

All of this escaped me at the time and during the subsequent seven lectures of C. S. Lewis I failed to notice him carefully *not* sitting next to Helen. He did mention her once, saying that he had seen Helen and her boyfriend gently stroking each other's faces at a party, but it was spoken not longingly but in an amused tone of 'Well, these young people, charming, charming.'

After worshipping her from afar, he moved to worshipping her from even further away, as his attendance at lectures of any kind diminished, for the reason that he edited the student paper. This meant that he was also not assiduous at supervisions, as tutorials are known at Cambridge. Since I shared supervisions with him, or would have done if he had turned up, I had to make various excuses, several of which, such as the one about an aunt's funeral, were nearly true. When Finals loomed up at the end of our three years, I took him round to introduce him to the academics who should have been teaching him and they were pleasantly surprised to see him at last. He was amazed by the knowledge I had picked up: 'You come out with all these difficult words like "Dickens", "Tragedy" and – what was it again? – "Romantic Poet".'

Years later he told me of a recurring dream. 'It's like my other dreams of going on air but not having my shoes on or not even being in the studio.' This was an anxiety dream and a half: 'I'm doing my Finals – and I haven't done any of the work.' Richard, that might not have been just a dream.

Geography classes kicking off at 7.30 a.m. would not go down well if Hugh Dennis's character suggested them to his onscreen brood in the clever sitcom *Outnumbered*. However, that was how he started the day in the sixth form at University College School, London, with three other Oxbridge scholarship candidates. 'All four got in; one got a scholarship and I got an exhibition to Cambridge,'

In his first year he was one of 700 men at St John's. In his second year there were 693 men and seven terribly brave women, who made the place much more civilised. It was at the end of the year that a friend, who went on to be an investment banker in Hong Kong, suggested they write sketches for The Footlights.

'Someone made the mistake of laughing.' He spent his third year mainly doing comedy. He became treasurer, Nick Hancock was president and the vice-president was Steve Punt, who later became 50 per cent of the Punt and Dennis duo. 'The Footlights also had the post of Falconer but no falcon.'

Meanwhile, back in the lecture room, geography was proving an enjoyable mixture of mountain ranges and post-Stalin economies, glaciers and New Towns. 'It involved a little bit of an enormous number of things; it was like doing a pub trivia quiz for three years.'

Hugh got 2.1s in his first two years and was surprised, what with the joke-making, that he ended up with a First in his Finals. 'Even though it was probably the result of monstrously good luck over five days in June 1984, no one can take it away from me – not unless they go back and mark my papers again.'

Having failed his A levels, Monty Don worked on a building site and retook English, this time getting it at an A grade. He then went to France and worked as a gardener. This might not have seemed like a smart career move but it – the gardening part rather than the French bit – turned out to be exactly right for anyone who was going to present a programme called *Gardeners' World*.

In France it occurred to him that it would be good to go to Cambridge and then become a thatcher. Cambridge academics do not teach degrees in weaving straw, at least not my father, who by chance was one of Monty's supervisors at Magdalene, the Cambridge college where Monty got a place.

'Arthur Sale was a huge influence on my life.' Apparently my old man used to point him towards rural writers who might not be much use for exam purposes but were right for Monty himself. The thatching never happened.

As might be expected of a future editor of the *Sunday Telegraph*, Sir Peregrine Worsthorne made Peterhouse his first choice in 1942 when taking his entrance exams purely because the invigilator for this group of Cambridge colleges looked 'very Brideshead'. Evelyn Waugh's saga was, of course, set in Oxford but what the young entrance candidate admired was that the interesting academic in question was wearing a soutane or cassock, purple socks and shoes with black buckles. 'He looked faintly satanic – no, worldly in a glamorous way.' It is just as well that Perry decided that 'satanic' was not the *mot juste* as this turned out to be the chaplain of Peterhouse.

Perry's first supervision was given by a historian who later became the Master: 'He thrust a rolled-up copy of *The Times* into the fire and tried to use this great burning brand to light one of the Wills Whiffs he chain-smoked, setting fire instead not only to his eyebrows but also to the quiff of grey hair overhanging them.'

Peterhouse had a tradition of social snobbery, which encouraged undergraduates to develop these tendencies, according to Perry, who added, 'not that I needed any encouragement.'

One evening at 10 p.m. he was crouching in his pyjamas in front of the gas ring to fill up his hot-water bottle, when in walked Princess Marina, wife of the Duke of Kent. 'The most romantic person on earth. She was in full regalia, tiara and all, having just attended some grand function at King's.' Apparently this royal vision had asked where there might be an amusing undergraduate and such was Perry's fame that his name was suggested.

'Simply too charming.' She *didn't* say that or anything at all. The Princess just glanced round and walked off without a word, presumably thinking to herself, 'If this cove with the hottie and jimjams counts as an amusing undergraduate, what are the dull ones like?'

With one A in English but two poor grades in history and Latin, Clare Balding was rejected by Christ's, Cambridge. It had been easier in her father's day; Ian Balding, who trained racehorses for the Queen, said he had got there with only O levels. Thrown by this, she then remounted, as it were, her academic career, taking history A level again and being coached in interview technique. She also started riding in races.

Two years later, she was a Cambridge student, at Newnham instead of Christ's. In her first week, she asked Jean Gooder, her director of studies, if she could have Tuesday off for a race: 'If I win the Lady Riders' Championship, I would receive my weight in champagne.' She added, 'And bring reflected glory on the college.' Permission was granted, provided that she explained the racing page of Jean Gooder's newspaper.

When Joanne Harris went to St Catharine's College, Cambridge, it was a very masculine environment. It was only the second year in its five-century history that it had condescended to allow women in. Correspondence from college authorities was never addressed to 'Miss Short' (her surname at the time) but to 'Mr Short'.

St Catharine's was at least ahead of Magdalene, which was the last male college to go, as it were, unisex. She was walking past there once when she was asked by some of its undergraduates standing outside if she would strip for them, for a fee of £300. She replied, 'Not if you were the last man on earth!'

The teaching at Cambridge made up for the chauvinists. She could not complain about being insufficiently stretched. Dr Lethbridge, her French supervisor, gave her a piece of Proust and remarked cheerfully, 'This is impossible to translate.' Alternatively, he would give her a sonnet by Victor Hugo and she would spend hours translating it into a sonnet in the style of *later* Wordsworth. In her last year she started her own novel, a vampire tale triggered by an inscription she noticed on a small monument with a metal door in the Grantchester graveyard: 'Something inside me remembers and will not forget.' Unlike most novels started while a student, *The Evil Seed* was both finished and published.

'In my Finals, I was stuck behind a boy who broke wind with much regularity and Chaucerian volume.' (Note the word 'Chaucerian' instead of 'really mega farts'. That's the benefit of a university education.) Despite the sound effects, she still got a 2.1.

Susan Greenfield was not a late developer, except in the area in which she is now a leading light. 'I hated science at school. At

Cavendish Primary in west London, science was "Nature Study", which consisted of having a book read to you about acorns.' At Godolphin and Latymer her O levels included Latin, Greek and maths but excluded science. As did her four A levels, which consisted of the same three subjects plus ancient history. She got into St Hilda's, Oxford, to read PPE (philosophy, politics and economics) but found the first P, philosophy, a bit of a disappointment. She remembers reading a whole chapter on 'the'. There's not a word missed out in that last sentence: the chapter was all about the definite article. Maybe the next chapter was all about 'a'.

It was enough to inflict psychological damage but instead she switched to experimental psychology; this was a science but the student did not need to know the basic sciences to study it. 'I certainly went in through the back door! I got what would now be classed as a very good 2.1 and my tutor said it would be a hoot if I were to become a scientist.' She became a scientist.

When Oliver James was at Eton, his father set out three options: 'Work on the railways at Swindon, which was not all unappealing to me; go to work in the City, which in our family was like going to a concentration camp; or go to Cambridge University.' Swindon's loss was Cambridge's gain, as he did well at the entrance exam to Magdalene.

'When I got there, I was horrified that there were eight other Etonians in my year – the eight Etonians you very much didn't want to bother with.'

The college had a beagle pack, which didn't seem cutting edge in 1973. Oliver was more in the spirit of the age when he smoked pot and took LSD in his first term and spent the rest of the year recovering. 'In my second year I became very diligent and got very interested in academic subjects – and have been ever since.' He then went on to an MA at Nottingham. 'Out of my seventeen years being educated, I worked for six years and ten weeks. I don't think that's too bad.' Not too bad! It's about five years and ten weeks more than many of us.

Clive James (absolutely no relation to the Oliver above) did not after all become a scientist. At the age of thirteen he thought he was heading for a career as an aeronautical engineer but it became apparent that he was not a rocket scientist. He went to Sydney Technical High School: 'Almost immediately, this started being miserable. I was not any good at mathematics.' At seventeen he was still not any good at maths. It may be true that nothing is ever wasted and that everything can add a flavour to the soup of one's experience. If not, these sound like four wasted years. Anyway, he was about to get back on course – an English course.

'I got to Sydney University and my career began.' He directed the university review and wrote for the student press. He achieved a 2.1 in English: 'This was generous of the university because I had started to leave lectures alone.'

He moved to England and got a place at Cambridge where he did many of the same things: university review, student magazines and English degree. He was lucky to get a 2.1: 'On one of the papers I got nothing at all and there was a suggestion that I should be sent down for it.' He must have done extremely well on the other papers, because he was allowed to stay on for a PhD on Shelley. This went the way of Clive's aeronautical career, abandoned forever. That was Shelley's loss but the poet, being dead, could handle it.

After leaving Rugby, Chris Brasher began a year's apprenticeship at Metropolitan Vickers in Manchester. This involved a five and a half day week which didn't leave much time for mountaineering and, worse, meant that during the winter you would cycle to work in the dark and cycle home in the dark. It was the dark cycling, plus a lovely sunny day in February, which made him decide that engineering was not for him: 'I had a tea-break outside for ten minutes and there was a lark singing his heart out. He was free and I wasn't.'

He went up to Cambridge in 1947 and read geology because there is a lot of geology in mountains. He also did mineralogy and crystallography.

Despite the lack of mountains in the Fens, Chris stayed on for a fourth year at university. The nearest thing Cambridge has to peaks is some tall, spiky buildings which roof-climbers in the student body were wont to ascend. He and his fellow 'stegophiles', as they are known, planned to celebrate the end of their exams by decorating the Cantabrian pinnacles with hydrogen balloons. Chris added these accessories to the 'Wedding Cake' or cupola of New Court in St John's College.

'As dawn broke, there was the marvellous sight of coloured balloons tugging at strings attached there and on King's College Chapel – but by seven o'clock there wasn't a single one to be seen, only sorry bits of string and rubber. We had bought ordinary balloons and the hydrogen had diffused through the rubber.' Perhaps he should have kept up with the engineering after all.

While Chris Brasher is as outdoor a kind of guy as you could possibly meet, Caroline Hamilton has had at least as much fresh air on her face as he has, having led the first women's team to the North Pole and the South Pole. Her maths A level came in very handy for navigation on polar trips.

At Cambridge she was awarded a Blue in hockey, cricket and athletics. In her six Varsity matches against Oxford, her team lost only one. They even won the athletics match during which she was stabbed in the back.

'I was the only javelin-thrower to stab herself in the back with her own javelin – between the shoulder blades, very painfully. Then I fell over.' Despite the extreme privations, her polar expeditions involved less bloodshed.

Michael Frayn's father, who was an asbestos salesman, was upset by his son's choice of university. He didn't think Michael should have chosen a university at all, not when there could be a job going in his company if a word was spoken into the right executive ear. However, Michael went off for an interview with the senior tutor at Emmanuel College, Cambridge, who was a well-known anti-Semite and anti-Catholic.

'Suppose you have children who go to France and come back converted to Catholicism. What would your attitude be?' It could have been worse; the don could have asked how you would feel if your kids went to Israel and came back Jewish. Anyway, Michael believes he must have given a sufficiently intolerant answer, because he got in.

Fortunately the senior members of the university were not all like that. His wonderful moral science supervisor, Jonathan Bennett, would start at twelve o'clock. At one they would still be arguing, so would go to the pub and carry on there, sometimes returning to his room for the rest of the afternoon, stopping only when it was time for the evening meal in Hall. It was a very good way of learning philosophy and, in Michael's case, getting at 2.1.

It also left time for extra-curricular activities: 'I wrote the Footlights May Week Review. This was the only time it did not go on to the West End.' Still, he did get there very soon: 'Bamber Gascoigne, a friend of mine, used two numbers in his revue *Share My Lettuce*.'

He also wrote a humorous column in *Varsity*, the student paper. A decade later, when I was writing a supposedly humorous column there, I found Michael's series in the back numbers. It was a kind of dry run for the column he was by then writing every week in *The Observer*. The student paper once masochistically printed a letter from a cross reader listing its faults, one of which was me, 'a third-rate (very third-rate) Michael Frayn'. It was the bit in brackets that particularly rankled: did that mean three times three? Ninth-rate? On the other hand, perhaps I shouldn't knock it: it was good to be in the same sentence as Michael Frayn.

Despite his harmonious times with his supervisor, there was another Fellow with whom he had a bumpy, not to say un-Christian, encounter. Emmanuel was sporting and he was not.

'Are you a rowing man?' asked the chaplain.

'No.'

'Rugger man?'

'No.'

'Athletics?' (Growing disbelief.)

'No.'

'Boxing?' (The chaplain must have clutching at straws by now.)

'You *are* a member of the Church of England, aren't you?' (Latent hysteria detected.)

'No.'

'There doesn't seem much point in continuing this conversation,' he said. A sentiment with which Michael could only have agreed.

'I was used to being the bee's knees.' Mike Newell is the bee's knees now, of course, as he buzzes busily around film studios directing *Harry Potter* and other big-time movies. But he didn't feel as if he was delivering much honey to Cambridge when he arrived in 1960: 'I walked in feeling I was really clever – but I found everyone else was cleverer. I had an exhibition; everyone else seemed to have a scholarship.' He was overwhelmed by the massiveness of the subject you had to digest: 'English literature from soup to nuts.'

His tutor (moral as opposed to academic) was a descendant of Charles Babbage, the English mathematician who devised a precursor to the computer in the nineteenth century. Babbage once asked, 'Apart from work, what do you want to do with yourself?'

'I want to play around in the theatre.'

'Oh God, you'll get a 2.2.'

He got a 2.2.

In his first year Mike was auditioned by Trevor Nunn, then a grand old man in his third year at Cambridge, later to be even grander as the director of the National Theatre. 'I did a piece from *Hamlet* and a little bit of Pinter. He had his head in his hands. I knew I would never be an actor.' He would, though, be a director, and proved it with an excellent production of Noël Coward's *Hay Fever* at the end of his third year. One of the student stars was Miriam Margolyes, 'As crazy then as she is now'.

Peter Hall set his heart on directing and in his first term at Cambridge booked the student theatre for the first week of his last year. In the meantime he did some acting, which ranged from understudying a part in a Greek play that had only one line even if he actually got to speak it, to a big duel in *Romeo and Juliet* with John Barton, later to be his co-founder of the Royal Shakespeare Company. Barton had already wrecked his back in a swordfight in *Macbeth*; now he had one of his fingers split by Peter and ended up in hospital.

The accident-prone Barton added to the potential for damaging himself by eating razor blades. As his fellow thespians asked nervously, 'Do you think that's wise?' he would put them in his mouth and turn them over with his tongue. There was a story about an actress fainting as blood trickled from his mouth.

Richard Mabey was rejected by Cambridge. He got distinctions in his physics and chemistry A levels but failed his maths, being awarded an O level grade. His maths may have let him down but his maths teacher did not, pointing him towards his old Oxford college: 'I'll put in a good word.'

Richard went up to study biochemistry but in his first biology experiment he was meant to extract the contents of his own stomach with a tube. In his third week he applied to switch to PPE and ended up with what he was assured was 'a good Second'. One of his tutors was Iris Murdoch, who used to moonlight as a famous novelist. The philosopher and professor Isaiah Berlin delivered a course on Marx that became a big university event.

'There were 2,500 to 3,000 present – a third of the student population, with people standing on tables for his heroic, electrifying performance.'

Adrian Mitchell did pretty well in his A levels and got into Oxford. His college was Christ Church but he spent most of his time at Balliol, mainly for the Balliol Communists' wine-and-cheese parties. 'John Cornwell, now John le Carré, who was thought to be a police spy, used to write down our names in a little book.' My own theory is that this was in fact research for his forthcoming novels, though Tinker, Tailor, Soldier, Balliol Student and The Spy Who Came in from Christ Church never did get written.

Adrian was Fourth Man in Crowd in an 'existential' production of *Julius Caesar* and one newspaper compared him to Harpo Marx. Presumably the First Man in the Crowd would have been Groucho.

On the work front, Adrian decided to read and write what he wanted. He practically reduced his Anglo-Saxon tutor, Christopher Tolkien (J. R. R.'s son) to tears. 'I got a "Pass" degree, like Auden. That means you haven't done any work but you're a totally brilliant man.'

Jean Marsh did not go to university – she scarcely went to school and the closest she got to drama school was a course of six private lessons at the Central School, then located on the top floor of the Albert Hall – but she wished it had been possible.

An insult to Oxford once reduced her to violence. A boyfriend who had been at Christ Church took her there and she was looking admiringly around Tom Quad, the most impressive part of a spectacular college. The boyfriend chose this moment to give off about the place and express the wish that he had experienced a different life which hadn't involved the architectural glories in front of them.

She was furious at his rejection of this rich culture: 'I smacked him, the only time I've ever hit a man.'

Later she was involved with concerts put on in Christ Church at Christmas. 'I never leave straightaway but wander around the college and pretend I am a student.'

Pam Ayres had similar glimpses of the charmed Oxbridge life. In her case it was Cambridge that she didn't go to, as it were. Leaving school at fifteen, she went into the civil service, took two O levels, went into the Women's Royal Air Force and did three A levels.

When she was stationed near Huntington, she used to take the bus to Cambridge, look through the gates at the beautiful colleges and think, 'If only I had the chance!' To her it was like a foreign country.

As it happens, I would have been at one of these colleges during this period and it could have been mine, situated as it was near the bus stop at the centre of town, through whose gates she peered. This induces a vague feeling of guilt. It could also be a scene in one of those state-of-the-nation television plays: I bump into her while rushing off to the student paper, apologise briefly and then, decades later when she is 'Britain's favourite poet', I jump at the chance of an interview about her schooldays. The second part is certainly true.

Jean Marsh and Pam Ayres, being deprived of the three years at university which they deserved, have a kindly, wistful view of student life. Others on the outside see these young people as a lot of layabouts. Many students are in fact extremely active. Admittedly, only some of these activities concern their academic work; others do not. There are students who combine curricular with extra-curricular activities and achieve great success in both. I take off my mortarboard to them.

CHAPTER 18

RIGHT HONORARY DEGREES

ichard Griffiths had three marvellous years in the drama department at what is now Manchester University, but it was Durham University that gave him an honorary degree at the same time as the novelists Pat Barker and P. D. James.

'We were walking in procession' – with his portly frame, I expect Richard did a mean procession – 'up Stockton High Street behind 200 undergraduates and forty teaching staff.' Together with the then Chancellor Peter Ustinov, the three of them were the tail-end Charlies, splendid in their red gowns. Ustinov heard a woman asking, 'What on earth is going on? I'm trying to get across the road to Littlewoods.' And her friend said, 'I think it's a gypsy funeral or wedding.'

Harry Secombe was knighted and, in view of his wide and short stature, used to refer to himself as Sir Cumference. (His motto was 'Go On,' as in 'Goon'.) Having left school at fifteen, he was also gratified to receive an honorary doctorate from the University of Wales, Swansea. He was particularly pleased to be told that he was being dignified with the highest honour they could offer, but this dignity was somewhat chipped away by the reception he received when he strode up to receive it from Prince Charles, the Chancellor – and the most royal, loyal Goon fan. The Prince of Wales collapsed in hysterical laughter.

Harry saw the joke: 'In my gown and mortarboard, I looked like a Toby Jug waddling up. A Goon in a gown.'

So many honorary awards have been bestowed upon Trevor Baylis, the inventor of the clockwork radio, that he has a standard acceptance speech for when he turns up to receive them.

'I was so stupid when I left Lady Margaret Infants in Southall, Middlesex, that I couldn't spell my own name. Two short planks!' Endearingly, he thought that 'Miss' was the Christian name of his peach of a teacher in Form One, Miss Batt. 'It puzzled me that most of the other women teachers seemed to have been given exactly the same first name.'

No one in his childhood would have prophesied this kind of academic glory, any more than they would have guessed that he would be an underwater escapologist in a Berlin circus, which he was for a time. He is a man of many parts, few of which were picked up by his schools. This was not entirely their fault, as he was uncooperative: 'Teaching me must have been like trying to communicate with a slab of tripe.'

Yet when he left school at fifteen for an engineering apprenticeship with a one day a week release scheme, his studies in hydraulics, hydrostatics and mathematics went like clockwork, if not a clockwork radio.

Since John Peel never got further than his five, or six, O levels, university was not an option. However, he was extremely proud of his honorary degree: 'An MA from the University of East Anglia in one of those modern subjects which I can't quite remember.' He also liked to mention another notch in his academic CV: 'I once helped the daughter of a friend with her art course – she was very good but not at the writing – so I feel I have a share in her degree.'

To someone revising desperately for Finals, it seems a wonderful way of achieving a degree: wait for someone to give it to you. Of course, you have to do something impressive in life to make them want to award it but you don't have to bother about the nasty business of exams.

CHAPTER 19

BAILING OUT

'Shouldn't you be in your Finals exam?' my father asked one of his students when he bumped into him in a Cambridge street.

'No, I'm giving up university,' was the answer.

That was in the laid-back 1960s, when even dropping-out was left to the last minute. Today's speeded-up students mostly make the decision to abandon ship in their first year, often over Christmas. As the student intake has been rising over the years, 'non-retention' numbers have risen with it.

It doesn't look too good on the CV of the droppee or the record of the institution. However, my father wasn't too bothered about his 'non-continuing' student who had done the work but not the exam. One of his colleagues definitely approved of anyone making the positive choice of saying goodbye if they thought their university course was not right for them. Dropping out can lead to dropping in to a more congenial institution or occupation. Some students have always plumped for an early bath and something better may be waiting for them when they take a short cut out of the groves of academe.

There was a moment when Rick Wakeman, keyboard player of Yes, said No. He came down to earth with a crash like the final chords of a Wagnerian opera. Throughout his schooling he had enjoyed fourteen years of musical education and now had a scholarship to the Royal College of Music. His experience of musical competitions had been like this: 'I was entered, I learnt the music, I played and I won.' The competition here was different. 'I was with 100 performers who had won scholarships from all over the world. On the first day I walked past a practice room where a pretty Korean girl was playing some stunning Schoenberg. I realised I was a fish out of water.'

He was complaining one day to his clarinet teacher that students were banned from moonlighting as session musicians. His teacher, the wonderfully named Basil Tchaikov, gave him a dramatic piece of advice: 'I suggest you walk out of the building, don't look back and don't come back. There are doors open to you now that may not be open when you finish the course.' This is what Rick did. Looking back, he does not regret that he went to the College in the first place: 'I realised that their teaching gave me more jigsaw pieces for my picture.'

Thirty years later Rick was featured on *This is Your Life* and Basil Tchaikov was one of the guests. Rick took the opportunity to ask why he, as a professor at the Royal College, had given that advice about bailing out. The answer was: 'I did the same thing.'

It wasn't a good year for A levels at Tony Hawks's school and no one achieved what they wanted. His hoped-for B, B and C grades turned out to be B, D and E but that was enough for a place on the drama course at Manchester. He lasted only a term and a half: 'I didn't like the students and I didn't like being a student or the course. I realised that I didn't want to be a straight actor.' This didn't leave much, plus it rained a lot in Manchester.

He told his tutor he wanted to leave and was met with dismay: 'But *Paul*, you're doing so well!' For someone called *Tony*, that was the final nail in the coffin of his student career.

By the time Rosie Boycott had finally achieved her two A grades and an S at A level, the ratio of good to bad (for her) educational institutions was running at an unsatisfactory two to four. Kent University, where she went to read maths, would count as neither, just neutral.

> I trotted off to Kent University to read maths. Kent was quite hip at the time but it was a very druggy place and I found myself taking a lot of drugs. I suppose I should have made some different friends.
>
> I'd proved that I could get into university and I knew I'd get a degree – but so many exciting things were happening in London in 1971.

She was about to become one of them. 'At nineteen, two-thirds of the way through the second term, I packed my car and went to London. I lived in my car for two weeks.' At twenty she was co-founder of the radical feminist magazine *Spare Rib* and later of publishers Virago Press. Several stages of her life should have had a government health warning: Don't try this at home, kids, or indeed at school! And other stages of her life provide a reassuring example to show worried parents that young folk can turn themselves round, buckle to and make the grades. And if not, they could always borrow the car. To live in.

When LBC, the first commercial radio station, started up in 1973, I used to pop in to record a 'What the Periodicals Say' slot about different types of magazines. How did the motor magazines see the world through their windscreens that week? Bird-lovers' publications – did they just parrot the same views? The extracts would be read out by whichever reporter was wandering past the studio at the time. The most competent reader was a tall young man who left to work in television and now presents *Channel 4 News*.

Jon Snow should not have been opposite me in the studio at all. He should have been in the early stages of the legal career begun a few years earlier when he went to university.

'Student life at Liverpool University was a magical time and not in my wildest dreams did I imagine that I would be thrown out after five terms.' That is in fact what happened to him. Being on the student union executive, he was at the cutting edge of protest over, among other issues, the university's investments in apartheid South Africa.

Two and a half thousand students occupied the Senate House but, when everyone went home at the end of term and the dust settled, only ten were punished, including Jon. Thanks to his having looked after the building and cleaned the loos, he received the most lenient sentence; he was sent down but only for a year.

'I never went back. I felt to some extent that I had to work my passage, make amends and gain my life experience in some other way.' He went for a job as the director of the New Horizon Youth Centre for homeless teenagers (one of the interviewers turned out to be John Profumo, the disgraced defence minister who went into charitable work). Barely out of his teens himself, he spent three emotionally draining years as director before moving into the media. 'Presenting *Channel 4 News* is not a doddle – but I know which is the tougher job.' Meanwhile, two of his fellow protestors continued their legal careers, becoming barristers and QCs. But Jon has no regrets: 'I would have become a very indifferent lawyer.'

Carol Smillie went to Glasgow School of Art when she was eighteen and then, as befits the presenter of *Changing Rooms*, renovated her life completely. 'I spent the first year thinking I didn't know if this was what I wanted to do. There were people with green hair and pink shoes, on another planet to me. The tutor I got was very much into abstract art – throwing paint at the wall – and I wasn't.'

Carol then took up modelling, which fitted conveniently around her study time. This prompted another tutor, a lovely man with whom she got on well, to advise, 'If I were you I should stick with this modelling malarkey. You can do your art at any time.' She thought this may have been a kind way of saying, 'I don't think you've got what it takes.'

She left at the end of the first year. 'My parents were horrified. They thought modelling was a very dodgy career choice. Was I going to go on the game?'

Stephen Poliakoff found Cambridge a stuffy place and its history course shockingly bad, so left after only two years. 'In my penultimate term I announced grandly to my supervisor that I was going to spend the whole term writing about the French Revolution.' The usual deal was that you wrote about one subject per week. 'After I had been reading out my essay for about three hours, he suddenly rushed off and vomited.' This was nothing to do with his student; he'd over-indulged the night before. Having tidied himself up, he said, 'Very good – but now you've got to catch up.'

Stephen did not even begin to catch up. In his last term he moved on from the French Revolution to write a very long essay about the rise of Fascism in a single town in Germany. 'This was very interesting but it didn't get me far in learning about the Black Death. I didn't take the exams.'

Maybe the course isn't delivering the goods or the student made the wrong choice in the first place. Alternatively, they may not fit in comfortably with fellow students and senior members. Or perhaps they feel that their studies, however agreeable, will not help with what they want to do afterwards and so don't justify the fees. Bailing out may be the right choice for those who are struggling with the work or for those who are so bright and sure of themselves that they see the work as really beneath them. The students who are somewhere between those extremes are best advised to keep their heads down and write the essays. It beats working for a living – and there are forty more years of that ahead.

CHAPTER 20

PARENTAL GUIDANCE

Someone who played at Wimbledon once challenged me to a game of tennis – and I won, despite not having picked up a racket for years. The reason that I won was that the lad, a second cousin of my wife's, was seven at the time and it was some years before he featured in an All England Lawn Tennis Club junior championship. I played as well as I could to give him a decent game and I only just won after lots of deuces.

I mention this because he was lucky to have parents who gave him the chance to make the most of his abilities. Without questioning the innate skills of my small opponent, it has to be said that his natural talents were encouraged by the fact that a large part of his garden was taken up by a proper tennis court. The challenge for parents is to come up with the right opportunities for their children; it would have been annoying for my relatives to have gone to the trouble of providing this fully equipped tennis court for their son, only to observe him becoming a world-class glider pilot instead. In this case they would have faced another challenge, which is to encourage a child setting off in a quite different direction to the one they thought of. There must, for example, be couples who go to great trouble to introduce a kid at an early age to the soaring glories of gliding, only to be asked if there is any chance of a tennis racket for the next birthday.

Like Prince Charles and the Queen, children often follow in their parents' footsteps. As with the Prince of Wales, we cannot know how much their career and success is by force of example and how much is down to their DNA. The novelist Martin Amis had a novelist as a father; if Kingsley Amis had been a greengrocer, would his son have gone into the writing trade? Television historian Peter Snow works with his son Daniel Snow; what if Snow Senior had been an insurance adviser? Asking this question does not deny the talent of those two sons, who, having chosen those careers, still have to deliver the goods; I just wonder if they would necessarily have headed for literary novels and historical battles if they had been born with different backgrounds.

Then there are children of outstanding parents who make a success of something completely different. A man whose mother is novelist Margaret Drabble and whose father is actor Clive Swift could have followed either or indeed both, as a novel-writing actor. In fact, Joe Swift is a garden designer and presenter of *Gardeners' World*. It is as if there was talent floating around to be encouraged and used – and this was the way it emerged in him.

'Why don't you write novels?' his agent asked him.

'I don't want to write a novel,' he replied. 'My mum writes novels!'

Brian May's seventh birthday was a sort of Big Bang, creating for him two parallel universes: stardust and stardom. This was when he was given his first guitar, which set him off in one direction. Being allowed to stay up to watch Patrick Moore's *The Sky at Night* set him off in another direction: 'That made me want a telescope. My father and I made a 4-inch reflector and it was amazing what you could see with it: the moons of Jupiter, the rings of Saturn. I projected sun-spots on to paper and saw them moving across.'

The neighbours were more than amazed; they were frightened by the sight of someone standing in the middle of the road at odd hours. Was it burglars? No, that would have been young Brian, stargazing as usual.

Brian May's late father would have been very proud to know that his son has been a guest on Moore's astronomical programme. Brian told me of his father's worry when, with his PhD practically complete, he was faced with giving it up for the vagaries of the music business.

'It was a big risk but when a certain door opens, you either walk through it or you don't. It won't open again.'

Since Queen's *Greatest Hits* became the bestselling album ever, financial insecurity was to be the least of his son's worries. It occurred to me that, had Mr May Senior been alive when Brian decided to turn from rock to doctorate, this might have been another moment when he advised his son not to give up the day job, i.e., abandon music for the wild uncertainties of an academic life.

Dr Fox had much the same discussion with *his* dad. (The doctorate differs, of course, from Brian May's, which was awarded by the University of London; Neil Fox's is a DIY version that he awarded himself for his services to DJ-ing.) 'I had my only fight with my father, who never wanted me to go into broadcasting. He thought that the entertainment business was ridiculously insecure – or overpaid; it irritated him that the actor who played Captain Birdseye in the ad was paid more than the chairman of the company.' But before he died his father changed his tune, conceding, 'I bet you're glad you didn't take my advice!'

Chris Boardman remembers throwing away the stabilisers of his blue Raleigh Chopper at five one morning and going off with his father, a racing cyclist who had been shortlisted for the Tokyo Olympics in 1964 but chose to marry his mother instead.

Mr Boardman Senior's hand behind his saddle, both metaphorically and physically, must have steered Chris towards his cycling career. But we are in the old nature versus nurture debate here. He was also propelled by the high gear of his mind-set – and not necessarily in a good way. 'I think you'll find that other riders may be mentally healthier than me; I'm very intense about what I do. Some riders want desperately to win; some *need* to win. I fall into the latter category.'

The twelve-year-old James Caan could not have been picked as a potential *Dragons' Den* investor because the programme was not even a twinkle in a BBC2 producer's eye. But he could have been spotted as a potential entrepreneur by the way he acted as a retailer for the family leather garment business: 'I went to Forest Gate School, London, in one of my father's jackets, a different one every week, and I would sell them. In one transaction I get double my pocket-money of £1.50 a week.' Three quid a go was not a bad profit and all was proceeding smoothly for young James until he realised his father was cottoning on to the fact that there was a mark-up being quietly made from dad's wholesale price to son's retail figure. Mr Caan enquired casually what price the jackets were going for in the comprehensive's playground.

The poor lad was as nervous as someone asking the *Dragons' Den* team for investment in a scheme to sell snow to supermarkets inside the Arctic Circle but he was relieved that his father was absolutely delighted: 'I was showing a bit of initiative.'

No one from the top stream had ever left before O levels but this was what James did. He now funds a school in Pakistan. I wonder if the kids sell jackets to each other in the playground and what the profit margin is?

His fellow Dragon Duncan Bannatyne was less fortunate, as was his mother. On his first day at Clydebank High School, he realised immediately that he was going to find it tough. There were 600 children at this 'posh school' – i.e., grammar – and 598 of them were wearing the school uniform. He was one of the other two.

With her large brood, his mother found it difficult to provide the right clothes. Uniforms were expensive and it seems that she'd borrowed a blazer and made some trousers herself; it was not a proper uniform. She told Duncan to explain to the teachers that he would have his proper uniform for the second week of term but everybody knew he was poor and so they teased or avoided him. Understandably, he declared 'I'm out,' and like James Caan he left as soon as he could, without any exam qualifications.

'Sports days at Bridgetown School in Stratford-on-Avon were for my mother the beginning of a long period of embarrassment.' (Lord) Sebastian Coe, who first won gold medals at the 1980 and 1984 Olympics and then helped organise the 2012 Games, was as a nipper the nippiest on his feet. 'For years she found it disconcerting that I was winning.' Oh dear – all that competitiveness! Sebastian would walk off with all the first prizes, amid murmurs from disgruntled mums and dads of 'Oh, it's that Coe boy again.'

The parents of his Olympic competitors would probably have said the same thing, though in different languages.

Paula Radcliffe did well out of her parents. 'My dad got into running to lose weight and when I was six I used to run with him in the nearby forest.' She went on to break records and he, well, lost weight. When at eleven she found herself moved to the middle of a middle school where the class had started French two years earlier, her mother, a French teacher, got her to the same position in the language as she was in athletics: back on track. 'I caught up and did French at university.' She got a First.

'My dad was very hard, and my mum,' said darts champion and commentator Bobby George, adding, 'I did hold a grudge against them when I was young but I realise they did me a favour: they made me get off my arse.' He is generously giving them the benefit of the doubt and attributing their behaviour to a 'Boy Named Sue'-style scheme aimed at toughening him up. It worked in one way at least: 'I would go to school to get away from all the shouting at home but when I got there the teachers would shout at me too.'

Bobby had a problem that is surprising for someone who grew up to be a commentator. He had suffered from a stutter before going to school and in class he would put up his hand and stand up to ask a question – and stutter. The teacher's helpful response would be to tell him, 'Sit down, George.'

At junior school he had a friend named Eric who also stuttered. 'I knew what he was saying but in public we came across as a right pair of idiots. My old man said, "Keep away from him," and Eric's father said, "Keep away from *him*."' Bobby drifted away from Eric and at sixteen, two years after leaving school, he realised that he was no longer stuttering.

Bel Mooney was very lucky in her parents. They applied for

a council house transfer so that they could be in the catchment area of a very good primary school, Northway, which they had read about in the *Liverpool Echo*, 'My father worked overtime to pay for the more expensive rent for this larger flat.'

With fifty in a class, learning by rote, a strict regime and a spelling test every week, it does not sound immediately attractive, but it delivered the goods. 'I was very clever, a little bespectacled swot.' It sounds as if her parents were very lucky too.

In the case of the Roux family, the DNA and the cooking background are so entwined that the jury will always be out on the nature vs nurture debate. To explain it one really needs to be pointing at the family tree but here goes: Michel Roux Senior is the co-founder of Le Gavroche in London and The Waterside Inn at Bray. He was born in Charolles in central France, where the best cattle are reared. They – the Roux family, not the cattle – lived above the delicatessen of his grandfather, a *charcutier* who made sausages and pâté. ('My father was a naughty man and left home; my mother had a very tough time.') He attributes his interest in food to helping his mother at home. He loved shopping for bread, Camembert and carrots.

His older brother Albert was his minder at school when he lost his marbles. Literally – he would win marbles fairly from the other kids, who would try to nick them back. Michel followed his brother into the pastry business and into England, where together they founded the two restaurants, each of which became loaded with Michelin stars. They then split up, taking one restaurant each, which seems very fair. Michel kept The Waterside Inn, which he handed on to *his* son Alain. Albert retained Le Gavroche, which he passed on to his son, who, confusingly, is also named Michel. It must be tricky for Michelin when they have to work out where to post all those stars.

Novelist Celia Brayfield is a prime example of what can happen when parents try to steer children in the wrong direction. 'My father was fifty when I was born. He was very pigheaded and bad-tempered to me; it was like living with Ian Holm's *King Lear*.' (But without, presumably, the nudity, which was one of the talking-points of Holm's memorable performance.) She credited him with sending her to what he considered a good school. In this he differed from most of the families in Wembley Park, Middlesex, who didn't bother with their daughter's education, which made St Christopher's Preparatory School 75 per cent boys, the 25 per cent girls being beaten up on a regular basis.

'My father wanted his children to follow him into dentistry and he planned my education with that in view.' The fact that she is known for novels such as *Wild Weekend* and not for her skill with a drill indicates that Celia for one did not fulfil this destiny. The signs of her deviant path were there from the start. At St Christopher's she won the English Prize and received a *Complete Works of Shakespeare* and *Fowler's Modern English Usage*.

It got worse when she passed the exam to St Paul's. This is a leading girls' school but she was not a leading girl, certainly not in science. Her top O level grades were in English and French. 'Look, Daddy,' she said, 'the teachers think they could get me to Oxford with my English.' His response was to make her specialise in four science A levels: botany, zoology, physics and chemistry. 'It was immensely cruel. I did enjoy physics but chemistry was black magic; none of my experiments worked. My copper sulphate crystal fell off my string; I used to write stories in the back of my experiment book.'

Predictably, her A levels were a disaster: 'I failed chemistry and physics, ending up with two not very good A levels and a very angry father.' She did a secretarial course with air-headed debs in London and a French – or, to be honest, skiing – course in Grenoble.

Years later, *Pearls*, her first book, came out and was sent to Anthony Burgess for review. To her joy, the great novelist declared, 'Her grammar is impeccable.' And he wouldn't have said that about her extraction of wisdom teeth.

With far fewer resources, the parents of another writer, Geoff Dyer, were touchingly supportive. 'There were no books in our house, apart from Second World War books such as *The Three They Couldn't Kill*, which my mother, a dinner lady at my junior school, described as "hard going".' Thanks to the free education he received – Cheltenham Grammar School, Oxford on a full grant and then reading Russian literature on the dole – he has written four novels and six 'genre-defying' titles that include *Yoga For People Who Can't Be Bothered To Do It*. He has won the Wodehouse, Somerset Maugham and E. M. Forster awards.

This is not bad for someone whose father advised him, 'Never put anything in writing.' Geoff did, though, follow another piece of paternal advice when choosing A levels: 'Don't do history, that's all in the past.' He chose English, economics and geography.

His badly paid parents spoiled him as much as they could. When he was in hospital with tonsillitis, they bought him a Beatrix Potter book every day. They gave him space and time: he had no siblings to compete with. They went on about how other people's children left school to bring money into the house but they were excited about his exhibition to Oxford; his mother made a cake in the shape of an open book with his college's name iced across the middle.

This is the familiar story of the one enthusiasm that has the kid forging ahead – in Geoff's case it was English – and pulling the other subjects in its wake. There was the other familiar story of the gulf between him and his family as he moved on.

'I had no idea of class until I went to Oxford. I was becoming unpleasant and precocious, speaking differently from my parents. I tried to improve their lives, get them to read a different book or drink a different tea.' On a visit home in his third year at university, his mother opened the door to him while wearing her dinner lady's blue uniform; they embraced and both started crying. 'We knew this was something about class and the different world I was about to move into.'

His parents hoped he might get a proper job in the civil service but he moved into a house in Brixton with fellow Bohemians on the dole. 'There was all this Russian and French literature to read.' He may not have quite finished it yet.

Gina Yashere's mother, who came to England from Nigeria, was always on her daughter's case. In a good way. Gina was the class clown and did mini performances in assembly but was never allowed to do school plays, as she had to go straight home to get on with her homework.

'She had told me when I was a child that I was going to be a doctor and she chose my exam options. She said I was going to get ten GCSEs at good grades. My A levels were going to be physics, chemistry and biology.' Unfortunately she hated chemistry and it was the subject she failed at GCSE. So on to Plan B: physics, French and biology.

Mummy Yashere, who had been fluid in switching from Catholic to Church of England when necessary in the choice of Gina's successive schools, now showed a similar flexibility when her daughter had to dissect a rat during the biology course. Gina decided, 'I don't like the sight of blood. There's no way I can be a doctor.' Forget biology: hello, maths A level.

She passed her A levels but had another announcement: 'I told my mother I wanted to become an engineer: to get dirty, work with my hands and wear a hat and overalls. My mother didn't like it but I said I would study to degree level at the same time. I started with British Telecom as an apprentice engineer and then worked for Otis, who make lifts, for four years. I was one of the crew that built Canary Wharf. It was hard – working a twelve-hour day and studying for my B-tech in electronic engineering. I am a qualified engineer.'

Myself, I wouldn't have liked to have been in the room when Gina informed her mother that she was taking voluntary redundancy and going into stand-up. Presumably it was all resolved when Gina, having got to the top in Canary Wharf, did the same in the world of comedy.

Celia Brayfield's father could have done with lessons in parental guidance from Gina's mother on when to keep a firm grasp on the reins - and when to use a light touch. For a graphic demonstration of how not to do it, let's return to Monty Python again. In a clever sketch about parental miners and writers, Michael Palin plays an aspiring young son who appals his rough, down-to-earth father – a novelist – when he breaks away from the family business of writing and escapes to Barnsley in order to have a more fulfilling life hewing coal. 'Hampstead wasn't good enough for you, was it?' sneers his outraged father.

CHAPTER 21

SPECIAL INTERESTS

The twelve-year-old son of a friend was just ticking over at school, cruising happily without undue – or any – exertion. Suddenly he discovered birds, as in the Dartford Warbler, and his life was transformed. His leisure time was spent spotting, ticking off and researching. He started to see his hobby in school terms and set his mother an exam on identifying different types of birds; due to lax revision, she achieved only 3 per cent. Finally, this energy spread to his school work and his marks took wing.

Faced with an under-performing boy, a teacher at my son's school managed to harness his interest in football in an academic way. When the lad showed signs of life in class, he would be rewarded with a photograph of a player in his favourite team. This would get him showing further signs of life and the idea was that his schoolwork would become a perpetual motion machine that would keep going after the teacher had run right through the entire first and second teams.

Only a tiny proportion of teenagers kicking a ball around actually get to play professionally. Similarly, most people who want to be writers are advised not to give up the day job if they hope to pay the rent. However, in these and other areas there some lucky young people whose hobby becomes a career. They manage to do for money what they would be doing for pleasure anyway.

'I should always advise people to have some hobby at university, which may turn out to be more useful in the long run than the subject they're actually reading.' Richard Whiteley had a hobby that was close to a full-time job. We were in the same college reading the same subject and spending our time on the same student paper but (as with his passion for Helen Drabble) I had no inkling that his student journalism was part of his plan for a career in television. In 1962 the BBC had a single channel and ITV had been transmitting for only seven years. Television was what people a long way away did – and not many of them – but Richard had been bitten by the broadcasting bug when he was seven.

When he was being driven over Ilkley Moor to his prep school in Bingley, Yorkshire, he saw a BBC Outside Broadcast van with the proud slogan 'Nation Shall Speak Peace Unto Nation' on its side. In 1950, this was like a spaceship that had touched down on the Moors. Richard was very excited. His father stopped and asked if his little boy could have a look inside.

'Yes,' said the BBC technician – and immediately slammed the door in their faces. They drove sadly away. Richard always wondered what went on inside that mysterious van.

'I went to Cambridge with the sole aim of becoming a BBC general trainee,' he told me when he had become a fixture on the television screen. 'I thought the best way was to distinguish myself in the world of drama.' Having once sold tickets for his school play, he now volunteered his services as director of a 'nursery' production involving one act of Arnold Wesker's *Roots*. That did not distinguish him: 'I didn't really get on with the actors, who seemed to know everyone – except me.'

He credited me with his next move. I was already on the student paper and apparently I said, 'Come to *Varsity*,' which he did, to great effect, eventually becoming editor and producing the first student colour magazine. This led to a job offer from the *Daily Mail* but he was strangely reluctant to sign the contract.

It turned out that when he had been on Anglia Television to talk about the colour supplement, the interviewer asked afterwards if he had thought of trying to get one of the ITN traineeships. Richard had not thought about this because he had never heard of the scheme but next day his letter was in the post. Fourteen years after that encounter on a Yorkshire moor, he became a scriptwriter on ITN. I never asked him if he finally got to see the inside of a BBC OB van.

There was one point during her journey to primary school when Ellen MacArthur would be peering desperately out of the window. 'There were too few of us for a school bus in the early days at Wirksworth County Infants in Derbyshire, so Mr Chadfield's taxis used to pick us up, going down little lanes past farms. We went past a fantastic little lake with an island; I used to try to catch a fleeting glimpse of it – and dream. At Wirksworth Juniors I used to "sail" with my friend Sarah round 'islands' in the playground.'

Dame Ellen, as she now is, does not come from a sea-faring

or indeed lake-faring family but when she was four her grand-mother took her and her brother on a trip up the East Coast in an old 27-foot boat. 'We did it again the following summer and after that our family holidays were spent there. It was designed for two or three but there were seven of us and the dog.' All very *Swallows and Amazons*, no doubt – Ellen still has all twelve of Arthur Ransome's wonderful series – but you can see why she might want to specialise in *solo* circumnavigation of the globe.

Ellen MacArthur's grandmother, incidentally, sounds like Super Gran's brainier sister:

> She was the most incredible lady who had won a scholarship to university as a girl but her father couldn't afford to let her go. As a result, education was very important to her and she was very keen for her children to go to university. She came to our school, Anthony Gell Secondary in Wirksworth, to study for her GCSEs and A levels – I used to have lunch with her – and went on to get a degree in European languages in her eighties.

Ellen owes her nautical career, and her chance to win the record for fastest solo navigation of the world, not only to her enterprising grandmother but also to glandular fever. Because she caught this enervating disease just before her A levels, she ended up with low grades. Having worked at the local vet's every Saturday morning for three years, she had aimed to be a vet herself but that ambition was sent straight to the knacker's yard.

However, there can be an upside even to glandular fever. It was while she was still off school that she saw a programme about a round-the-world race. 'I realised that it was possible to sail as a job.'

She hoarded her school dinner-money to make this career possible. 'I saved everything. I used to take bananas from home and then would buy just a 5p flapjack or baked beans (4p) and mash (4p). Gravy,' she adds, 'was free.' OK, there may not be such a thing as a free lunch but she has showed us that you can, with enough determination, get one for a mere 8p.

Lib Dem MP Sarah Teather derives her interest in science, and her 2.1 in natural sciences, to the family shopping. When Sarah was nine, her mother brought home a fresh mackerel and, being an optician, dissected its eye.

'My brother said, "Disgusting!" but I took the other eye to school in a jar for a show-and-tell.' Presumably half the class would have said 'Disgusting!' and the other half would have begged, 'Please bring one of your dollies next time.'

You could tell that five-year-old Ranulph Fiennes had been playing in the sandpit: 'There was a lot of blood on the sand.' The school near Cape Town had a small sandpit with a four-foot concrete apron round the edge and a small fence round that. Somebody dared the little boy to jump over the fence and summersault before flying into the sandpit. Predictably, his head hit the edge of the concrete.

'Take your son away before he kills himself,' the kindly sisters who ran the school begged his mother. He learnt this early lesson and has kept well away from danger by climbing the towers at Eton by night, by climbing the north face of the Eigar, by climbing Everest, by climbing Everest again, by being the first person to reach both Poles by surface travel…

Bradley Wiggins never cycled to school. 'Cycling wasn't a cool sport; you wouldn't be seen dead in Lycra.' This, of course, was in the days before Bradley Wiggins himself made cycling cool. 'I always walked to St Augustine's Church of England Primary and St Augustine's Church of England High next door to it in Kilburn, north London.'

His mother said he would have a talent for cycling, though even maternal pride would not have made her dream that he would in 2004 become the first British athlete to win three medals in the same Olympics. She bought him a 'home trainer' or exercise bike, which was safer for a child – or indeed anyone – than cycling on the roads, until at about twelve he would race at the Herne Hill velodrome. Unlike most uses of that over-used expression, it can be said that cycling actually was in his DNA: 'I grew up having a father who was a professional cyclist, although I never saw him cycle; he left us when we came to England from Belgium when I was two. I didn't have any contact with him for seventeen years but when I was eighteen he got back into contact because he had seen my name in the press.'

When he was fifteen or sixteen he would leave school at lunch-time and head out on his bike for three or four hours up the A40 to Denham and Beaconsfield. 'I never really told the teachers what I was doing and they just thought I was a waster. They thought I was bunking off but I wasn't just going down behind the bike sheds and smoking.' In fact, normal lessons and games would have been a doddle when compared with the full-on burning of energy required for pounding away on the pedals.

> I wasn't very good at school. I wasn't a *bad* kid; I knew the difference between right and wrong but I struggled with the whole authority thing. I felt the teachers were doing the bare minimum but I can understand why: the kids weren't the best-behaved pupils and it was a vicious circle.

Would he be happy for his children to go there? He is certainly happy for his brother to be there. As a PE teacher, that is. 'It is actually quite a good school now.'

He was literally a hands-on kind of student: woodwork, PE, sport. He wasn't lazy but didn't really concentrate. Even in French he couldn't see the point, saying to himself, 'I'm going to move to France and be a professional cyclist and learn French there. You think you know it all when you're eleven.'

It all worked out for him but it wasn't the best way to experience school. 'I got six or seven GCSEs. I didn't revise. During the weeks of study leave I just used to go out on my bike.'

These days, he feels, the teachers would be more encouraging. When they asked what he want to be, he would say, 'I want to be an Olympic champion,' and they would tell him he was crazy: 'Be serious!'

As a performance poet, John Hegley thinks it was 'possibly auspicious' that he lived in Byron Road. This is not to say that Byron published a collection entitled *Glad to Wear Glasses* or *I am a Poetato* [sic] but John is definite that he has always been interested in wordplay, to the extent of making up his own words to play with when the English language has failed to come up with the goods. He came up with a name for a little bit of paper which he had spat on and flicked from a ruler (don't try this at school, children). It's a 'flobby-gobby', of course.

When he wrote a poem called 'Witches' Dell', a little boy enthused that 'It sounds like a real poem.' And the teacher said, 'It is a real poem.'

Now that's what I call a *real* teacher.

And here's another real teacher. No, not G. M. Ford, though he has taught part-time as well as writing crime novels (such as *Fury* and *Black River*). It was Mrs Becker, a teacher from his past, that Gerald was telling me about.

'I have had former students stop me in the mall and say that I really turned their lives round.' Since his pupils would have been thrown out of conventional schools in Seattle by the time they reached the special institution where he taught, his achievement would have been pretty crucial; it wouldn't just have been a matter of someone dropping history and taking extra maths. However, while they are expressing their heartfelt thanks, he will be racking his brains, trying to remember who they are.

He does, however, recall *the* teacher in his life and the precise moment in which a page of his own life was turned over to begin a new chapter. He could still picture the classroom and the dress that Mrs Becker was wearing when she gave him an A-plus for his essay on *Golden Boy* by Clifford Odets. He was a ten-year-old in the fifth grade and this story was the first thing he had read in which he perceived what the author was getting at. At the bottom of Gerald's paper Mrs Becker had written: 'This is way above what you would expect from a fifth-grader.'

He went on: 'When I was forty-five I had occasion to take stock of my life – my divorce – and I remembered how good I had felt about that A-plus.' He resolved to compile a 'bucket list' of things to do before he kicked it.

He remembered that after the death of his father he had bunked off school (intercepting the letters which would have tipped off his mother about his truancy) and discovered the mystery section in the public library where he went to get warm. Now in his mid-forties he could put all that snatched reading to good use: number one on the list was to write a mystery novel. *Fury*, starring sacked journalist Frank Corso, was the result. It would be nice to think that today kids sneak out of school to read his stories in public libraries.

In 1979, when he was in his mid-teens, my accident-prone nephew Jonathan Sevink grabbed someone's knife – as an uncle, one doesn't like to ask too many questions – and cut a tendon in his finger rather badly. For the terminally unmusical such as myself, any local hospital could easily have glued it together again perfectly well but the lad played the violin and so needed a really pukka repair job to restore sophisticated control over the wounded digit. His grandfather asked around and pulled a few strings of the non-violin variety to find the best finger-surgeon in the business.

Although he was well over six foot by this time, Jonathan was booked into a children's ward at the London Hospital (maybe he crouched when he went in) and the operation was performed successfully. He was just coming round from the anaesthetic when I popped in on my way home from the office. I brought the latest issue of *Punch* to fan his hot brow; he could always read it later if desperate.

I was also carrying with me a special greetings card. When I had mentioned my errand of mercy back at the *Punch* office, a passing cartoonist offered to dash off a rapid gag – at absolutely no charge. Ken Mahood was the go-to guy for customised cards for colleagues: no event too big or small – birthdays, bar mitzvahs, marriages and, as in my case some time later, sackings.

He now came up with the most encouraging cartoon a youthful violinist could be given. Decades later, I can still visualise his drawing of two smartly dressed men walking past a large building with a vaguely familiar dome. One of them is saying, 'I hear Jonathan Sevink is playing the Albert Hall these days.' And just behind them is a young lad with a violin – busking on the pavement.

Years afterwards, I interviewed my nephew about his musical interests. 'I did have a brief flirtation with the French horn,' he said. 'I never played it, I just took it to bits.' (He is good with his hands.) 'Then I returned it to the school, still in pieces.' (But not *that* good.)

For me the music came from Tany's Dell, my primary school in Harlow, Essex. The deputy head, Mr Miller, was a fantastic violin player, and when he played at assembly, it was one of the few times that there wasn't a single person talking. I was convinced that this was the thing for me and began having private violin lessons.

In general, it was mainly sport on the menu for him, with a side dish of fighting until he was beaten up by a tougher kid. There followed two moves and couple of inharmonious schools on the south coast, until at fourteen he settled down in Brighton.

'I went to Dorothy Stringer, a comprehensive that had the most amazing music teacher, Heather Cowl, who was given an MBE for her services to music. That's when my music really took off.'

He became leader of the school orchestra in his final year and also went on tour in Canada with the Brighton Youth Orchestra. Music was not one of his O levels: playing it was what he liked. Also he hated classical music and was listening to Led Zeppelin and Pink Floyd. Unfortunately Led Zep was not going to be advertising for a violinist any time soon.

As soon as I got to the end of my A levels, I put the violin in its case and didn't play it for six years. I must have been about twenty-three when I picked it up again. My sister's boyfriend said to me, 'We want a fiddler for our new band and you're the only person I know with a violin.'

After jumping out of his fine art course at Manchester University before he was pushed, Jonathan had been doing unmusical things like making furniture for dolls' houses (maybe he was good with his hands after all) but was happy to tune up with the embryo band. He switched from 'Jonathan' to the grittier 'Jon'.

His soaring fiddle gave its distinctive sound – well, as his uncle I would say that, wouldn't I – to what was and still is The Levellers. The radical folk-rock band has notched up fourteen Top 20 hits and its albums have reached No. 1.

They are notorious for, among other things, being a hardworking group that are always on the road, often a European road. It took some time before Jon could find a window of opportunity for an interview with his Uncle Jonathan. This was in 2008, when The Levellers were on the tour that celebrated their (first) twenty years in business.

The last gig of that tour was in the Albert Hall.

Despite its highly industrial location next to a Newcastle slaughterhouse, there were beehives at Wharrier School and Eric Burdon joined the Bee Club, complete with the protective hat and smoke apparatus. This gave him some status: 'Leave him alone – he might set the bees on you!'

He was also in the Comic Club. In those post-War days, English comic books were printed in bleak black-and-white, so he used his artistic skills to colour them in and exchange them for American comic books, which were printed in colour. 'Two English comic books for an American one: my introduction to currency.'

As a boy, James Naughtie always had the idea of writing for a newspaper and did so: in his own newspaper. He found an old typewriter and with it produced a couple of issues, which he hawked round the village. He quite liked the idea of doing something with books, too.

'One day when I was about nine I found some old books in the attic and put up a notice saying that I was opening a lending library. A lending library – in a village with about twenty houses!'

Arlene Phillips had bad luck – and I'm not referring to her being dropped from *Strictly Come Dancing*, a decision that Harriet Harman denounced in Parliament as blatant 'ageism'. Her uncle paid the school fees at Broughton Prep in north Manchester but she couldn't afford to take Quality Street sweets to school like the other kids. At her grammar school she was in the lower-to-middle stream and consequently treated as remedial by the girls in the top set, despite the fact that she had passed the Eleven Plus to get there in the first place. Just before O levels, she left to look after her dying mother and never went back. Not a good hand of cards: thank you, fate!

Fortunately she was all this time dealing herself a better hand from another pack: 'I wanted to dance, that's all I wanted to do.' She had started at three, going to a little class which at first she disliked because the teachers were too strict. (No one wants strict; you can get that at school.) She stayed with the dancing and by eight or nine it was an obsession.

There was netball at Manchester Central High School for Girls but no dancing – does it *sound* like the kind of educational establishment that would have pirouetting and twirling on the syllabus during the 1950s? – but on Saturdays and after school Arlene nipped off to the splendidly named Muriel Tweedy School of Dance. At sixteen she went on its full-time course and at twenty was a teacher there.

Her Hot Gossip group had three years of rejection on account of being too sexy, and was about to pack it in until suddenly 'too sexy for television' became 'just what we are looking for on *The Kenny Everett Television Show*'.

'Passed/Failed?' laughed Diarmuid Gavin when I told him the name of my interview series. 'Just call it "Failed" in my case.' Well, he didn't win the reality competition *Splash!* but that wasn't playing to his strengths, which are horticultural, and his 'Irish Sky Garden' did land first prize at the 2011 Chelsea Flower Show.

'Everyone worries when you're the only one in the family who shows no academic leaning. One evening, my dad came into my bedroom and threw at me papers containing every result I had ever had at school. I had been a let-down to him.'

Diarmuid had loved every second of his time at Loretto College in Dublin, having a lot of fun in its noisy playground and farm, run by nuns, with cows grazing. Sadly, when Diarmuid was six, his younger brother was knocked down and killed on the way to school.

The nuns were very caring – one of them wrote a little book about the dead child – but, to escape the painful memories, his parents moved him to another local school where, despite some great teachers, he felt like a fish out of water. It was much the same at Templeogue College, his secondary school. He was good at English, the art teacher was an inspiration and Diarmuid was usually first in religious studies: 'I found it easy to write a pleasing essay for a priest.' But otherwise, as the exam results in his father's hand demonstrated, he was not doing at all well.

The careers teacher asked him to bring in the Lego buildings that he had been assembling. How about engineering? But Diarmuid had another thought.

'When I was twelve, I had marched my little sister into the park and under the bushes and we had landscaped the side of the hill with my father's gardening tools.' Landscape gardening was territory worth exploring. The College of Amenity Horticulture in Dublin did not ask for any qualifications and he was soon dug in. 'I loved every moment of my three years there and came out of my shell.'

One of memorable moments was a strike. Horticulturalists are not known for their militancy but the students at the College were annoyed because the qualification that they would receive was downgraded from a Higher Diploma to a mere Certificate. As it happened, he wasn't bothered about the words on the piece of paper but did enjoy drinking Guinness on the picket line.

'I failed the Eleven Plus,' said Pam Ayres. 'I'm not saying I would have passed but I remember being terribly irritated when the headmistress, who was invigilating, was gossiping with the vicar throughout the exam.'

Still, it was at her secondary modern that she saw the first publication of her work. The school wasn't much to look at, over-flowing as it did into various outposts. There were 'The Huts', a displaced persons' camp with corrugated-iron roofs (well, no one said it was going to be Roedean) and an old Marines' camp where they used to do their needlework.

'The teaching was chequered.' One of the English teachers wasn't mad. In fact, Bill Reeves was gorgeous. 'He encouraged me to write stories and we put together a little book called *Ayres and Graces*.' This was the first recorded sighting of that particular play on words. He started a paper called *The Conquest* in which she wrote stories – very Monica Edwards, this – 'about ponies and escapades'.

Rather different from those of Pam Ayres, 'Runaway planets and frogmen emerging from the Sargasso Sea' were the themes of the yarns told by Brian Aldiss to the other boys in the dorm. They were based on what he had read in *Modern Boy*, the maga-zine for what passed as modern boys in the 1930s, and he generally ended with a cliff-hanger. This was at a comparatively advanced stage of his story-telling career.

'As soon as I could read, I could write. I used to write lit-tle stories and illustrate them.' Like Pam, he saw his words in book format, thanks to his mother, who bound them up in floral wallpaper.

'I was six when I was sent away as a boarder, an age when one is still on good terms with one's teddy bear, to the pretentiously named St Peter's Court at Bacton on the north-east coast of Norfolk.' There was an upside to what sounds a most unpleasant experience.

'I regard that school with gratitude because at night I would tell ghost stories in the dormitory and when one of the boys yelled out, "Shut up Aldiss, you bastard!" it was such a sign of success.' He would also give lectures on dinosaurs and the other boys would listen patiently and even take notes.

The runaway planets and frogmen became part of his repertoire at Framlingham College in Suffolk, a name he could never utter afterwards without a sense of loathing. The masters at the school where he was sent at nine were bad enough; a speciality of French teaching, for example, was to set long lists of irregular verbs that were hard to memorise and so laid one open to the punishment of the twisting of the short hairs above the ears.

The nights were for initiation rites. The new 'squit' would have to stand on his bed and tell a story and if the older boys did not like it they would throw shoes. 'But not a shoe hit me! I'd become a dab hand. I've never feared criticism since. This is how storytelling – the oral tradition – began: out of fear.'

Brian became the champion storyteller of the dormitories but he was stuck in the Odysseus dilemma; by giving the yarn lots of welly to avoid the Scylla of the flying shoe, he risked disturbing the Charybdis of the walloping cane. The housemaster would rush in to demand, 'Who's talking?' and the bard of the dorm would hold up his hand to receive six of the best on his nearly bare bottom.

He was saved by the outbreak of World War Two, which made the east coast of England a dodgy location: 'My father made one of his rare wise decisions: we moved to Devon.' In terms of schools, it was a case of third time lucky. Brian deserved a break and he got it in the shape of West Buckland, on the edge of Dartmoor. It was a marvellous school, particularly when he reached the class of 'Crasher' Fay (the nickname related to his big boots, not his driving). Mr Fay let him write a short story instead of the weekly essay.

'I diversified: some crime, some science fiction, some pornography and some stories which were all three. Copies were circulated round the school.' Brian Aldiss the grown-up writer was being formed. He was also coming across a perennial problem for authors: 'It was meant to be threepence a read but I never got any money.'

Gary Rhodes, who won his first Michelin star when he was twenty-one, has a lot to thank his school meals for. It was terrible muck. Twydale Juniors in Rainham, Kent did not cook its own food and had the nerve to be very strict about pupils finishing up the unappetising grub: 'You were forced to eat those overcooked Brussels sprouts. I couldn't wait to go home for the home-cooked food. This inspired me to help in the kitchen and my career was born.'

Although he has been back to demonstrate his skills, they were not ones to be revealed at the time. 'In those days, cooking was for the lady! You certainly did not tell your friends, "I made some fancy potato to go on my mother's shepherd's pie".' (Michel Roux Senior, co-founder of Le Gavroche, also derived his interest from his mother's kitchen: 'I used to mash the potatoes. The steam coming out and over my face was lovely.')

In was only when he was about to leave secondary school that he revealed his culinary secret to his best friend, Steve Grant: that he had been cooking the family's Sunday lunch since he was thirteen. At this point there was a *Billy Elliot* moment: Steve replied, 'You're going to be even more shocked; I've been going to the Ballet Rambert. I've been dancing since I was six.' The lads had known each other for ten years, each living a double life.

Gary could come out happily as a chef when he went to the superb catering course at Thanet Technical College. 'In my first year, I achieved a pass level; in the second a credit; and in the final year a distinction.' He also clocked up Chef of the Year and Student of the Year, which gave a feeling as good as the first Michelin star. Catering college had something else to offer.

At fifteen, he spied 'the most gorgeous young lady' on another platform on Chatham station. 'I hid behind a pillar to watch her, as I was in my scruffiest clothes for my cleaning job. When I'd been at college a month, I discovered she was there too.' In their third year, they were among the fifteen chosen for the advanced cooking class. They have been sharing a kitchen ever since.

Richard Whiteley's advice, that a hobby at university may be more useful than the subject studied, applies to school as well. Quite apart from the pleasure of doing something which doesn't involve homework, the interest shared with friends could lead on, directly or indirectly, somewhere useful. Eric Burdon looked after the school's bees; as it happened, he went on to be the bee's-knees of the British Blues world but, in an alternative universe, he could be the leading light among English apiarists and pur-veyors of honey.

CHAPTER 22

CHANCE WOULD BE A FINE THING

L ife's a lottery and some are presented at birth with losing tickets. John Bird, the founder of the *Big Issue*, was
made homeless twice by the time he was seven. When
the family did have a home, it involved him sleeping in
a room with two brothers, while in a corner of the room his parents were drinking with friends.

The pieces were, for him, to some degree picked up, first by
a Catholic orphanage and then by the 'approved school' where a
teacher introduced him to H. G. Wells, since which time John's
nose has always been in a book.

He was fortunate to encounter these institutions but they were after all doing what they were set up to do. For others I interviewed, the turning points in their schooling were much more random, often resulting from outside forces that had in themselves nothing to do with education. Some involved decisions and some just happened. Here are some of those people who got lucky.

'I am one of the few people who can say "Thanks" to Hitler.' On the whole, Andrew Sachs would join the rest of us in saying 'No thanks' to Adolph but it is a fact little known to historians that the rise of Fascism created the career of the man best known for Manuel in *Fawlty Towers*. 'If we'd stayed in Germany, where I was born in 1930, I would probably have gone to university there and never become an actor.'

He pointed out that if Hitler had left his political activities until three years later, he – Andrew – would not have escaped to England and thus would not have started to learn his second language at the young age of eight and three-quarters when his mind was still flexible enough to pick up English easily.

It is a fascinating alternative What-If of history. Suppose the Führer had gone off the idea of goose-stepping, ranting at Nuremberg rallies, persecuting people and invading countries, then Andrew would not have learnt fluent English, wondered what to do with it and realised that 'You don't have to learn much to be an actor.'

Andrew can make light of it now but, as he told me, he was coming home from school one day in 1938 when he saw the smashed windows of the Jewish establishments attacked during Kristallnacht. It got worse: 'My father was Jewish, which wasn't very helpful. He was arrested in a restaurant where we were having supper but released after a few days because of a business contact in the police who pulled some strings.' The family immigrated to England a few weeks later.

Note the English understatement there about it not being very helpful to be Jewish during a Fascist takeover. 'I tried to speak the King's English and develop what I thought was beautiful diction – and the producers cast me as French jockeys, Russian POWs, Japanese scientists … and Spanish waiters.'

Fats Waller used to complain that 'Your feet's too big' but Steve Redgrave has no complaint about his own large 'pedal extremities'. He owes his career and five Olympic golds to the size of his own feet and hands – and to the fact that Francis Smith, his form teacher at Great Marlow Secondary Modern, noticed them. Mr Smith was captain of the Marlow town rowing club and was looking for a few individual boys who wanted to join the school rowing team.

Rowing is not like football. You need water, for a start, and most schools don't have it. Marlow has the Thames; Steve's first school was on a street that went down to the slipway where cabin cruisers were launched. Even then, it is not plain sailing, or rowing; instead of the space for twenty-two lads to gamble about provided by a football pitch, the largest boat has room only for eight – eight big bodies to power the craft through the water.

'He chose me because I had big hands and feet and so was liable to become a big person,' explains Steve. Francis Smith chose well. 'Of the twelve in the school rowing club, three of us got to the 1988 Olympics, coming fourth or better.'

Chris Owen, Martin 'Zippo' Burton's English teacher, pointed him towards the Oxford Playhouse. When Martin was applying to the English course at King Alfred's teacher training college, now Winchester University, Chris Owen wrote an unexpected reference: 'Don't give him a place on the English course but on the drama course.' That is why Chris, instead of being an English teacher, makes his living from clowning around in a red nose and big feet.

All the other people on the course had been in the National Youth Theatre and knew difficult words like 'downstage' and referred to the curtains as 'tabs'. To make up for his lack of practical experience, he joined a local fringe theatre that used to do clown shows on Brighton beach. He once did a three-month tour of Amsterdam which cut right across term time and no one noticed, except that when he returned, someone asked, 'Were you ill last week?' He could always have blamed his absence on an exploding car.

'It was a complete fluke that I got into RADA.' Towards the end of his time at school, two of the teachers – take a bow, Mr Reader and Miss Woods! – said to David Harewood, 'What are you going to do when you leave? We think you should be an actor.' A light bulb went on in his head and he applied to several drama schools and got a place. It was not at a particularly good drama school but he wrote to the others cancelling his application. He then had a phone call from RADA asking him to come in for an audition in a few days' time. He realised that his letter to this prestigious drama school had never arrived. Changing his mind, he rapidly learnt a speech for his audition. His success there launched a career that has included the film *Blood Diamond* and the TV series *Homeland*.

According to a theory well above my pay grade, it is a matter of pure chance that I am around to tap out these words and you are around to read them. Apparently, if the laws of physics had happened to be slightly different, the universe would be very different. Or not exist. Or something. Anyway, it is therefore fitting that the Astronomer Royal, (Lord) Martin Rees, suggests that he has benefitted too from the workings of chance. That sounds like a gross libel on himself but it is the account that he gives of his career in science.

At Shrewsbury, the public school he went to a few years after Richard Ingrams and the *Private Eye* generation, boys who did Classics were top dogs and sat in the front row of the kennel, or chapel.

'It was my lack of facility at languages that drew me towards science. The teaching was good enough to get me into Cambridge, with physics and double mathematics at A levels.' *Double* mathematics is a concept to give most of us nightmares. Plus he got a scholarship, which he qualifies as being only 'minor'.

He then achieved a First but – astonishingly, there's a 'but' coming – 'I wasn't one of the outstanding people in my year at all. I had *some* [my italics] mathematical skills but I wasn't cut out to be a professional mathematician.' That left a choice between economics and astrophysics.

'Luckily I got a research studentship, I think only because someone dropped out. My research focused on trying to make sense of some puzzling new discoveries about very distant cosmic objects.' He added that he was lucky in starting his research when the subject of 'observational cosmology' was just beginning and thus able to make his mark at an early age.

'The first evidence for black holes and the Big Bang both came along at that time and my PhD related to both.' Sounds like quite a thesis.

He concluded with a reminder that 'Astronomer Royal' is an honorary title given to a senior academic: 'People sometimes think it's "Astrologer Royal" and want their horoscopes read but I have to tell them that they couldn't afford my fee.'

Heather Couper is another astronomical success and she too had her lucky day or, to be precise, night. She has had an asteroid named after her: 'Heather' is a much nicer name than boring old 'Asteroid 3922'. She has lectured at the Greenwich Observatory, been President of the British Astronomical Association and made television programmes on cosmic phenomena like black holes. And it all started by chance.

'One night when I was seven or eight I was looking up at the planes – my father was a pilot – and I suddenly saw a bright green shooting star. My parents said there was no such thing; in the paper next day there was a small headline saying, "Green Shooting Star".'

The least her father could do was to buy her a little telescope, which he did, a series of them, and Heather used to take them out into the garden, even when it was chilly enough for her mother's washing to be frozen stiff on the line. 'Being plump and well-padded I didn't notice the cold.'

She was not what could be called a model pupil: 'I was top of the class but disruptive.' Her nature diary differed from the usual entries on the lines of 'Today I saw a tweetie-bird and a sort of brown leaf.' Heather's was less earth-bound: 'For my nature diary I put down all my astronomical observations.'

Her initial interest lasted until she was around thirteen: 'I gave up astronomy, which I thought was for old men.' She switched to gazing at another type of star and followed rock groups, pretending she knew The Searchers to impress her friends. The sixth form was an academic black hole. She dropped two of her four A levels.

Astronomy was not quite off her agenda, because it came up in her conversation with the careers teacher, who asserted, not very helpfully, 'You can't be an astronomer unless you make a discovery.' Heather then consulted Patrick Moore, concluding her letter with, 'PS, I'm a girl.' His reply came by return: being a girl was no handicap but you did need maths.

Her A levels were geography at A grade and an E in physics. At nineteen she rediscovered astronomy and joined the local society.

Then she decided she wanted to be a professional astronomer and had a job analysing data at the Cambridge Observatories. Studying one night a week for six months, she managed to get maths A level at the lowest grade. Now she was ready for the lift-off to Leicester University and astrophysics – the physics of the stars.

As an actor, Tom Conti gives the impression of knowing precisely what he is doing. This was clearly not the case when he was a sixteen-year-old in Scotland about to take his Highers and Lowers which are required for university entrance.

'On the first day of the exams, I decided, in a moment of insanity or as an act of silly rebellion, not to take them. My parents were absolutely shattered.'

His Plan B was music. He had been given piano lessons from the age of four, until one day he was told that the teacher had suddenly gone to America.

> When my mother thought I was old enough – I was about thirty-five – she told me that this woman, who gave me lessons for a pittance and played the organ at the local church, was 'taking in' men at night. They were local worthies and when this got out there was a witch-hunt – and *she* was the one who had to leave town.

Another teacher was found, this time a lady with a quieter night life. Unfortunately she had long fingernails that clattered against the keys. 'I took against her – and lessons – but now, with an eye on being a professional musician, I intended to go to music college, so I went along to the Royal Scottish Academy of Music.'

Here again he diverted himself from the chosen path but this time in a good way: 'I noticed a brass plate with an arrow pointing to the College of Dramatic Art.' He followed this flying fickle finger of fate to an office where a nice lady explained all about the place. Meanwhile, back at the Royal Scottish Academy of Music, they would either have been asking, 'Where's that Mr Conti got to?' or they would have been totally unaware of the talented student they were going to lose.

Tom decided that drama sounded wildly exciting and was lucky that a couple of places were left for late entrants. He returned in a week's time with two speeches for his audition. After he had performed, the head of the college said, 'While you were doing the speeches, my colleagues and I looked at each other and nodded, so we'd like you to start at ten o'clock tomorrow.'

On the way out, Tom saw another arrow, this one pointing to the Department of Sculpture, so he ... Just joking. It was a great drama course and he has been acting ever since. He told me that he still plays the piano. You never know.

CHAPTER 23

DID IT ALL WORK?

Education takes between a decade and a decade and a half but work – that's assuming we are lucky enough to have it – occupies us for much longer. My interviewees were fortunate in being able to match what they wanted to do with what they could be paid to do. This is a great privilege.

A friend of mine wrote off for an internship to a company that received ten such letters every day. The executive flicking through these applications was understandably hard pressed to make a choice among many strong contenders for the one unpaid post that was up for grabs. She noticed one of the applicants came from the same university as her, so that was how my friend got her foot in the door, first as an intern and then with a salaried post that has her more familiar with far-flung airports than her local railway station.

'Oh no, the Bahamas again,' she complains. It was complete luck that her letter did the trick – but it was down to her to get it under the right pair of eyes in the first place.

Nicholas Tomalin, the great *Sunday Times* journalist killed in the 1973 Yom Kippur War, alleged that he got his first job in Fleet Street because of an eye defect that caused him to hold his head slightly to one side. The effect was emphasised by the heavy black spectacles that he wore. Having previously sold the paper a number of stories, he arrived for his job interview just as the office was having a conversation about how they needed some-one with a new angle on the world. Enter Nicholas, head on one side, to be greeted by cries of 'Yes! That's him!'

At university William Donaldson decided that he was an inferior being when compared to serious intellectuals like his con-temporary Jonathan Miller. 'I thought that because I had money and drove a sports car, I was going to be an impresario.' He did indeed become precisely that, bringing Miller and co. to London in *Beyond the Fringe* while paying himself a far larger share of the takings than the four performers on stage.

Later a young American with a guitar kept hanging around in his office and wouldn't go away until finally Willie fixed up the first UK tour of none other than Bob Dylan. He – Donaldson not Dylan – was later to be penniless, or rather peseta-less, in Ibiza. There was also a story that the *Mail on Sunday* hired him but he never turned up for work. The editor couldn't tell him he was sacked for ages; he couldn't find him.

'A dirty old man' who picked up Jean Shrimpton at the polo in Windsor Great Park suggested modelling (of what type she didn't specify). Then she was approached by a film director who tried unsuccessfully to get her into his film. 'He told me I should be a model, so I went on a Lucie Clayton course which lasted about a month. It's a short course because there's not much to learn – just how not to have a brain.'

Konnie Huq's director of studies at Cambridge used to recommend high-flying students to the Bank of England. Having got a 2.1 in economics, she counted as a high-flyer, so she popped round to Threadneedle Street and found herself facing a couple of Bank executives, both wearing brown suits. 'It turned out to be dress-down day. I remember thinking, "If this is dress-down day, what are ordinary days like?"' There was an aptitude test; she turned out not to have an aptitude for it. She went into television.

Having already appeared on *Blue Peter* and presented a cable television programme while at school, and a quiz show on GMTV in the vacations of her first year, she was making a natural career move. However, it was not the end of her involvement with the Old Lady of Threadneedle Street: 'For years after that they used to write to me at Robinson College, addressing me as "Dr Huq" and asking me to recommend students for interview. The paperwork had obviously got mixed up.'

So here we have someone who, however talented, was not thought suitable for the Bank of England but who was credited with a doctorate she did not have and asked to recommend a fresh generation of students whom she had never taught. This could explain a lot about the economy.

'My father wanted me to be a boxer but my mother wanted me to be a solicitor,' explained Lionel Blue, the first openly gay rabbi. Neither of these careers appealed. One day he realised that there was no erotic charge with his 'sort of girlfriend' and that he was homosexual. As he was sheltering in a doorway from the rain, an old lady took him by the hand into a Quaker meeting for farmers, which led to a religious experience. A spiritual path and career opened up. When he told his mother he was going to be a rabbi, she was furious: 'You're only doing it to spite us; we've worked our fingers to the bone to get you out of the ghetto!'

Glenda Jackson had a hugely admired acting career, with films that included *Women in Love* and *Sunday Bloody Sunday*. She then made her exit and entered the House of Commons stage left. Before either of those careers, she had left school at sixteen to work in Boots: 'It was wonderful, going home with my wages and giving them to my mother.' During this period, a friend was acting in a drama group based at the YMCA and she joined too.

'I felt there was more to life than working in Boots and that I had more to offer.' She had heard of only one drama school, RADA, so that was the one she wrote to. Someone from the amateur dramatic group coached her and she got in, with the local authority stumping up for the fees.

Later, when consumed with fear on a first night at the theatre, she would say to herself: 'If I'd played my cards right, I could have been a regional manager for Boots by now!'

When the teenaged Brenda Dean started work as a secretary at a major printing concern, the Father of the Chapel – as the chief shop steward is known, or Mother of the Chapel if applicable – asked if she would be interested in working for 'the union'. 'Was this something religious?' she wondered. He was, after all, called Father.

If it is true that you get what you pay for, David Bailey's parents shouldn't have expected much, as the fees for the school he went to in the 1940s were only £7.50 a term. 'The teachers thought I was an idiot, although when I was twelve there was a woman art teacher that liked me.' He could draw and paint. His mother always said, 'My Dave, he's going to be a commercial artist,' but the head told her patronisingly, 'Somebody's got to dig up the roads.' Somebody also had to be the outstanding photographer of the age and this was the vacancy David filled.

Phil Cool's secondary modern remained more secondary than modern right up to the very end, when he left at fifteen without taking any O levels. The careers advice sending him out into the world consisted of him bumping into the headmaster on his last afternoon.

'What are you going to be?'

It was nice of the head to ask.

'I'm going to be an electrician.'

'You've got to be good at maths to be an electrician,' was the encouraging response.

Phil did become an electrician, though he didn't really like it. What, one wonders, do you have to be good at to be a headmaster? Empathy was clearly not a box that had to be ticked. The head was right to take a gloomy view of his pupil's prospects. Phil gave up the day job and afterwards was forced to scratch a living as one of our best-known comedians, appearing in the *Royal Variety Show* and his own BBC series. Still, if a boy doesn't have the maths, what can you expect?

If Gary Lineker had known how difficult it is to be a professional footballer, he would have worked harder at school. 'I did OK but my mind was elsewhere.' His last report said something like: 'He concentrates far too much on football. He'll never make a living at it.' He now accepts that these were wise words; a huge proportion of boys do not make a living from it. It's not something he said to me but it is a fact that, when your playing days are over, there are only so many people who get to be a *Match of the Day* anchorman.

While his fellow 'Salopians' (it means Old Boys from

Shrewsbury public school, for the benefit of those who didn't go there) went to posh universities, Christopher Timothy left at seventeen to work at a local gentlemen's outfitters for three years, during which he gained a professional qualification in how to measure a suit (and not in a *Fast Show* 'Suit you sir' kind of way). Knowing that the young employee's heart was set on the stage, his boss gently advised, 'Why don't you concentrate on gent's outfitting and do amateur acting? Otherwise you'll spend the rest of your life cadging drinks off other out-of-work actors.'

However, the master who directed *Hamlet* at school had once told Christopher, 'We'll get you to the Old Vic if it kills us,' and, after three years at Central School of Speech and Drama, he did indeed get to the Old Vic. His parts were mainly of spear-carriers but the Old Vic was at the time host to the National Theatre under the auspices of Laurence Olivier. And, despite his helpful teacher's words, nobody died, although sometimes they dried.

John Simpson applied to the BBC for a job before his Finals results came out. A kindly don wrote a letter saying that he thought his student was First material. When John finally appeared before the BBC selection board, the results were out but were not mentioned.

> Ten years later the man who had given me the job made a remark about 'You university Double-Firsts'. He was most put out when I said I had a 2.2. By this time I was a foreign correspondent and had been shot at in fox-holes and it was a bit late for them to do anything about it.

'I was told that the secret of happiness was a job for life with a pension,' Terry Deary recalled. 'One came up at the Electricity Board, where they said, "We've got a big backlog of filing."

It was death. After a year of "death", I went to Sunderland Teacher Training College, where I studied drama. I then did a couple of years in a junior school and two years in a huge comprehensive as head of drama. Yes, I've got to be honest. I have been a teacher.'

One wouldn't want to wish a moment's unhappiness on Terry, who is in person as agreeable a man as one could wish to meet, i.e. not like the characters in his books. However, it does seem that the horrible history of his schooling may have been worth it for everyone except the teachers who got up his nose. The aggravations he suffered, from the first walloping at kindergarten to the E in history A level, must have acted as the sword up the bottom that propelled him towards *The Terrible Tudors* and the rest of his scurrilous creations.

Imagine a parallel universe in which teachers, instead of hitting him for playing with his Dinky Toy, said: 'Do make your little car go vrrmm vrrmm on your desk,' 'Please take your report home to mummy and daddy,' 'Third out of fifty-two? Smashing!' 'Seventeen and a half out of twenty – that's what we call talent,' 'Let me guess which you'd prefer – tedious old maths with the boys – or history with the girls?' and 'No dates of battles or kings in your essay, Terry – but that really isn't a problem!'

In this alternative universe he could have ended up as a slightly older version of my brilliant college contemporary Simon Schama. But he wouldn't have ended up as Horrible Historian Terry Deary.

Barry Unsworth on his careers advice: 'When the headmaster asked us what we wanted to be, I couldn't possibly say I wanted to be a writer, not in Stockton-on-Tees at that time, so I said "journalist", because that was living by the pen. He nodded sagely.'

Mike Newell was struggling with a summer job as a progress chaser in a telephone manufacturing company. It was the summer that he left university and the job was driving him mad. Then Granada Television got in touch.

'Be in Manchester tomorrow for an interview. Here's a plane ticket.'

He joined as a graduate trainee: 'There were six places and around 800 applicants; there would be more today. We had it easy.'

At his auditions for RADA, Warren Mitchell did a speech by Morgan Evans from *The Corn is Green*: 'I had a pretty good Welsh accent from hearing Richard Burton talking about rugby.' The two had been friends in the RAF and the friendship was not wasted:

> I had two jolly years learning posh at RADA during the day and was duly de-poshed at the Unity Theatre, where we were all social-ists and communists, at night.
>
> Some of the teachers were not the best. When an Oscar Wilde play was suggested, the principal said, 'I don't want you doing that play: the man was a bugger!' And yet RADA was an excellent train-ing for the profession: bad plays with bad directors – and you used influence to get the part!

Libby Purves went up to the *Liverpool Post* for an interview. They said, 'You may have a First-class degree but you clearly know nothing about local government or football.' She got a job in radio.

As the Old Etonians took their places at the Cabinet table after their victorious 2010 election, they may well have breathed a sigh of relief that one of their fellow Old Etonians had left them in peace by standing down at the previous general election. Tam Dalyell had been the Father of the House, that is, the long-est serving MP, and was famous for pestering governments with awkward questions on tricky topics like the sinking of the *Bel-grano* during the Falklands war.

He was also for a long time the only Old Etonian in the Parliamentary Labour Party, having switched from the Conservatives at university, and yet remained on amiable terms with Parliamentarians on the other side of the House. He considered his housemaster at Eton, Tom Brocklebank, to be 'the most fickle, sarcastic, moody "beak"' but was still happy to join a group inviting him to dine in the Commons.

Looking around his old pupils – Cabinet Minister Nicholas Ridley, Newbury MP Michael McNair-Wilson, Winston Churchill (the grandson) and the Earl of Coventry – the housemaster observed that he was very pleased to have had more members of the House of Commons than any other housemaster at Eton.

'Tom,' replied Tam (he wouldn't have used the Christian name at Eton, certainly not) 'you were so difficult, so unreliable, sometimes so mendacious' – that's polite for lying – 'that you prepared us for public life.' Oddly enough, Mr Brocklebank did not set Tam the punishment of 100 lines. Instead, according to Tam, 'He purred with pleasure.'

A very good fishing river, the Deveron, ran through the village where James Naughtie lived. When he was six or seven, he heard that a famous man had booked a room in the local hotel. In the morning, the famous man would set off with a full bottle of whisky and a rod and in the evening he would come back with a few fish and an empty bottle.

'It was Jack de Manio, who presented *Today*. It is curious to look back and see that I'm doing what he did … without the whisky.' And, James might have added, without the plummy-voiced flannelling. A major achievement of a former editor of that flagship Radio 4 programme is that he persuaded Jack it might be time to move on.

It is no thanks to the careers office at Aberdeen University that James is one of the presenters now in Jack de Manio's old seat. He had never been in the gang of youthful hacks who produced *Gaudie*, the student paper, so his remark that 'I want to be a journalist' produced an inevitable laugh.

Then he said, 'A publisher?' and there was an even bigger laugh. 'I think you should be a hospital administrator,' declared the careers lady. Fortunately for the radio industry, he turned down that idea. People who know him say the NHS is pretty lucky too.

Gail Porter, who presented, among other programmes, *Top of the Pops* and *The Big Breakfast*, had been told by her careers teacher at Portobello High in Edinburgh that she'd be crazy to go into television in London. He was a 'Mr Sensible' type and said she should be a lawyer. She reminds him of this whenever she goes back and he says, 'Oh shut up!' This is the first time she has been known to wind a teacher up.

Benny Green's last formal education was when, at nearly thirty, he enrolled in an English and history course at the City Lit in London. The real spadework of his literary education was conducted by himself, when, as a jazz musician doomed to wander the country on the band coach, he could plough through lengthy novels by dead authors, interrupted only by drunken colleagues attempting to fight each other but being dragged down onto the metal floor by the bottles in their coat pockets.

One of the gigs involved passing near the Redruth home of the kind bank manager and his amiable wife who had looked after the lonely little evacuee and made up another part of the educational jigsaw of his life. Now an established musician with the most highly respected modern jazz band of its era, Benny was keen to show his two mentors that the former waif and stray had made something of himself. His time with them had not been wasted. Proudly he explained that he was now playing tenor sax with Ronnie Scott's jazz band.

The old lady burst into tears. Alas, poor Benny! Jazz – had it come to this?

Benny was going to get out of jazz anyway and he was soon earning a living as a freelance writer, a career that does not reduce one's friends to tears (though its ups and downs may have that effect on the freelance writer in question).

Harry Secombe had a similar Moment of Truth: 'I was very good at English and the teacher, Mr Corfield, used to get me to read my essays out in front of the class.' The teacher used to write to Harry after he had left: 'I went to see him with all the trappings of success: big car … Crombie overcoat … hat … shoes. He asked, "Harry, what went wrong?" He thought I was going to be a great writer.'

To be fair to the great Goon, his autobiography, *Welsh Fargo*, was pretty good. But it must be said it wasn't quite Walter Scott.

Shovell, alias Andrew Lovell, the percussionist and producer for dance group M People, went to see his careers teacher and said, 'I want to be a professional musician.'

'Are you taking music lessons?'

'No.'

'Can you read music?'

'No, because of not having music lessons.'

He left with pamphlets about lift engineering and plumbing. Shovell is not being critical: 'The best advice to give anyone is: "Please have something to fall back on." I've got a City and Guilds in plumbing and I was a plumber between the ages of sixteen and twenty-five. To make your living out of an art form is very hard. Education is vital.' He does criticise his teachers in general for not sitting him down and talking to him properly. 'OK, I was a pain in the arse. But their reaction was just: "Lovell, shut up!"'

Martin Sixsmith was portrayed by Steve Coogan in *Philomena*, the excellent film made of his book about babies sold off in Irish orphanages. He had previously been caught up as a civil servant in the Blair government's attempt to bury bad news by releasing it on the day when people were concentrating on Princess Margaret's funeral, which he was against (the burial of the bad news, not of Margaret).

He was slow to achieve membership of the Awkward Squad. At Manchester Grammar he was suspended several times but only for having long hair. More seriously, he was apprehended while attempting to leave the country. This came about because anyone taking Oxbridge exams had to stay on for an extra term. 'Four of us thought this was a waste of time and decided we'd go to France and come back later to sit the exams. We got as far as London but were caught as we were getting on the boat train at Victoria.'

He then spent a year at the Sorbonne studying French politics, rather too closely on one occasion when he was caught up in rioting by people who hadn't noticed that it wasn't 1968 anymore and the riots were supposed to be over. Demonstrators were throwing paving stones at the police and so long-haired lads were being locked up overnight. He found this good training for being banged up in Poland and the Soviet Union during his time as a BBC reporter. His exposé of the trade in Catholic babies has not so far resulted in him being on the wrong side of a cell door but he would be advised to watch his step when sightseeing in the Vatican.

There was talk of Bernard Hill being a priest, which would have involved staying on at school, but his father behaved like Yosser Hughes's father and said, 'You'd better leave and get a job.' Bernard went through the motions of training as a quantity surveyor but, like his friend and fellow-trainee Lionel, his heart wasn't in it as he wanted to be an actor.

On the first morning of the three and a half hour 'Intermediate' exams, they agreed that whoever finished first would go to the entrance of the exam room and call out the other's name. After a mere twenty minutes, a loud 'Bernie' echoed from the back of the room. There were three hours and ten minutes more left to answer questions on cement and subsidence. However, the stage directions, had this been a play, would have said 'Exit Bernard Hill'. His entrance into drama followed shortly.

Michael Heath failed his School Certificate and was thrown out of school. His parents were both illustrators, his father of children's comics and his mother of *Picturegoer* and *Woman's Own*. 'I had a feeling I could do that.' He could indeed. He had a brief eighteen months at Brighton College, where he said later that he was sent because he was useless at everything else – and he was useless there too, hating every moment. He was not useless at drawing the Thelonius Monk Trio, the subject of the first illustration he sold when he was still in his teens.

What with his lack of formal education and (presumably) dyslexia, Michael was never going to win any spelling bee championships. It has been said – but only by Michael himself – that an editor's hysterical laughter at his cartoons is caused more by the ludicrous spelling of the caption than the joke itself. When we were colleagues, I certainly never laughed at his spelling when he handed me his captions for checking. Just a little chortle, perhaps.

June Sarpong has been a presenter on Channel 4's youth strand. She was working on two A and two AS levels and was headed for university: 'Then I was offered work experience at Kiss FM. There was an uproar. Uncles I hadn't seen for twenty years turned up on the doorstep to say that I was ruining my life. My mum cried every day.'

Fighting her way through the throng of despairing uncles blocking the front door, she went off to work experience and then work at Kiss. She feels that she missed out on the university experience of making life-long friends and (as she fondly imagines) the growing up. But overall she is quite definite: 'The best decision I made was not going to university.'

Having said all that, she adds that she took a scriptwriting course and when we spoke she was working on a sitcom: 'It's a long process; never give up the day job!' Which is what her sensible uncles would say.

There is a kind of disclaimer or government health warning that I have left until this point. Yes, it's the penultimate chapter but better late than never. By interviewing well-known people one is open to the charge of fuelling the celebrity culture. Am I implying that the only jobs worth aiming for are those that involve staring into the lens of a television camera? The answer is: certainly not. The important thing is to have the career that suits. I know a former teacher who now works in television; conversely, there is a former television reporter who has chosen to become a teacher. It's a matter of horses for (teacher training) courses.

CHAPTER 24

AND TO CONCLUDE...

How do these interesting and well-known people come over after they have shared their recollections? They are not necessarily brainier than the rest of us, though the Astronomer Royal would take some beating. They are not necessarily more moral than the rest of us, particularly not in the case of William 'Henry Root' Donaldson, the self-confessed self-indulgent consumer of crack-cocaine. They are not necessarily rich, though they tend to be more prosperous than most of us.

They have achieved their potential, sometimes in two different spheres. With a few exceptions, they don't tell us how to do it, merely what they have done. The point is that we know they have harnessed their talents and perhaps we can learn from the courses they have followed. We each may draw different lessons.

You might, for example, notice that more surnames in this book begin with the letter 'M' than with a 'Z'. You might go on to change your name by deed poll accordingly. You might want to know that there is more to it than that.

There's fulfilling your potential – and then there's *really* fulfilling your potential. Take Charles Dickens, for one.

As a boy, he was removed from school by his bankrupt father and placed in a factory where he slapped labels on bottles. When the family finances improved, young Dickens returned to the classroom and then became a political reporter. This was a much better use of his abilities and many would have seen it as their ceiling. However, in Dickens's case it would have been a terrible waste of his talents if he had not indulged his Inner Novelist; fortunately he was able to give up the day job and give us Scrooge, the Artful Dodger, Mr Pip and the other characters from the cast-list of his fertile mind.

The trick, when navigating a route for ourselves or our children, is to consider where we are on the spectrum from bottle-labeller to political reporter to world-famous novelist. It can mean a glance sideways: a relative of mine hated teaching and moved into social work, in which he reached a senior level. Gina Yashere turned down the chance of university to wear a hard-hat and overalls as a qualified engineer, before stepping into the world of comedy.

If you don't try anything, you won't achieve anything. Some are forced to take up a new opportunity because their existing career went down the pan. You'd never guess it from his outdoor look but Monty Don had a jewellery business with his wife; when this collapsed, he stepped sideways into his garden.

Children need resilience too. They don't have financial disasters but they do, like Helen Sharman, get slagged off by a primary school teacher – and they remember the insult. Fortunately Helen also had the happy memory of the joshing words of her secondary school teacher and derived encouragement from them while performing her intricate task on the space station.

It is easy to knock schools and many of my interviewees knock their own schools for six. As the writer Hanif Kureishi put it, 'They say you can get a good education anywhere, except at school.' But where does that leave us? Home-schooling doesn't work in every home.

As for us parents, in the context of both food and studies, force-feeding children ends in tears. It is about as successful in the long term as herding cats. The 'Tiger Mother' theory is that children who do not win the Nobel Prize for Chemistry before they leave primary school should be left out on the mountainside to be torn to pieces by bears. (I confess I haven't read the book.) To my mind, the only creature that needs a Tiger Mother is a Tiger Cub.

A Pussycat Mummy and Teddybear Daddy approach is a much better bet. At the age of six Paula Radcliffe trotted along with her father on his runs through the forest and ultimately showed him and her competitors a clean pair of heels. Brian May's father gave his son two special presents: a telescope and a guitar, which let him have bites at two different cherries.

Trevor McDonald's father was pretty dubious about his son working in a precarious industry like television when there were safe careers in proper jobs like law and medicine. But, to his credit, Mr McDonald Senior let him go ahead and eventually accepted that Trevor appeared to be making something of it.

Some of my interviewees struck out on their own with little parental input. Others found parents to be a positive drag: Richard

Eyre's father paid the school fees but made a point of denigrating the cultural ideals of which his son became a standard-bearer as, eventually, the artistic director of the National Theatre.

Yet this negative force might have had positive results. Just as children follow in their parents' footsteps – Monty Don, for example, tried to impress his macho father by his (unsuccessful) attempts at boxing – they can also react strongly against them in their determination to take a different route. Perhaps parental disapproval pushes children on too.

To conclude with my own father. He was always very encouraging, both to me and to his students. Mind you, one of them, John Simpson, told me about visiting Arthur just after returning from a sticky tour of duty in Afghanistan; he was taken aback to be told off for splitting an infinitive in his report to camera. 'But I was under fire at the time!' John protested. As if that was any sort of excuse!

'It was very funny that a man so scathing about the media should over the years have taught so many students who were media orientated,' he said. Arthur's students included Bamber Gascoigne, Monty Don, *Guardian* editor Alan Rusbridger, drama critic Benedict Nightingale, Julian Fellowes of *Downton Abbey* and Michael Binyon of *The Times*.

Arthur always gave the impression that they should in fact have been poets starving in garrets but he always greeted them with a warm welcome when they returned to see him over the years. And he was proud of them, split infinitives or no split infinitives.

ACKNOWLEDGEMENTS

I am indebted to *The Independent* for allowing me to quote extensively from my series of interviews. In particular, to Wendy Berliner, who suggested that they could be raw material for a book, and to Lucy Hodges, who followed her as editor of the Education Supplement in which the pieces appeared weekly for thirteen years. Diana relentlessly revived the idea while it kept disappearing down the far end of my to-do list and, together with Rebecca, Peter and Jessica, cast a sharp eye over the eventual crop of words emerging from my computer.

I am including novelist and friend D. J. Connell in my acknowledgements because she included me in hers – and also because she tweaked my style and upped the levity level. Ian Jack, former editor of *The Independent on Sunday* and *Granta*, pointed out many important elements needed for a book, such as a title. Further invaluable advice came from the prolific Hunter Davies, who has had three books on the go while I have been tapping out this one.

INDEX